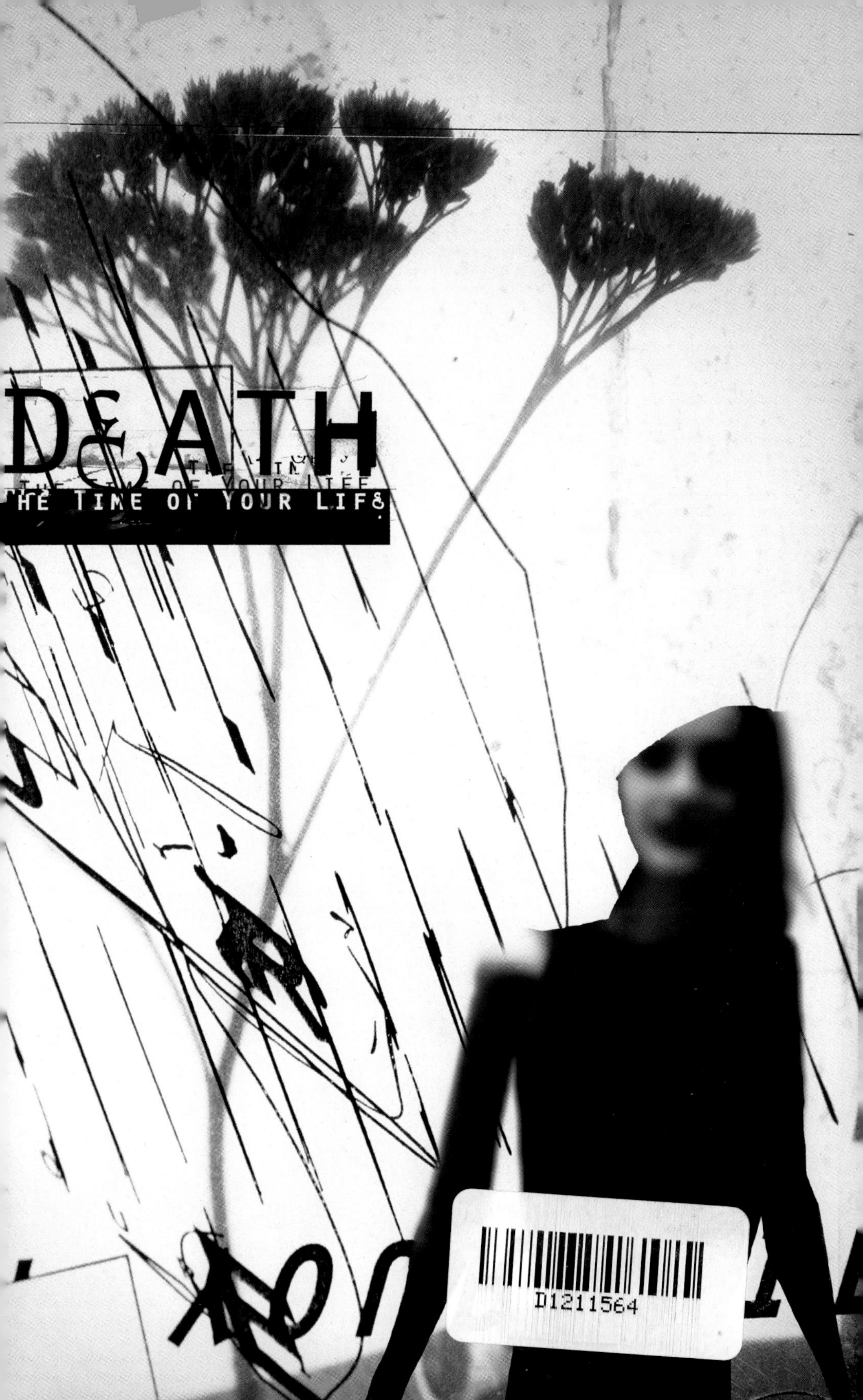
DEATH
THE TIME OF YOUR LIFE

writer neil gaiman

pencillers chris bachalo (pages 9-32, 35-47)

mark buckingham (pages 48-58, 61-88)

inkers mark buckingham (pages 9-32, 35-47)

mark pennington (pages 48-58, 61-88)

dedication - for ellen and delia, with love.

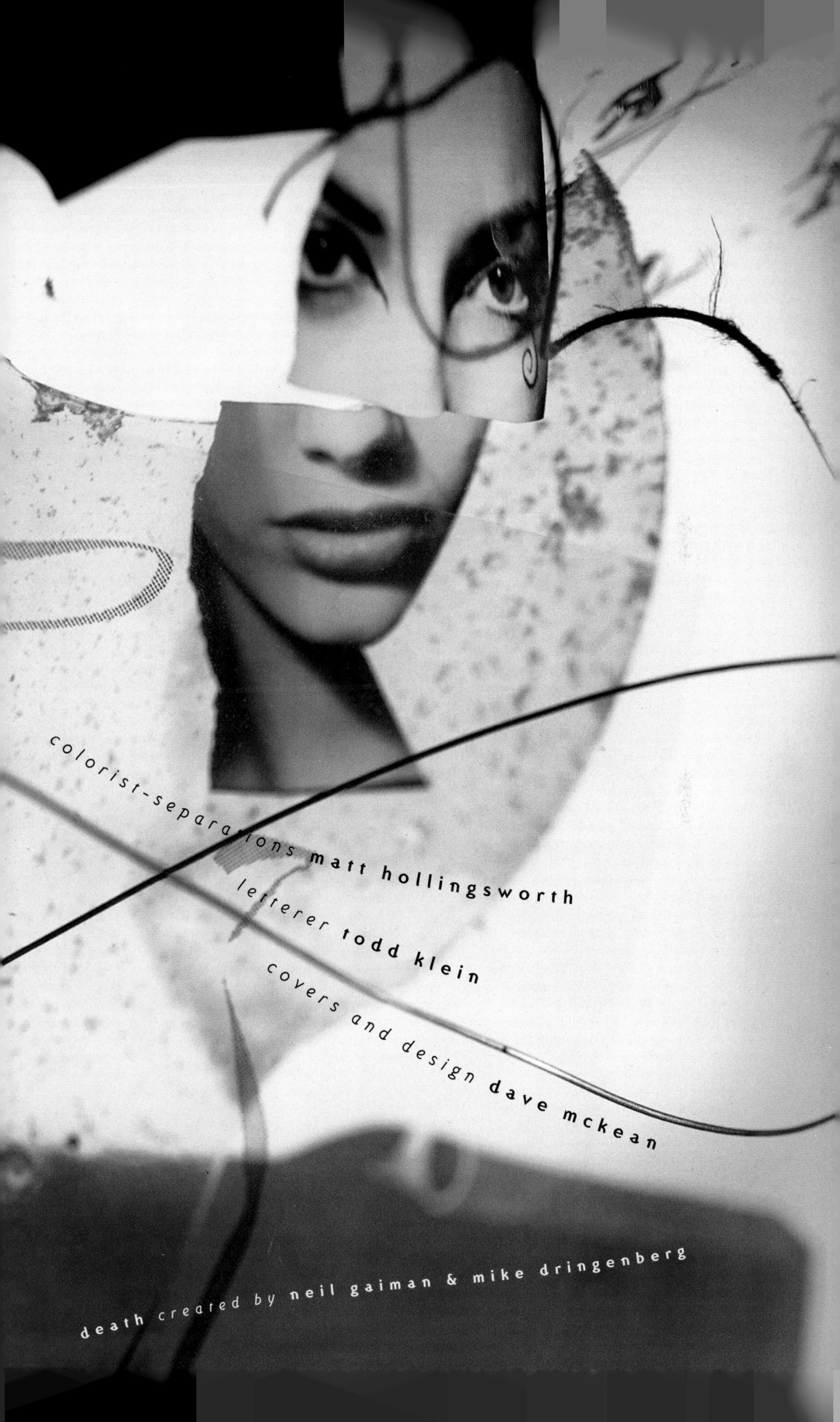

colorist-separations **matt hollingsworth**

letterer **todd klein**

covers and design **dave mckean**

death created by **neil gaiman & mike dringenberg**

con

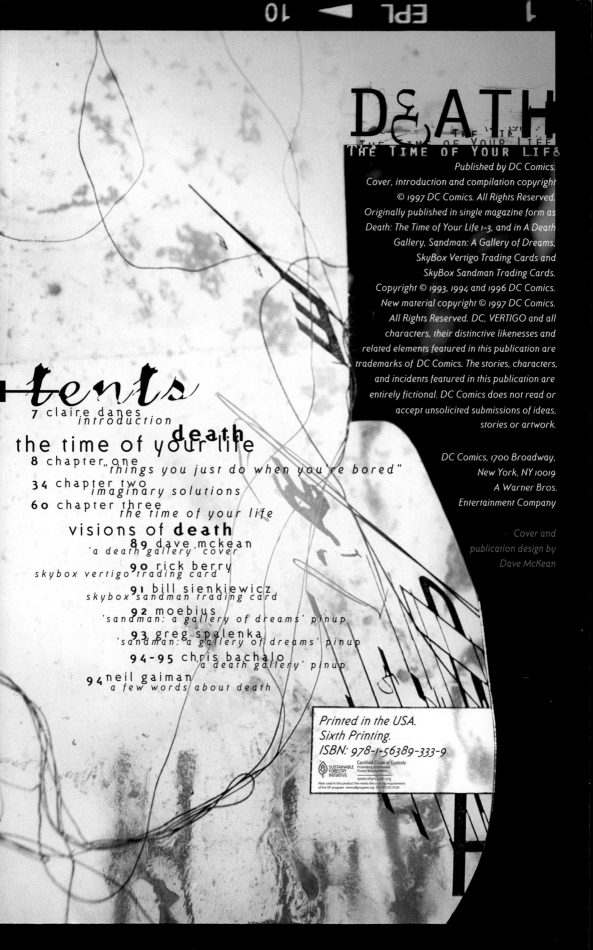

DE&ATH

THE TIME OF YOUR LIFE

Published by DC Comics.
Cover, introduction and compilation copyright
© 1997 DC Comics. All Rights Reserved.
Originally published in single magazine form as
Death: The Time of Your Life 1-3, and in A Death
Gallery, Sandman: A Gallery of Dreams,
SkyBox Vertigo Trading Cards and
SkyBox Sandman Trading Cards.
Copyright © 1993, 1994 and 1996 DC Comics.
New material copyright © 1997 DC Comics.
All Rights Reserved. DC, VERTIGO and all
characters, their distinctive likenesses and
related elements featured in this publication are
trademarks of DC Comics. The stories, characters,
and incidents featured in this publication are
entirely fictional. DC Comics does not read or
accept unsolicited submissions of ideas,
stories or artwork.

DC Comics, 1700 Broadway,
New York, NY 10019
A Warner Bros.
Entertainment Company

Cover and
publication design by
Dave McKean

+tents

Printed in the USA.
Sixth Printing.
ISBN: 978-1-56389-333-9

SUSTAINABLE
FORESTRY
INITIATIVE
Certified Chain of Custody
Promoting Sustainable
Forest Management
www.sfiprogram.org
Fiber used in this product line meets the sourcing requirements
of the SFI program. www.sfiprogram.org SCS-SFICOC-0130

YOUR

SELF

an introduction by

claire danes

Death has a body like a model, the clothes of a poet and the smile of your best friend. She wears a top hat for fun, her ankh necklace for power, and carries a big black umbrella for traveling to the "sunless lands." I wonder what she smells like? I'm sure it's fresh and clean and her laugh must be tinkly or maybe it's warm and chuckly, but whatever it is, Death laughs **a lot**.

We talk about the "miracle of birth" but what about the "miracle of death"? We have the science of death pretty much figured out, but death's magic and inevitability have been feared and ignored for a long time now.

What if Death is a person?

This friendly, people-loving Death I'm meeting here is not scary and far away; she's around every day and enjoying stuff. She's not here to punish us or kill us, she's here to help us figure out how to live before we need to go.

We think Death is a bad thing, but here she's the best kind of pal; she makes our choice clearer for us and tells us by her example that obsessing about things like violence and greed and prejudice and loneliness keeps us from being close to people and having fun and getting our good work done: it's wasteful of our time here.

What I appreciate is, is that Death never tells the people she is with what to do. She accepts everyone and understands why they are the way they are. She likes people (even if they are sad or old or young or nasty) so that they really begin to trust and like themselves too, and, liking themselves, instead of **ending** they can start beginning.

Claire Danes *is one of the most formidable young actresses on the scene today. She has been lauded for her work on television in* **My So-Called Life** *and her film work in* **William Shakespeare's Romeo and Juliet** *among others.*

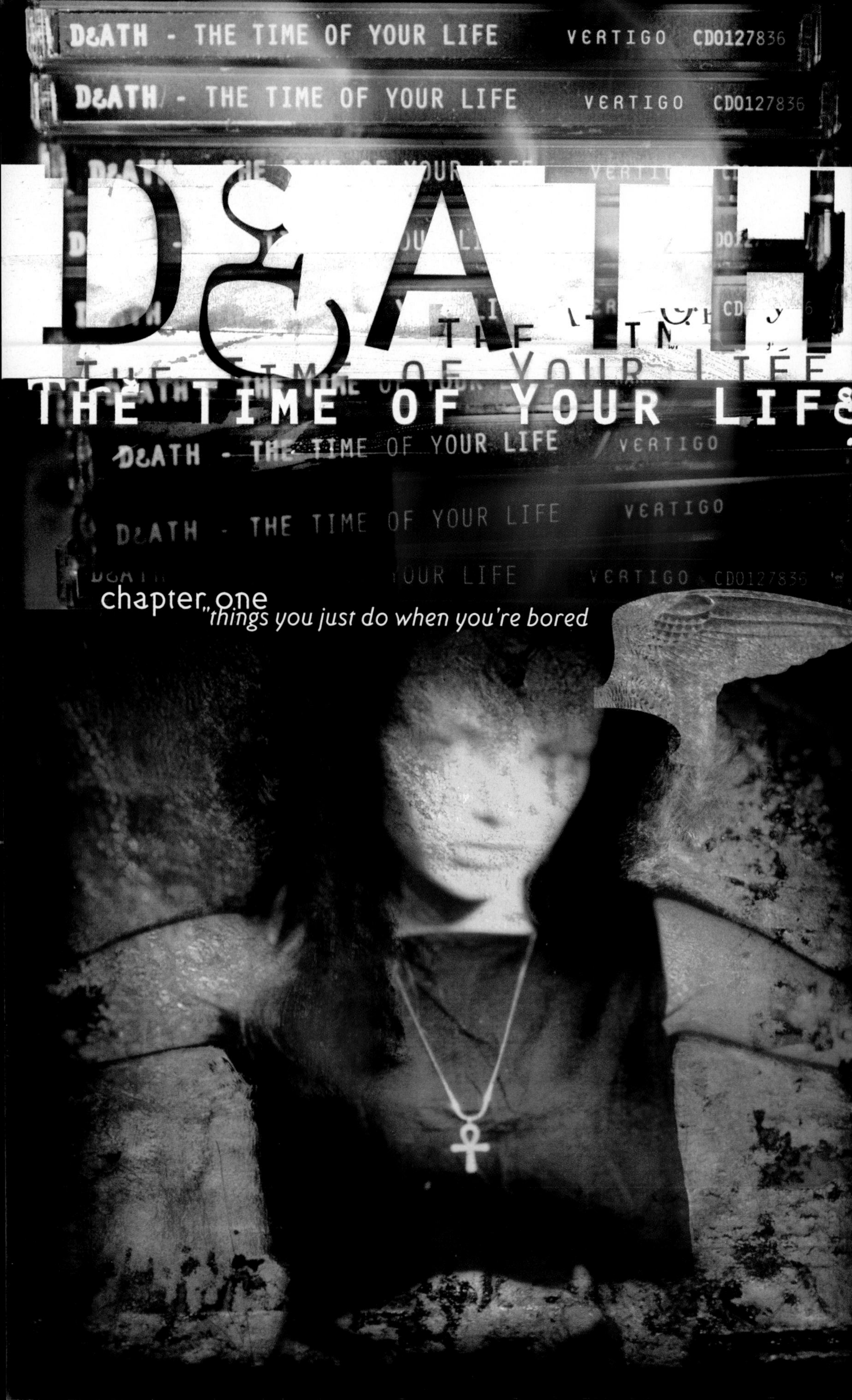
D&ATH - THE TIME OF YOUR LIFE VERTIGO CD0127836
D&ATH - THE TIME OF YOUR LIFE VERTIGO CD0127836
D&ATH
THE TIME OF YOUR LIFE
D&ATH - THE TIME OF YOUR LIFE VERTIGO
D&ATH - THE TIME OF YOUR LIFE VERTIGO

chapter one

"things you just do when you're bored

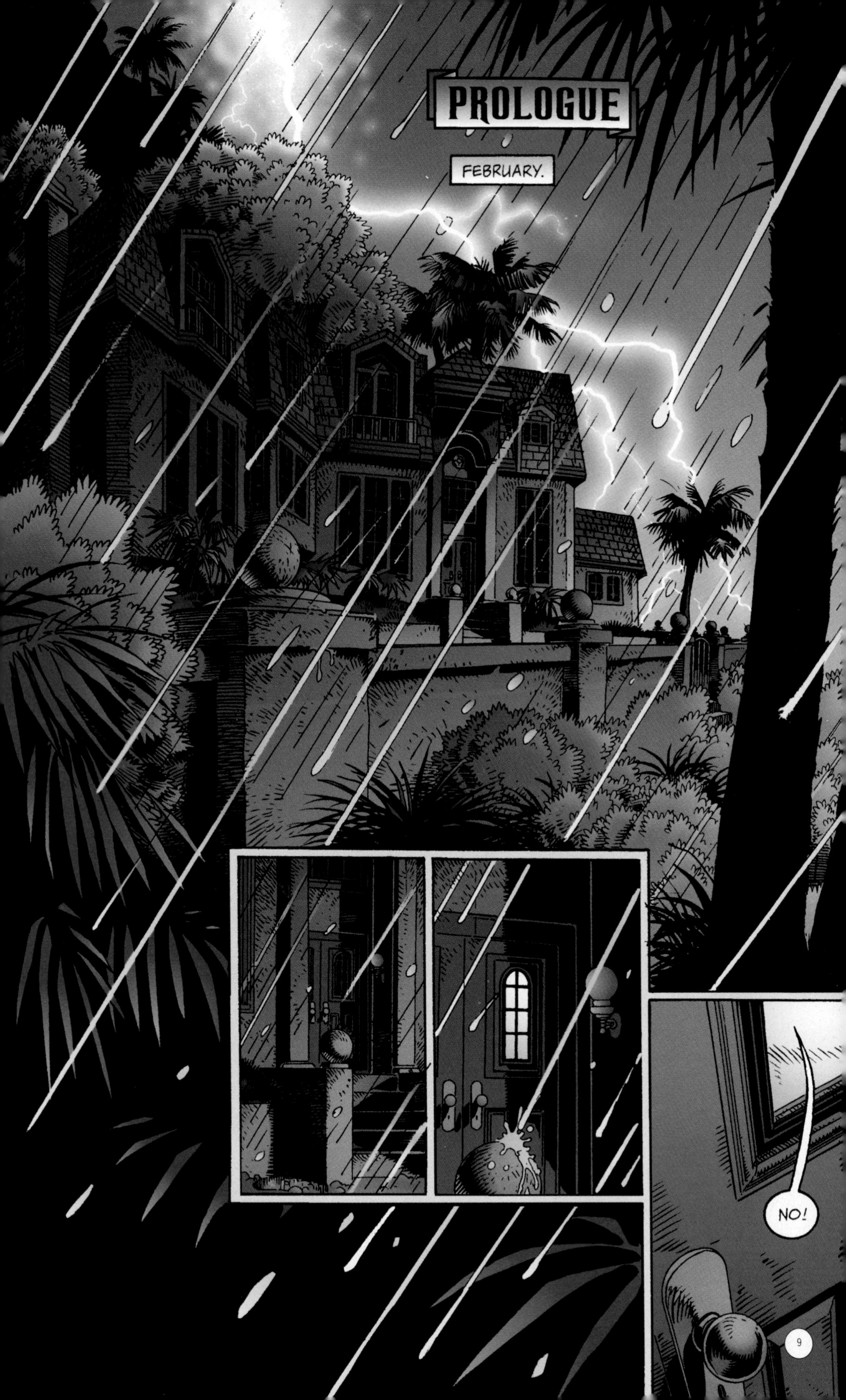
PROLOGUE
FEBRUARY.
NO!

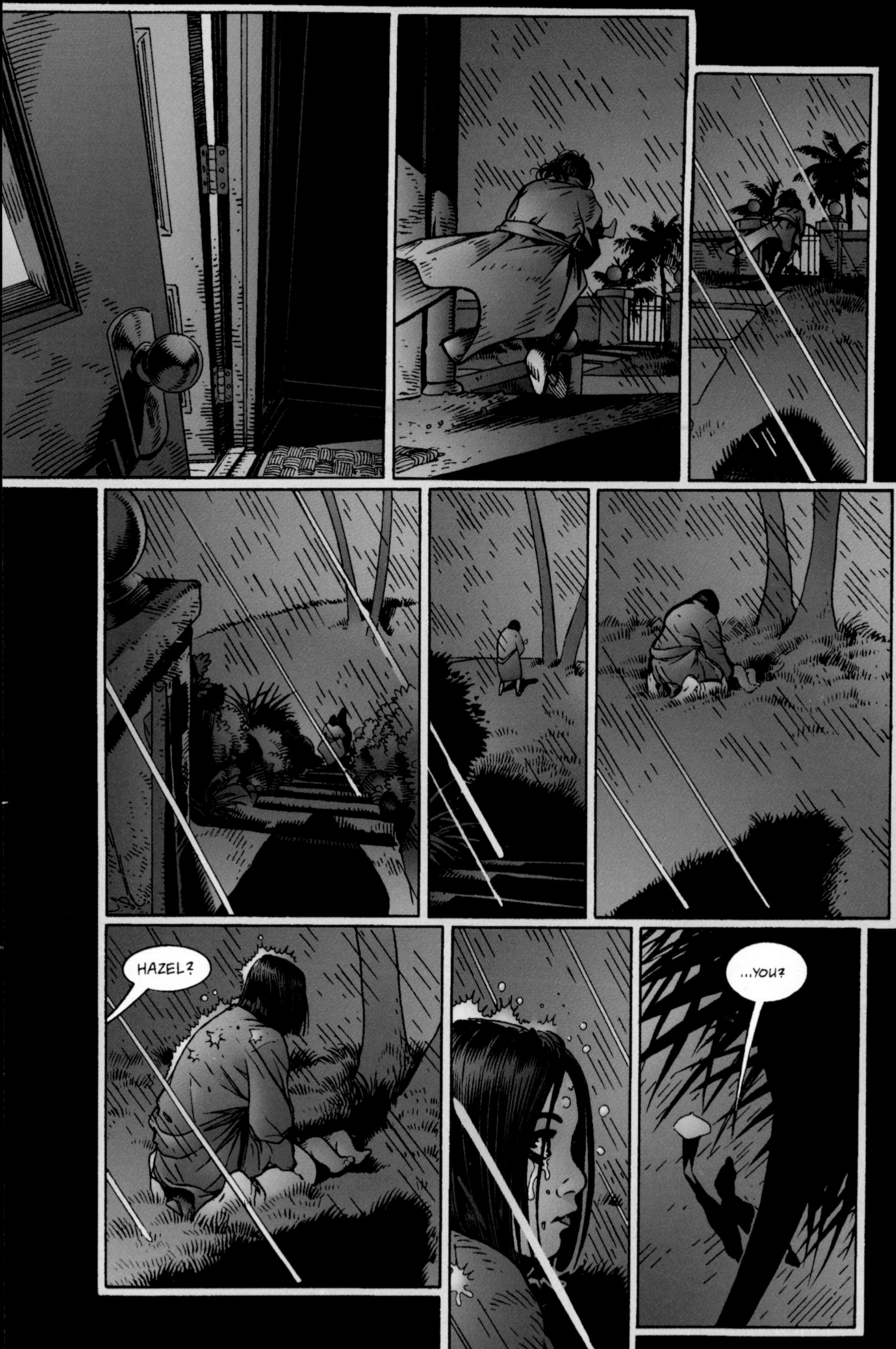
HAZEL?
...YOU?

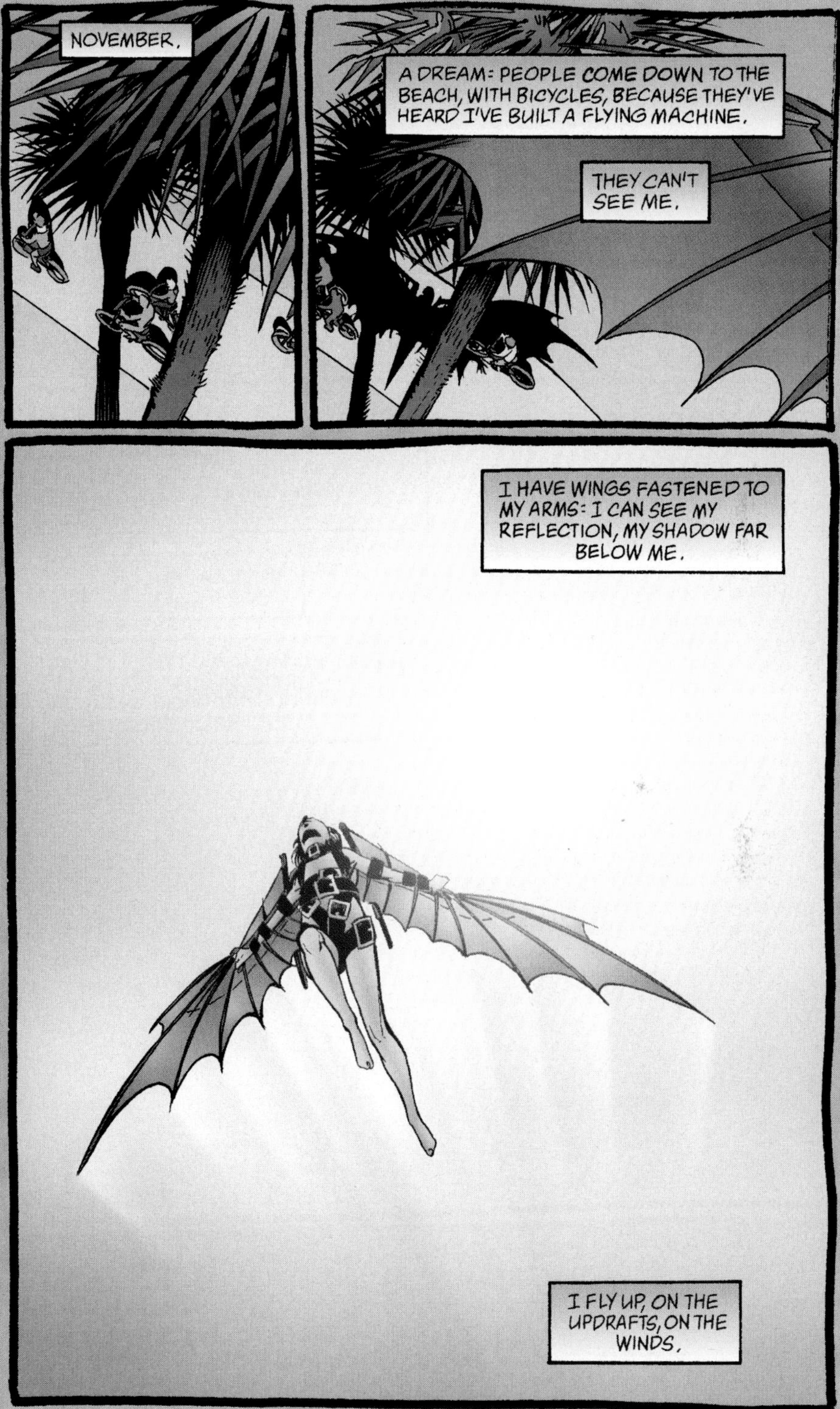
NOVEMBER.
A DREAM: PEOPLE COME DOWN TO THE BEACH, WITH BICYCLES, BECAUSE THEY'VE HEARD I'VE BUILT A FLYING MACHINE.
THEY CAN'T SEE ME.
I HAVE WINGS FASTENED TO MY ARMS: I CAN SEE MY REFLECTION, MY SHADOW FAR BELOW ME.
I FLY UP, ON THE UPDRAFTS, ON THE WINDS.

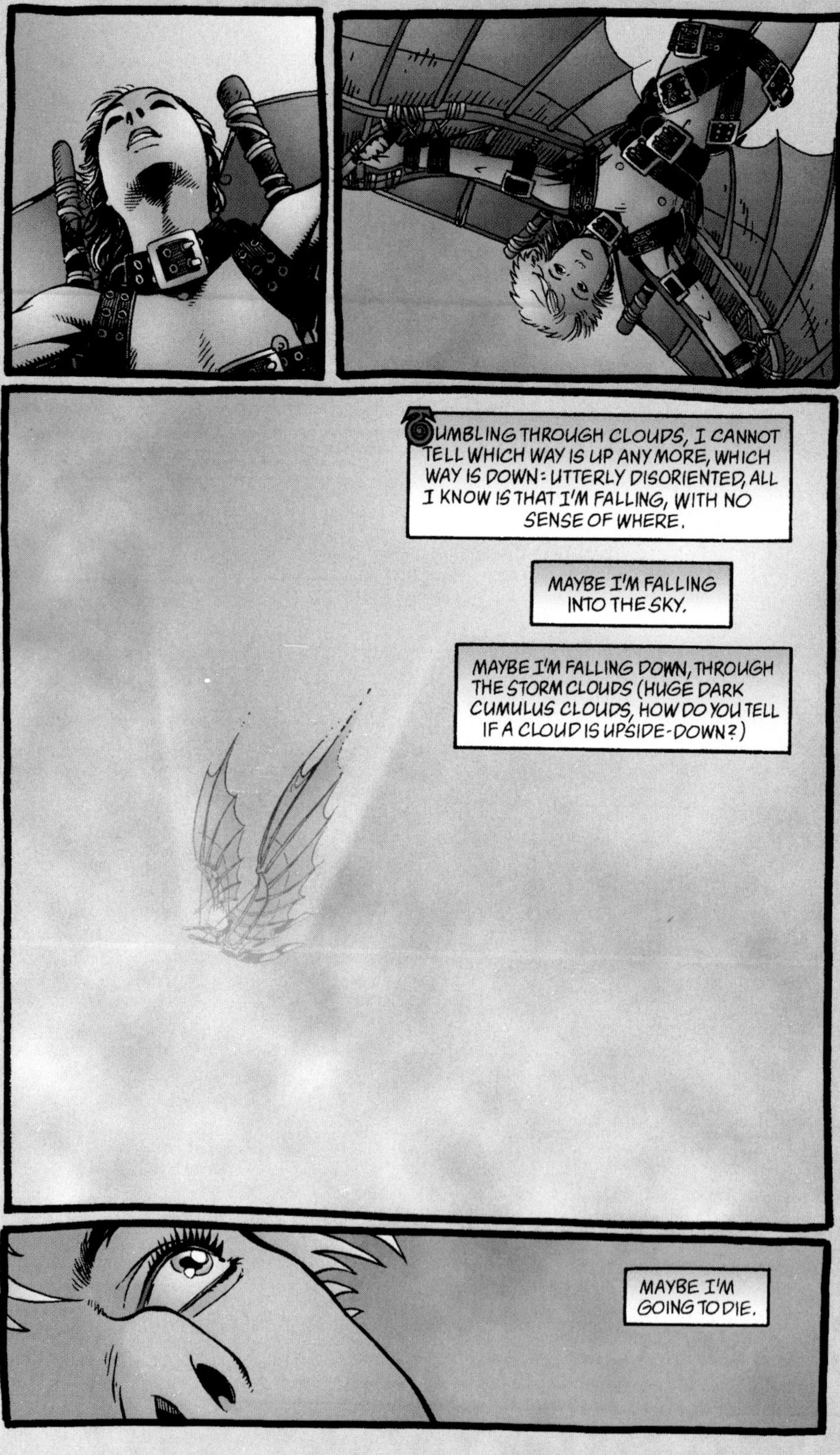
TUMBLING THROUGH CLOUDS, I CANNOT TELL WHICH WAY IS UP ANY MORE, WHICH WAY IS DOWN: UTTERLY DISORIENTED, ALL I KNOW IS THAT I'M FALLING, WITH NO SENSE OF WHERE.
MAYBE I'M FALLING INTO THE SKY.
MAYBE I'M FALLING DOWN, THROUGH THE STORM CLOUDS (HUGE DARK CUMULUS CLOUDS, HOW DO YOU TELL IF A CLOUD IS UPSIDE-DOWN?)
MAYBE I'M GOING TO DIE.

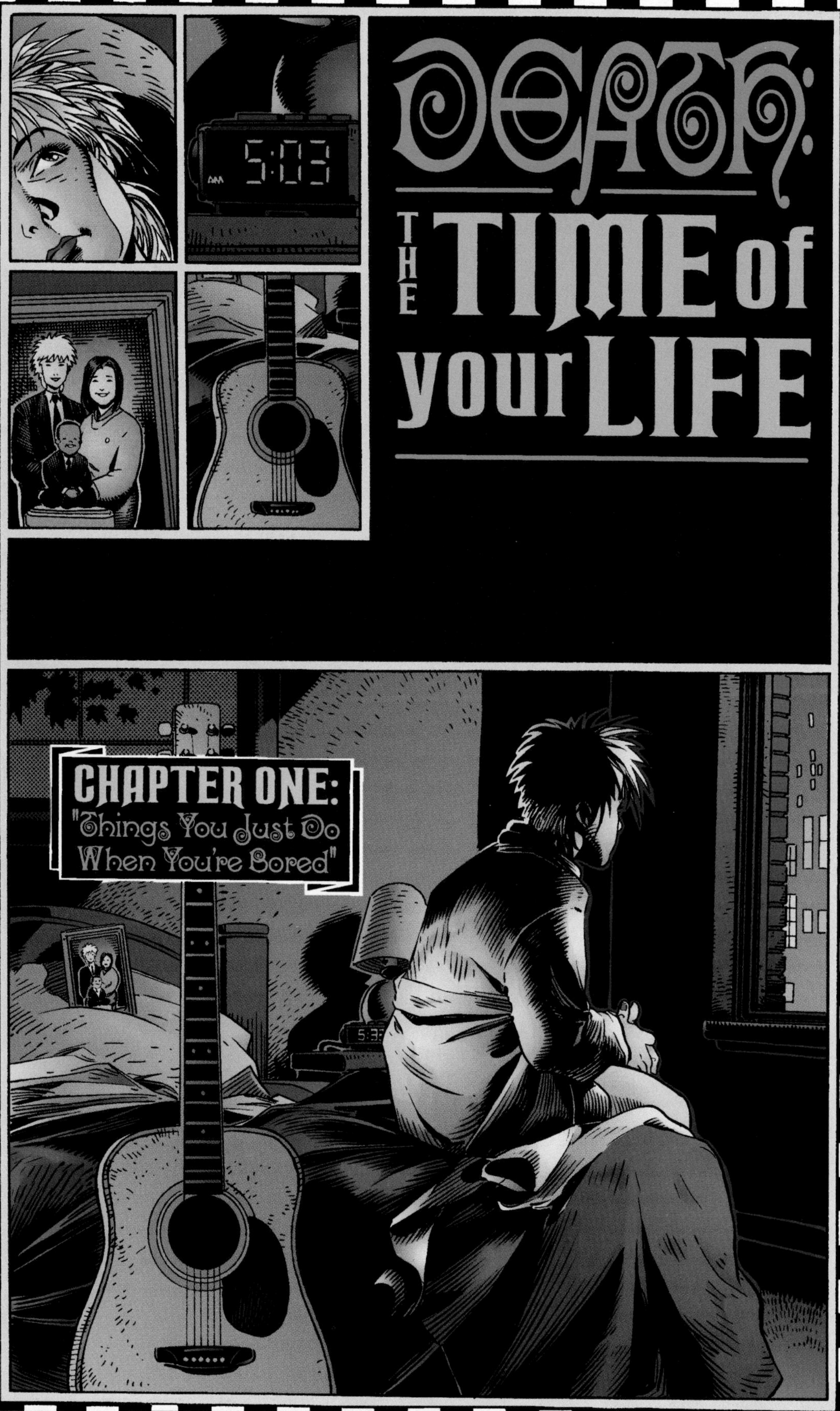
5:03
AM
DEATH:
THE TIME of your LIFE
CHAPTER ONE:
"Things You Just Do When You're Bored"

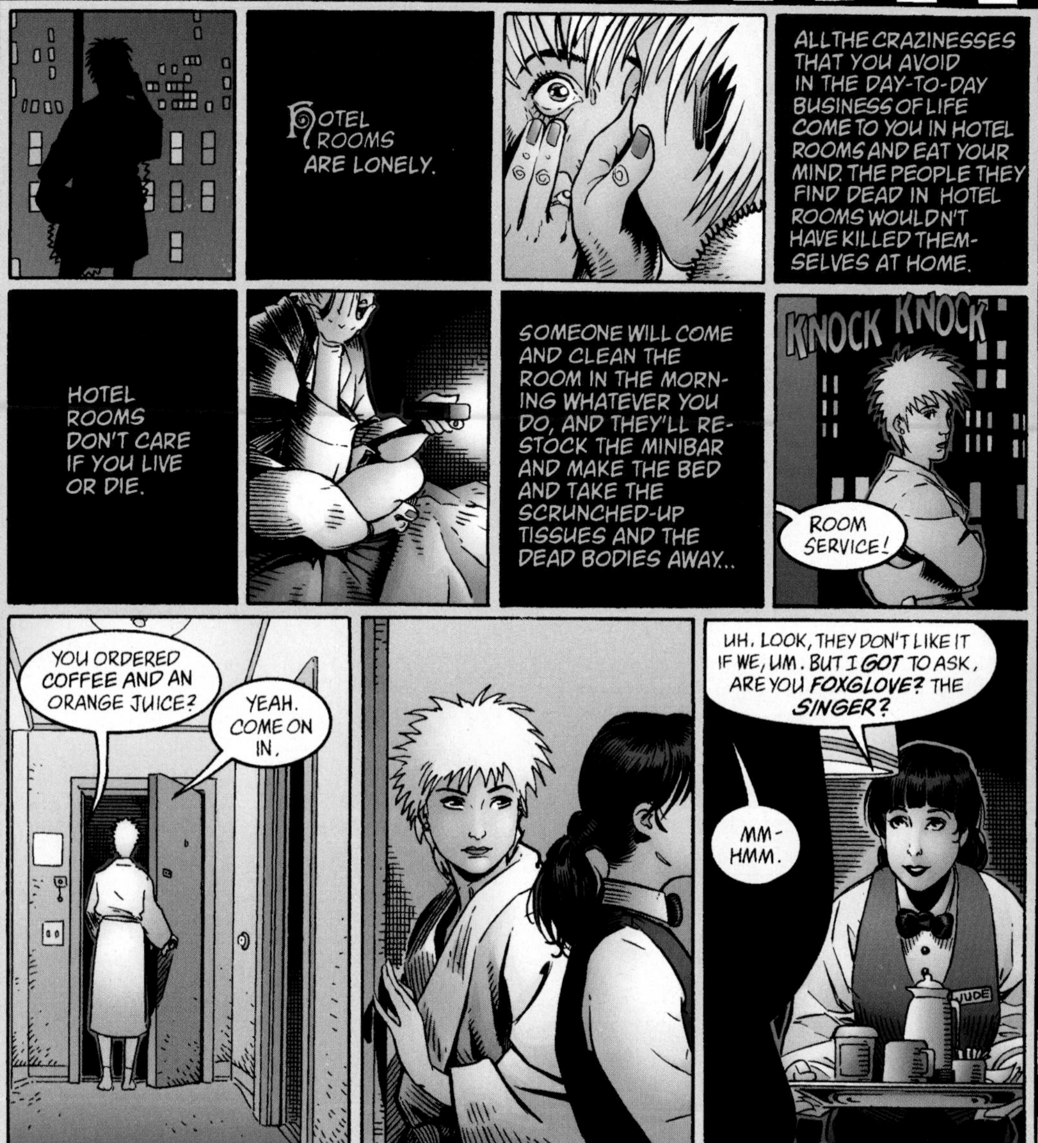
HOTEL ROOMS ARE LONELY.
ALL THE CRAZINESSES THAT YOU AVOID IN THE DAY-TO-DAY BUSINESS OF LIFE COME TO YOU IN HOTEL ROOMS AND EAT YOUR MIND. THE PEOPLE THEY FIND DEAD IN HOTEL ROOMS WOULDN'T HAVE KILLED THEMSELVES AT HOME.
HOTEL ROOMS DON'T CARE IF YOU LIVE OR DIE.
SOMEONE WILL COME AND CLEAN THE ROOM IN THE MORNING WHATEVER YOU DO, AND THEY'LL RESTOCK THE MINIBAR AND MAKE THE BED AND TAKE THE SCRUNCHED-UP TISSUES AND THE DEAD BODIES AWAY...
KNOCK KNOCK
ROOM SERVICE!
YOU ORDERED COFFEE AND AN ORANGE JUICE?
YEAH. COME ON IN.
UH. LOOK, THEY DON'T LIKE IT IF WE, UM. BUT I GOT TO ASK, ARE YOU FOXGLOVE? THE SINGER?
MM-HMM.
JUDE
OH GOD. I CAN'T BELIEVE THIS. I'M MEETING YOU. PLEASE DON'T TELL ANYONE THAT I ASKED YOU IF YOU WERE YOU, I MEAN THEY'D FIRE ME OR SOMETHING.
I HAD TO ASK.
"THE POETRY INSPECTOR" WAS LIKE MY FAVORITE CD OF THE WHOLE YEAR.
I JUST PLAYED IT AND PLAYED IT.
IT GAVE ME THE STRENGTH TO WALK OUT ON THIS GUY.
WHAT ARE YOU DOING IN NEW YORK? ARE YOU PLAYING ANYWHERE?
LETTERMAN TONIGHT.
I'LL WATCH. I'LL STAY UP AND WATCH. LISTEN, WILL YOU SIGN SOMETHING FOR ME?
WHAT'S YOUR NAME?
JUDE. LIKE 'HEY JUDE,' Y'KNOW?
AND THEN I SIGN A SECOND TIME, FOR THE ROOM SERVICE, AND SHE LEAVES.

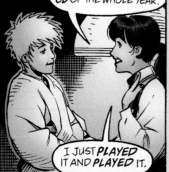

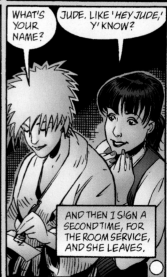

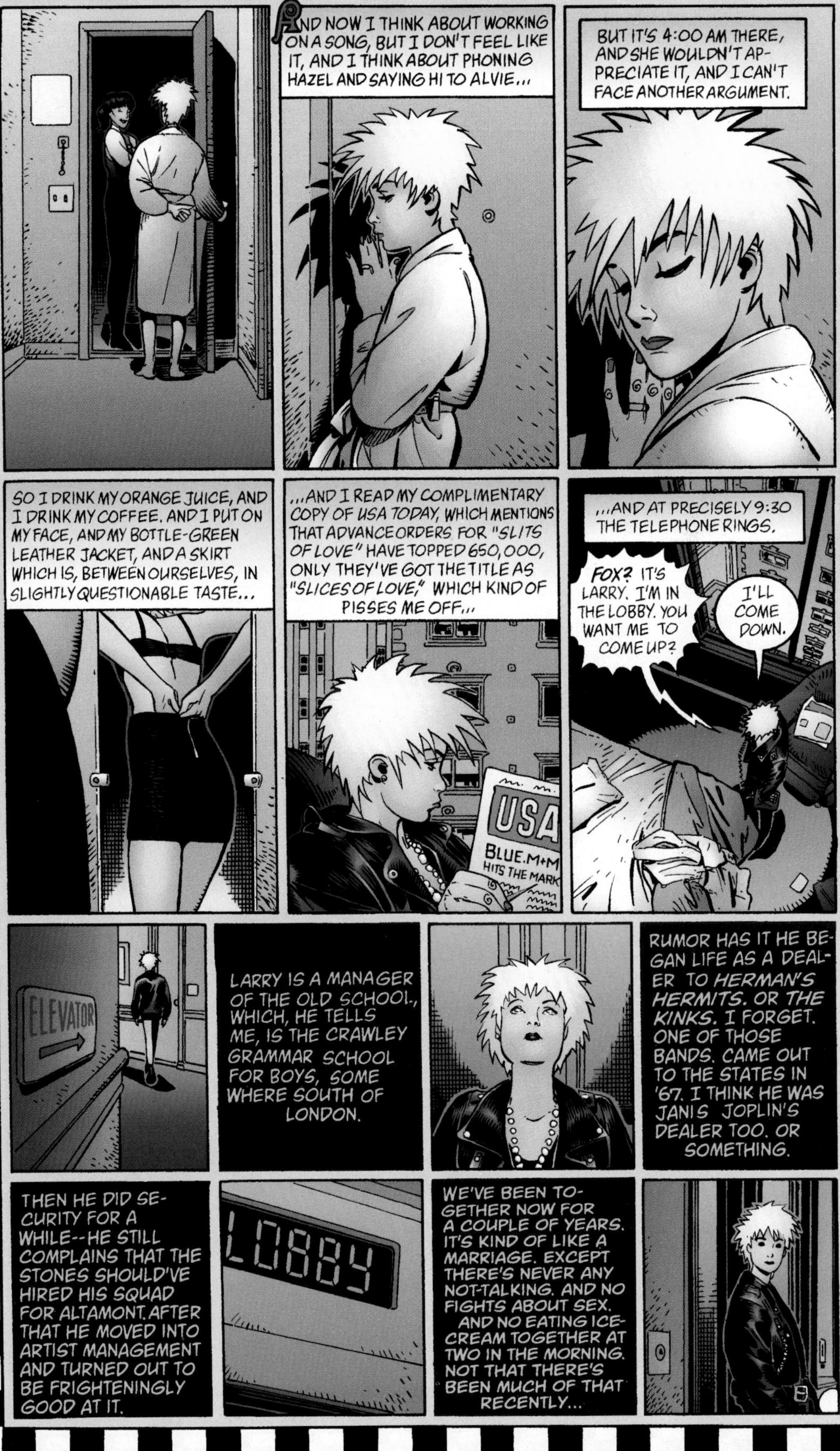
AND NOW I THINK ABOUT WORKING ON A SONG, BUT I DON'T FEEL LIKE IT, AND I THINK ABOUT PHONING HAZEL AND SAYING HI TO ALVIE...
BUT IT'S 4:00 AM THERE, AND SHE WOULDN'T APPRECIATE IT, AND I CAN'T FACE ANOTHER ARGUMENT.
SO I DRINK MY ORANGE JUICE, AND I DRINK MY COFFEE. AND I PUT ON MY FACE, AND MY BOTTLE-GREEN LEATHER JACKET, AND A SKIRT WHICH IS, BETWEEN OURSELVES, IN SLIGHTLY QUESTIONABLE TASTE...
...AND I READ MY COMPLIMENTARY COPY OF *USA TODAY*, WHICH MENTIONS THAT ADVANCE ORDERS FOR *"SLITS OF LOVE"* HAVE TOPPED 650,000, ONLY THEY'VE GOT THE TITLE AS *"SLICES OF LOVE,"* WHICH KIND OF PISSES ME OFF...
USA
BLUE.M+M
HITS THE MARK
...AND AT PRECISELY 9:30 THE TELEPHONE RINGS.
FOX? IT'S LARRY. I'M IN THE LOBBY. YOU WANT ME TO COME UP?
I'LL COME DOWN.
ELEVATOR
LARRY IS A MANAGER OF THE OLD SCHOOL., WHICH, HE TELLS ME, IS THE CRAWLEY GRAMMAR SCHOOL FOR BOYS, SOME WHERE SOUTH OF LONDON.
RUMOR HAS IT HE BEGAN LIFE AS A DEALER TO *HERMAN'S HERMITS*. OR *THE KINKS*. I FORGET. ONE OF THOSE BANDS. CAME OUT TO THE STATES IN '67. I THINK HE WAS JANIS JOPLIN'S DEALER TOO. OR SOMETHING.
THEN HE DID SECURITY FOR A WHILE--HE STILL COMPLAINS THAT THE STONES SHOULD'VE HIRED HIS SQUAD FOR ALTAMONT. AFTER THAT HE MOVED INTO ARTIST MANAGEMENT AND TURNED OUT TO BE FRIGHTENINGLY GOOD AT IT.
LOBBY
WE'VE BEEN TOGETHER NOW FOR A COUPLE OF YEARS. IT'S KIND OF LIKE A MARRIAGE. EXCEPT THERE'S NEVER ANY NOT-TALKING. AND NO FIGHTS ABOUT SEX.
AND NO EATING ICE-CREAM TOGETHER AT TWO IN THE MORNING. NOT THAT THERE'S BEEN MUCH OF THAT RECENTLY...

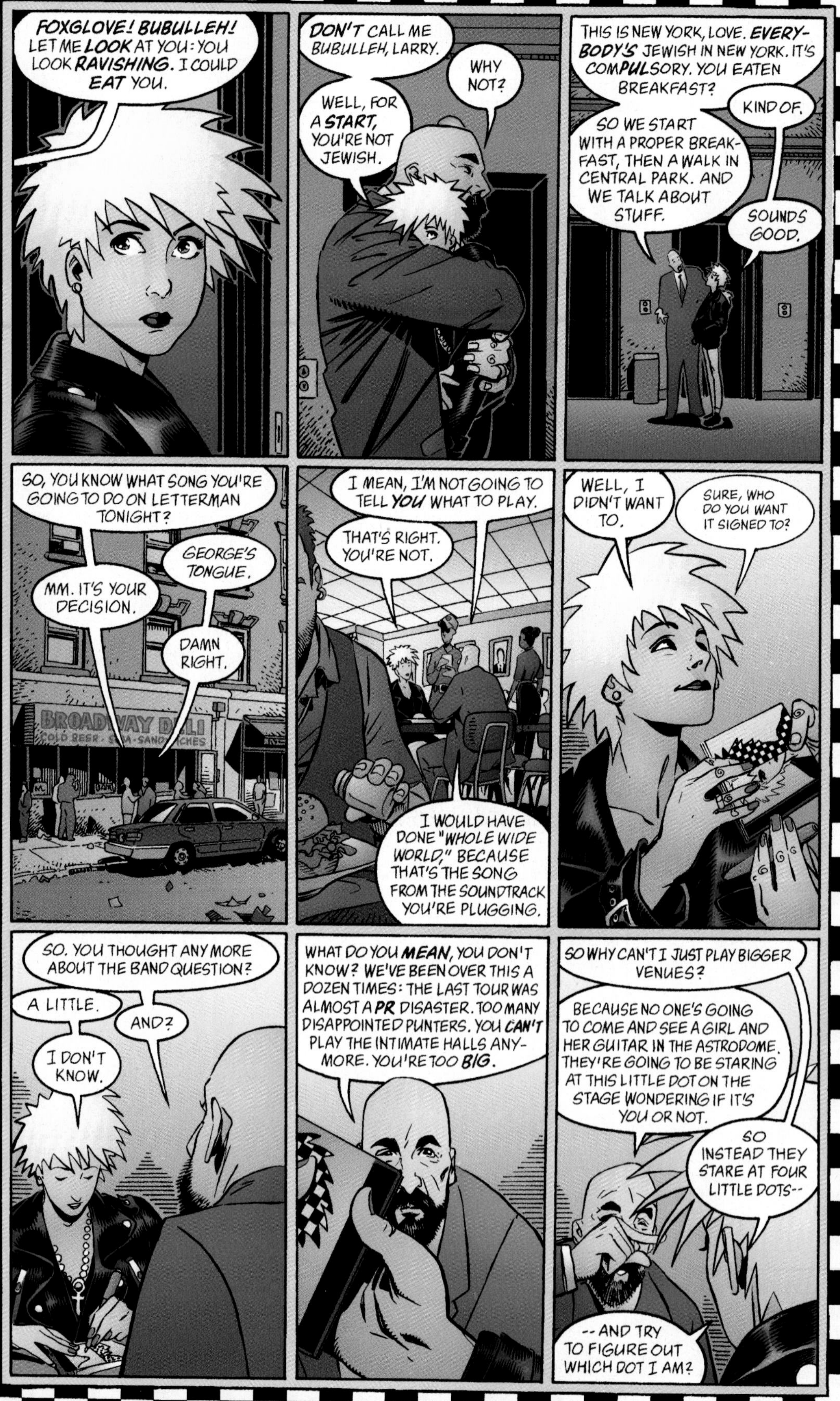
FOXGLOVE! BUBULLEH! LET ME LOOK AT YOU: YOU LOOK RAVISHING. I COULD EAT YOU.
DON'T CALL ME BUBULLEH, LARRY.
WHY NOT?
WELL, FOR A START, YOU'RE NOT JEWISH.
THIS IS NEW YORK, LOVE. EVERYBODY'S JEWISH IN NEW YORK. IT'S COMPULSORY. YOU EATEN BREAKFAST?
KIND OF.
SO WE START WITH A PROPER BREAKFAST, THEN A WALK IN CENTRAL PARK. AND WE TALK ABOUT STUFF.
SOUNDS GOOD.
SO, YOU KNOW WHAT SONG YOU'RE GOING TO DO ON LETTERMAN TONIGHT?
GEORGE'S TONGUE.
MM. IT'S YOUR DECISION.
DAMN RIGHT.
BROADWAY DELI
COLD BEER · SODA · SANDWICHES
I MEAN, I'M NOT GOING TO TELL YOU WHAT TO PLAY.
THAT'S RIGHT. YOU'RE NOT.
I WOULD HAVE DONE "WHOLE WIDE WORLD," BECAUSE THAT'S THE SONG FROM THE SOUNDTRACK YOU'RE PLUGGING.
WELL, I DIDN'T WANT TO.
SURE, WHO DO YOU WANT IT SIGNED TO?
SO. YOU THOUGHT ANY MORE ABOUT THE BAND QUESTION?
A LITTLE.
AND?
I DON'T KNOW.
WHAT DO YOU MEAN, YOU DON'T KNOW? WE'VE BEEN OVER THIS A DOZEN TIMES: THE LAST TOUR WAS ALMOST A PR DISASTER. TOO MANY DISAPPOINTED PUNTERS. YOU CAN'T PLAY THE INTIMATE HALLS ANYMORE. YOU'RE TOO BIG.
SO WHY CAN'T I JUST PLAY BIGGER VENUES?
BECAUSE NO ONE'S GOING TO COME AND SEE A GIRL AND HER GUITAR IN THE ASTRODOME. THEY'RE GOING TO BE STARING AT THIS LITTLE DOT ON THE STAGE WONDERING IF IT'S YOU OR NOT.
SO INSTEAD THEY STARE AT FOUR LITTLE DOTS--
--AND TRY TO FIGURE OUT WHICH DOT I AM?

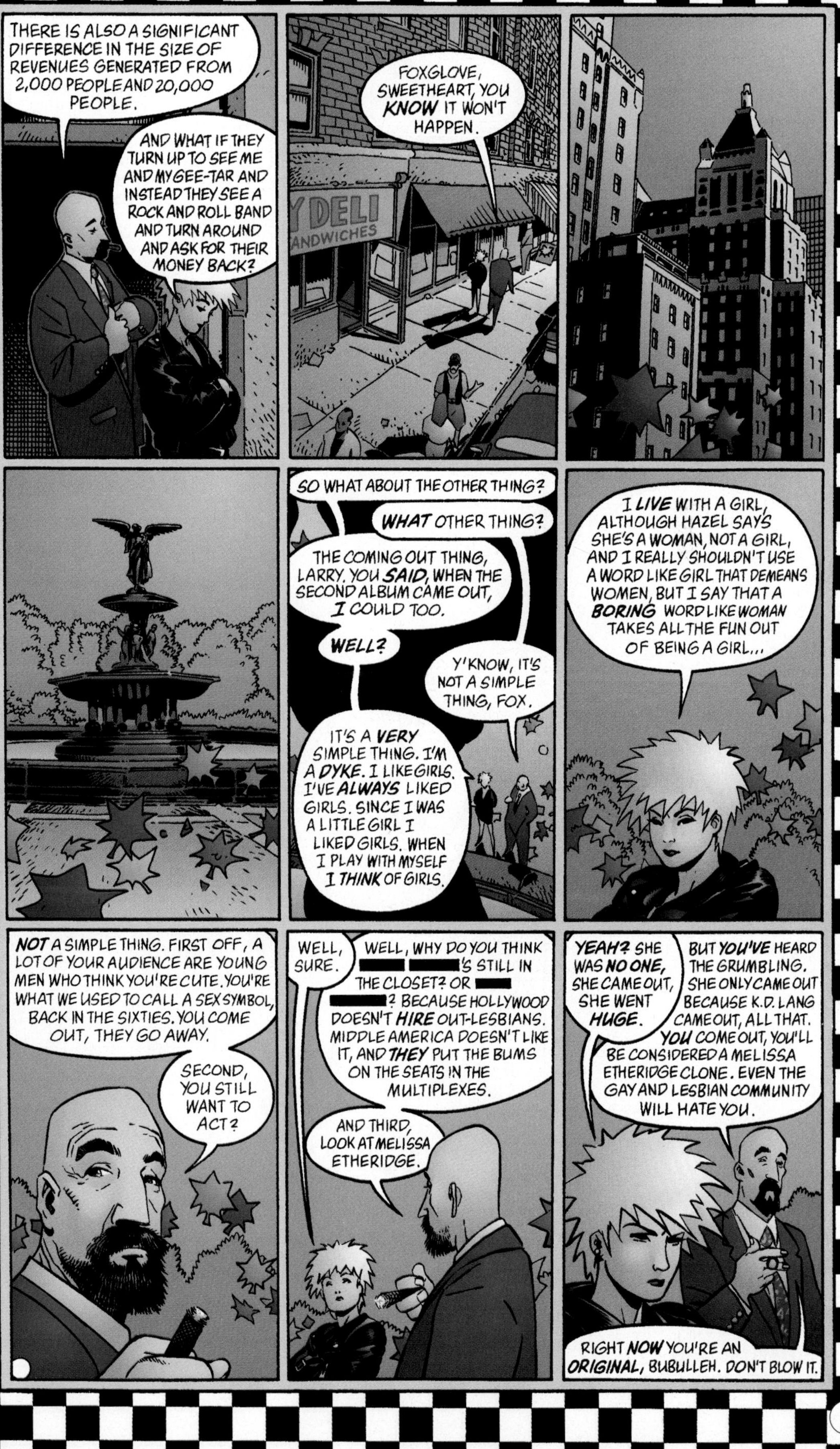
THERE IS ALSO A SIGNIFICANT DIFFERENCE IN THE SIZE OF REVENUES GENERATED FROM 2,000 PEOPLE AND 20,000 PEOPLE.
AND WHAT IF THEY TURN UP TO SEE ME AND MY GEE-TAR AND INSTEAD THEY SEE A ROCK AND ROLL BAND AND TURN AROUND AND ASK FOR THEIR MONEY BACK?
FOXGLOVE, SWEETHEART, YOU KNOW IT WON'T HAPPEN.
DELI
SANDWICHES
SO WHAT ABOUT THE OTHER THING?
WHAT OTHER THING?
THE COMING OUT THING, LARRY. YOU SAID, WHEN THE SECOND ALBUM CAME OUT, I COULD TOO.
WELL?
Y'KNOW, IT'S NOT A SIMPLE THING, FOX.
IT'S A VERY SIMPLE THING. I'M A DYKE. I LIKE GIRLS. I'VE ALWAYS LIKED GIRLS. SINCE I WAS A LITTLE GIRL I LIKED GIRLS. WHEN I PLAY WITH MYSELF I THINK OF GIRLS.
I LIVE WITH A GIRL, ALTHOUGH HAZEL SAYS SHE'S A WOMAN, NOT A GIRL, AND I REALLY SHOULDN'T USE A WORD LIKE GIRL THAT DEMEANS WOMEN, BUT I SAY THAT A BORING WORD LIKE WOMAN TAKES ALL THE FUN OUT OF BEING A GIRL...
NOT A SIMPLE THING. FIRST OFF, A LOT OF YOUR AUDIENCE ARE YOUNG MEN WHO THINK YOU'RE CUTE. YOU'RE WHAT WE USED TO CALL A SEX SYMBOL, BACK IN THE SIXTIES. YOU COME OUT, THEY GO AWAY.
SECOND, YOU STILL WANT TO ACT?
WELL, SURE.
WELL, WHY DO YOU THINK [redacted]'S STILL IN THE CLOSET? OR [redacted]? BECAUSE HOLLYWOOD DOESN'T HIRE OUT-LESBIANS. MIDDLE AMERICA DOESN'T LIKE IT, AND THEY PUT THE BUMS ON THE SEATS IN THE MULTIPLEXES.
AND THIRD, LOOK AT MELISSA ETHERIDGE.
YEAH? SHE WAS NO ONE, SHE CAME OUT, SHE WENT HUGE.
BUT YOU'VE HEARD THE GRUMBLING. SHE ONLY CAME OUT BECAUSE K.D. LANG CAME OUT, ALL THAT. YOU COME OUT, YOU'LL BE CONSIDERED A MELISSA ETHERIDGE CLONE. EVEN THE GAY AND LESBIAN COMMUNITY WILL HATE YOU.
RIGHT NOW YOU'RE AN ORIGINAL, BUBULLEH. DON'T BLOW IT.

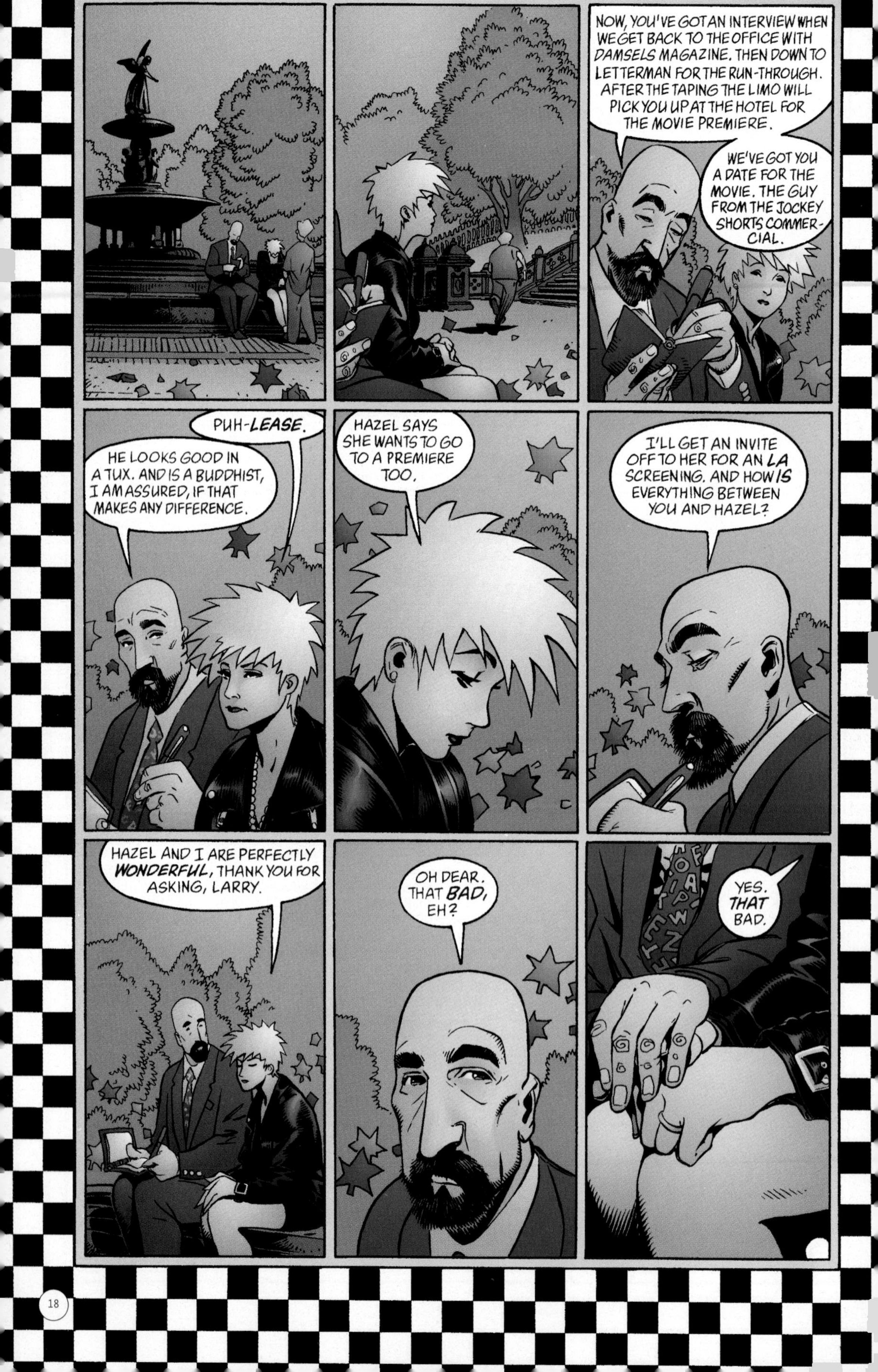

NOW, YOU'VE GOT AN INTERVIEW WHEN WE GET BACK TO THE OFFICE WITH DAMSELS MAGAZINE. THEN DOWN TO LETTERMAN FOR THE RUN-THROUGH. AFTER THE TAPING THE LIMO WILL PICK YOU UP AT THE HOTEL FOR THE MOVIE PREMIERE.
WE'VE GOT YOU A DATE FOR THE MOVIE. THE GUY FROM THE JOCKEY SHORTS COMMERCIAL.
PUH-LEASE.
HE LOOKS GOOD IN A TUX. AND IS A BUDDHIST, I AM ASSURED, IF THAT MAKES ANY DIFFERENCE.
HAZEL SAYS SHE WANTS TO GO TO A PREMIERE TOO.
I'LL GET AN INVITE OFF TO HER FOR AN LA SCREENING. AND HOW IS EVERYTHING BETWEEN YOU AND HAZEL?
HAZEL AND I ARE PERFECTLY WONDERFUL, THANK YOU FOR ASKING, LARRY.
OH DEAR. THAT BAD, EH?
YES. THAT BAD.

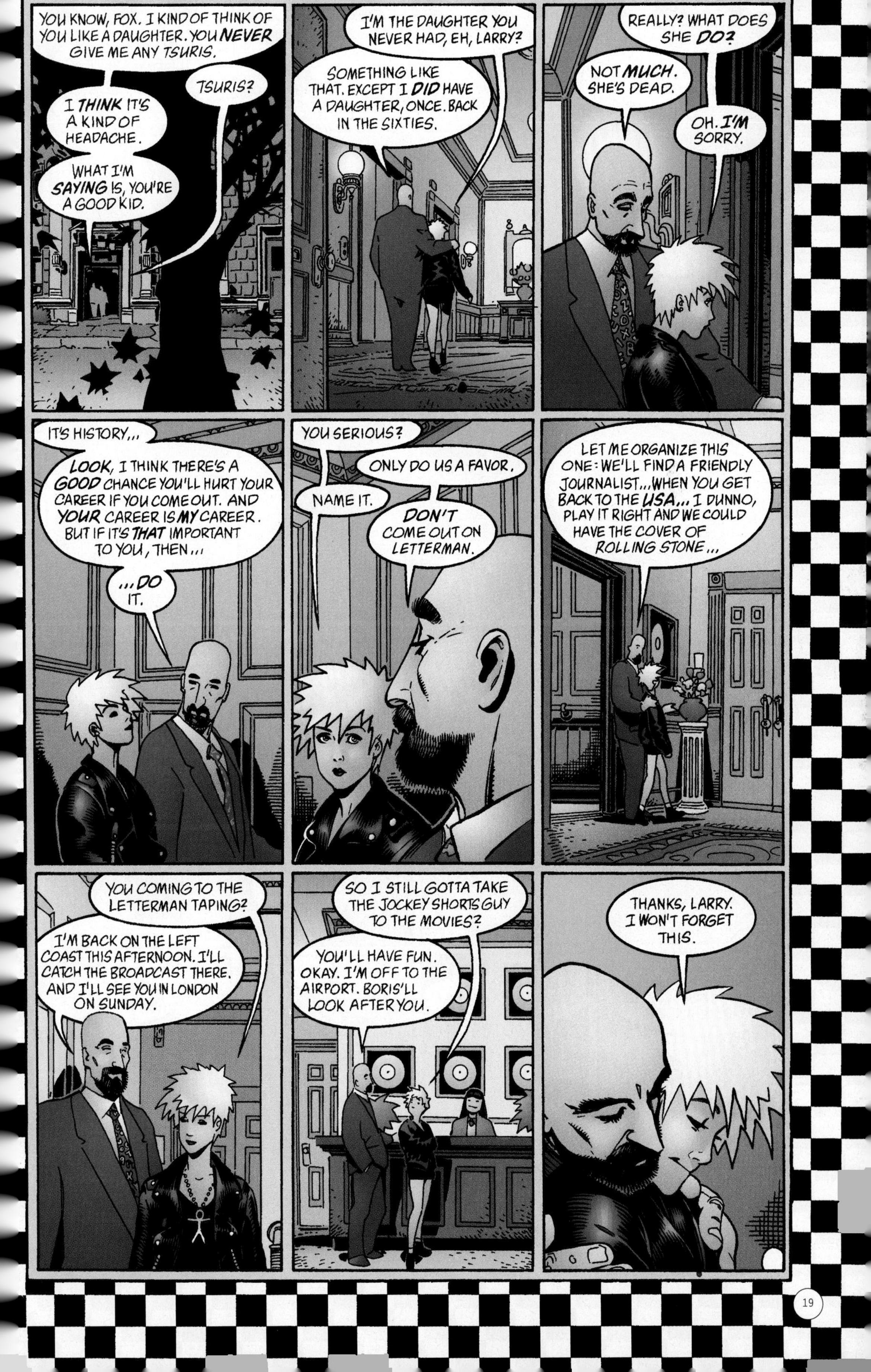
YOU KNOW, FOX. I KIND OF THINK OF YOU LIKE A DAUGHTER. YOU NEVER GIVE ME ANY TSURIS.
TSURIS?
I THINK IT'S A KIND OF HEADACHE.
WHAT I'M SAYING IS, YOU'RE A GOOD KID.
I'M THE DAUGHTER YOU NEVER HAD, EH, LARRY?
SOMETHING LIKE THAT. EXCEPT I DID HAVE A DAUGHTER, ONCE. BACK IN THE SIXTIES.
REALLY? WHAT DOES SHE DO?
NOT MUCH. SHE'S DEAD.
OH. I'M SORRY.
IT'S HISTORY...
LOOK, I THINK THERE'S A GOOD CHANCE YOU'LL HURT YOUR CAREER IF YOU COME OUT. AND YOUR CAREER IS MY CAREER. BUT IF IT'S THAT IMPORTANT TO YOU, THEN...
...DO IT.
YOU SERIOUS?
ONLY DO US A FAVOR.
NAME IT.
DON'T COME OUT ON LETTERMAN.
LET ME ORGANIZE THIS ONE: WE'LL FIND A FRIENDLY JOURNALIST... WHEN YOU GET BACK TO THE USA... I DUNNO, PLAY IT RIGHT AND WE COULD HAVE THE COVER OF ROLLING STONE...
YOU COMING TO THE LETTERMAN TAPING?
I'M BACK ON THE LEFT COAST THIS AFTERNOON. I'LL CATCH THE BROADCAST THERE. AND I'LL SEE YOU IN LONDON ON SUNDAY.
SO I STILL GOTTA TAKE THE JOCKEY SHORTS GUY TO THE MOVIES?
YOU'LL HAVE FUN. OKAY. I'M OFF TO THE AIRPORT. BORIS'LL LOOK AFTER YOU.
THANKS, LARRY. I WON'T FORGET THIS.

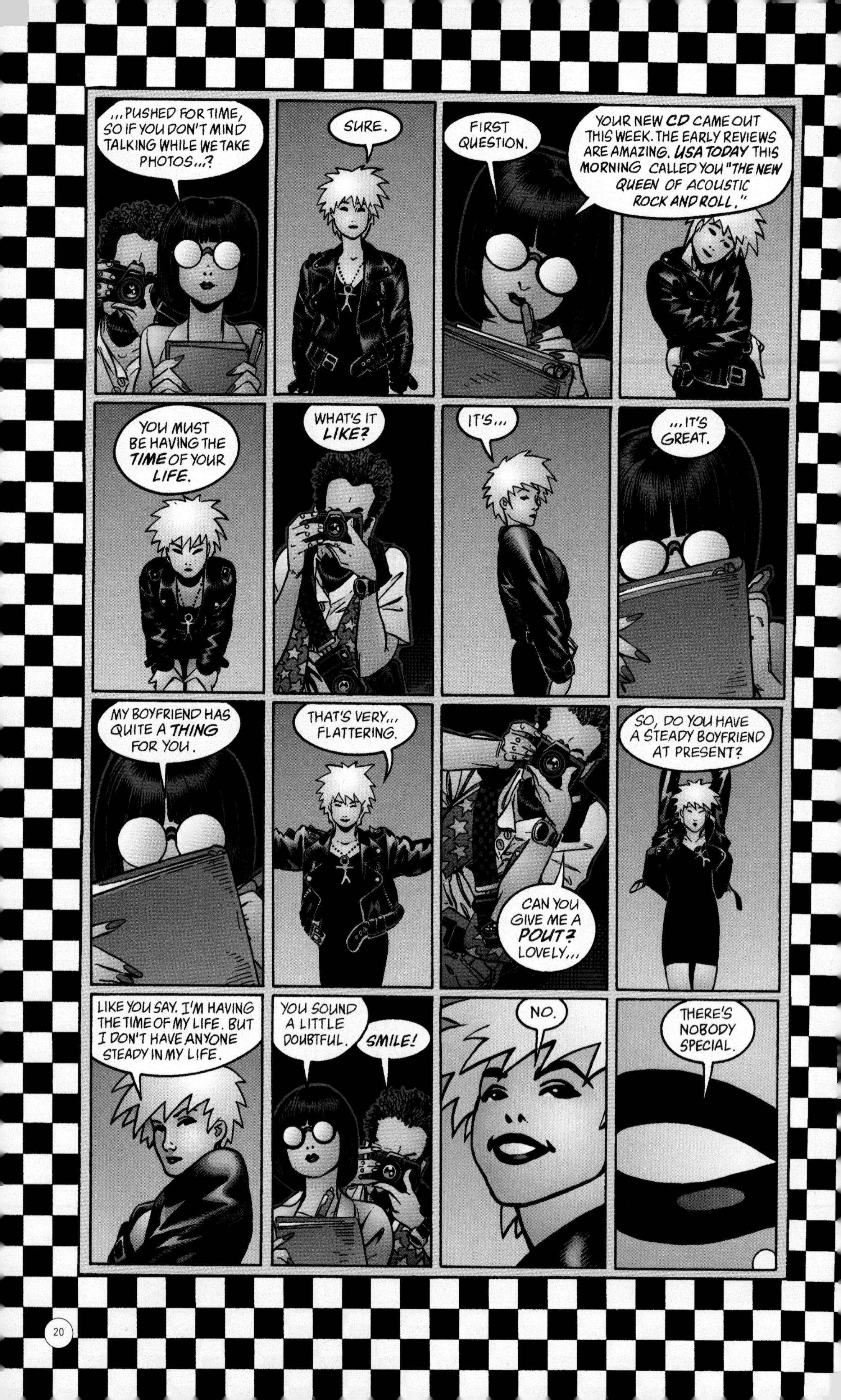
...PUSHED FOR TIME, SO IF YOU DON'T MIND TALKING WHILE WE TAKE PHOTOS...?
SURE.
FIRST QUESTION.
YOUR NEW CD CAME OUT THIS WEEK. THE EARLY REVIEWS ARE AMAZING. USA TODAY THIS MORNING CALLED YOU "THE NEW QUEEN OF ACOUSTIC ROCK AND ROLL."
YOU MUST BE HAVING THE TIME OF YOUR LIFE.
WHAT'S IT LIKE?
IT'S...
...IT'S GREAT.
MY BOYFRIEND HAS QUITE A THING FOR YOU.
THAT'S VERY... FLATTERING.
CAN YOU GIVE ME A POUT? LOVELY...
SO, DO YOU HAVE A STEADY BOYFRIEND AT PRESENT?
LIKE YOU SAY. I'M HAVING THE TIME OF MY LIFE. BUT I DON'T HAVE ANYONE STEADY IN MY LIFE.
YOU SOUND A LITTLE DOUBTFUL.
SMILE!
NO.
THERE'S NOBODY SPECIAL.

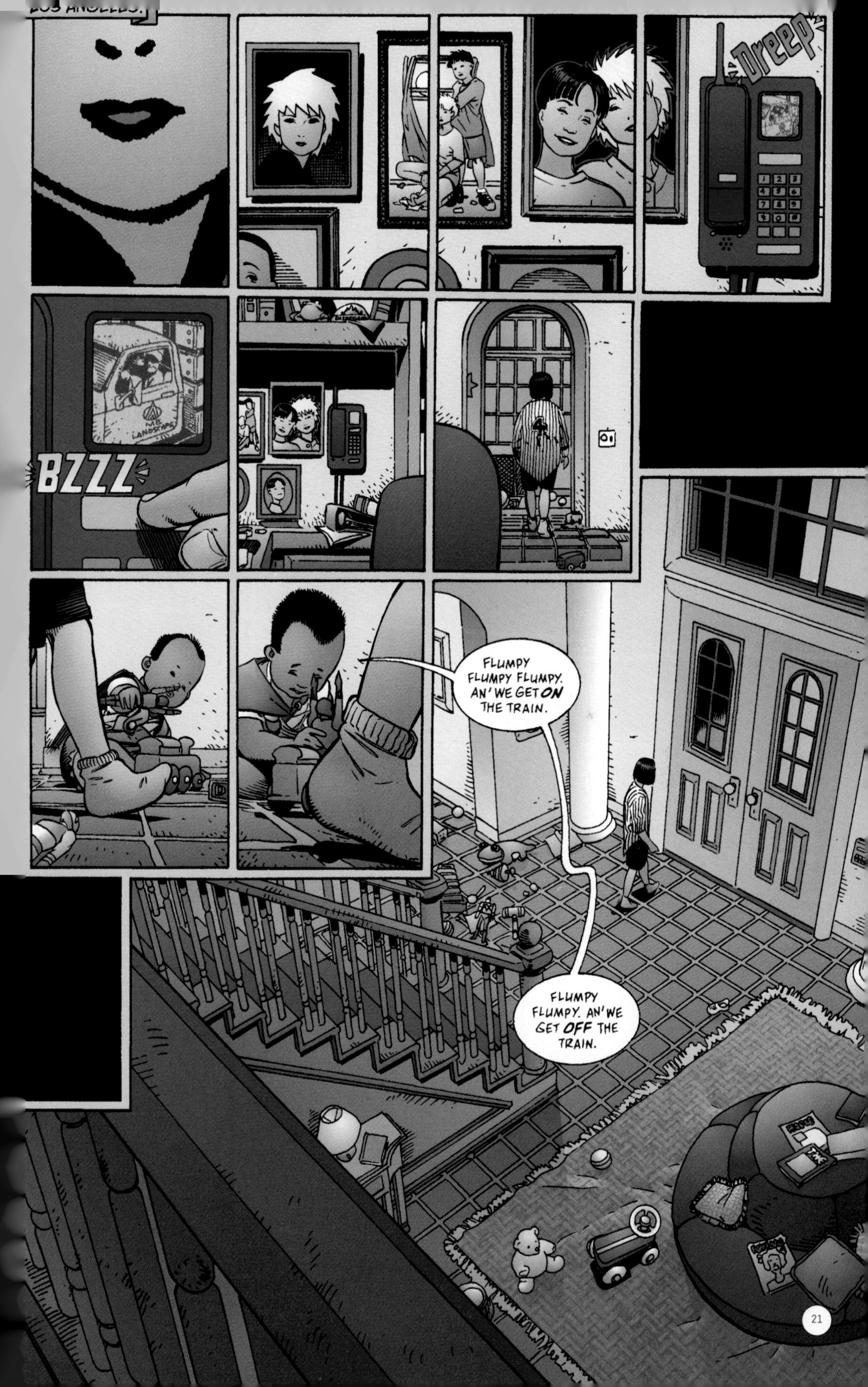
LOS ANGELES.
DREEP
BZZZ
FLUMPY FLUMPY FLUMPY. AN' WE GET ON THE TRAIN.
FLUMPY FLUMPY. AN' WE GET OFF THE TRAIN.

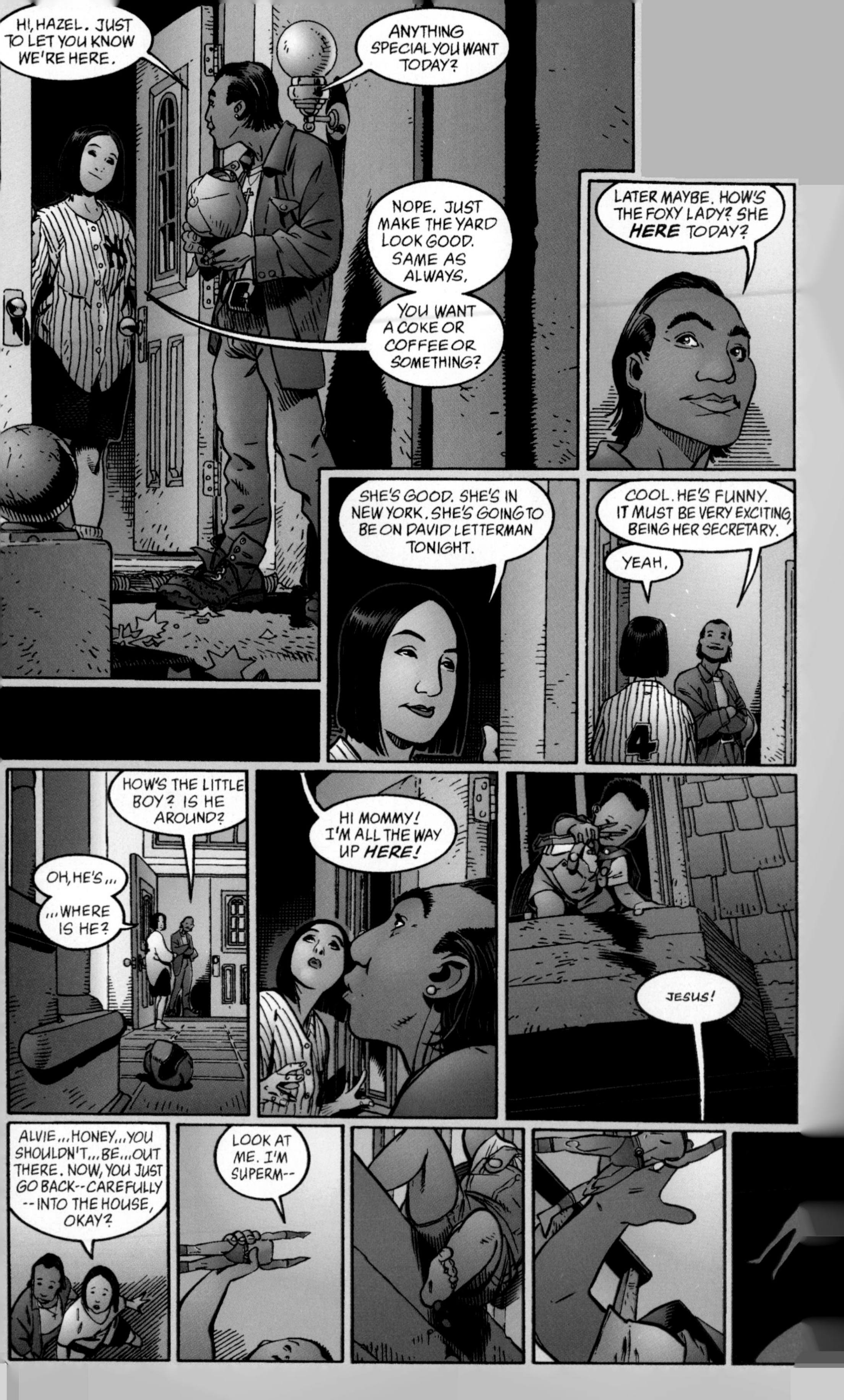
HI, HAZEL. JUST TO LET YOU KNOW WE'RE HERE.
ANYTHING SPECIAL YOU WANT TODAY?
NOPE. JUST MAKE THE YARD LOOK GOOD. SAME AS ALWAYS.
YOU WANT A COKE OR COFFEE OR SOMETHING?
LATER MAYBE. HOW'S THE FOXY LADY? SHE HERE TODAY?
SHE'S GOOD. SHE'S IN NEW YORK. SHE'S GOING TO BE ON DAVID LETTERMAN TONIGHT.
COOL. HE'S FUNNY. IT MUST BE VERY EXCITING, BEING HER SECRETARY.
YEAH.
HOW'S THE LITTLE BOY? IS HE AROUND?
OH, HE'S...
...WHERE IS HE?
HI MOMMY! I'M ALL THE WAY UP HERE!
JESUS!
ALVIE... HONEY... YOU SHOULDN'T... BE... OUT THERE. NOW, YOU JUST GO BACK--CAREFULLY --INTO THE HOUSE, OKAY?
LOOK AT ME. I'M SUPERM--

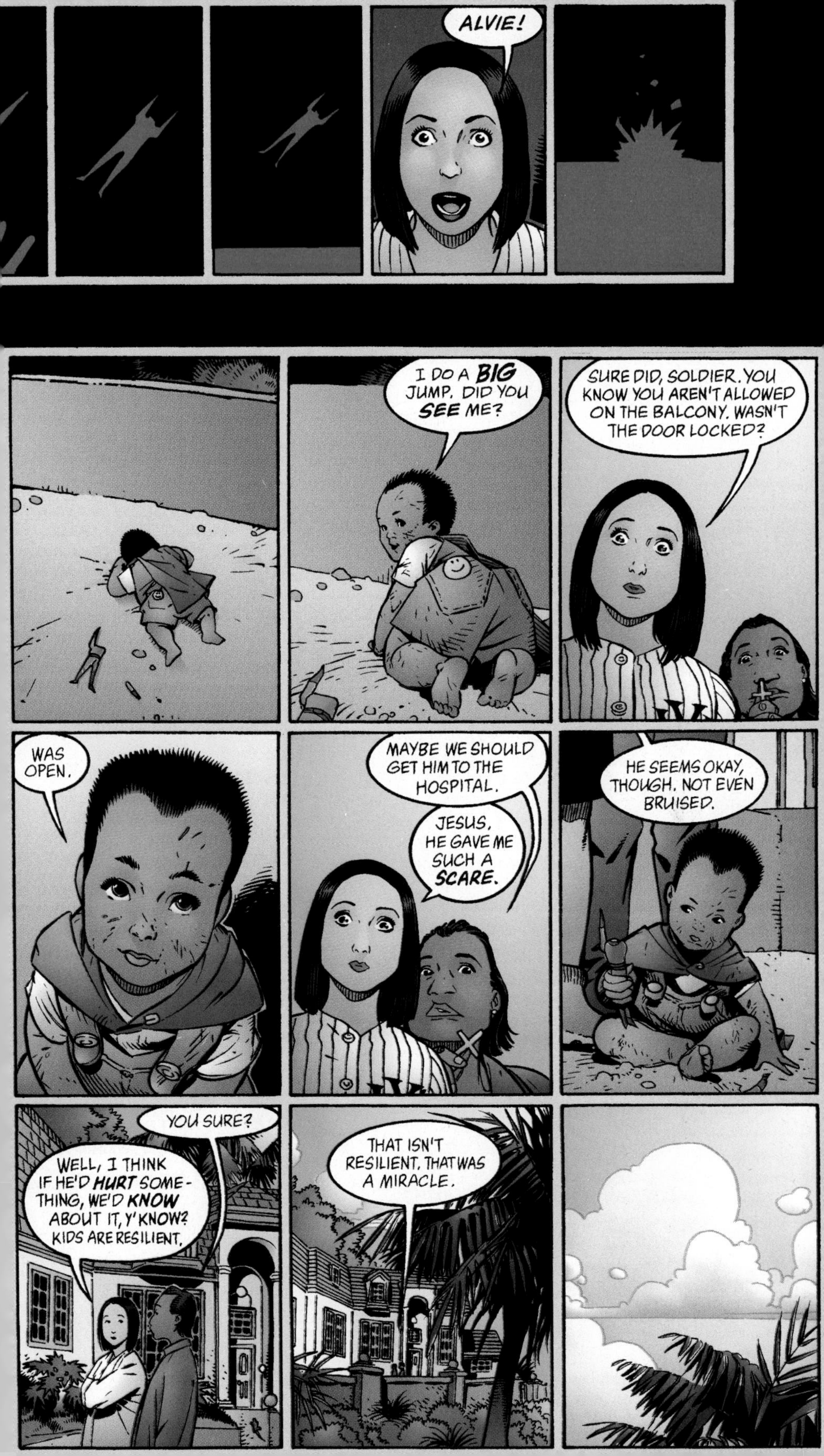
ALVIE!
I DO A BIG JUMP. DID YOU SEE ME?
SURE DID, SOLDIER. YOU KNOW YOU AREN'T ALLOWED ON THE BALCONY. WASN'T THE DOOR LOCKED?
WAS OPEN.
MAYBE WE SHOULD GET HIM TO THE HOSPITAL.
JESUS, HE GAVE ME SUCH A SCARE.
HE SEEMS OKAY, THOUGH. NOT EVEN BRUISED.
YOU SURE?
WELL, I THINK IF HE'D HURT SOME-THING, WE'D KNOW ABOUT IT, Y'KNOW? KIDS ARE RESILIENT.
THAT ISN'T RESILIENT. THAT WAS A MIRACLE.

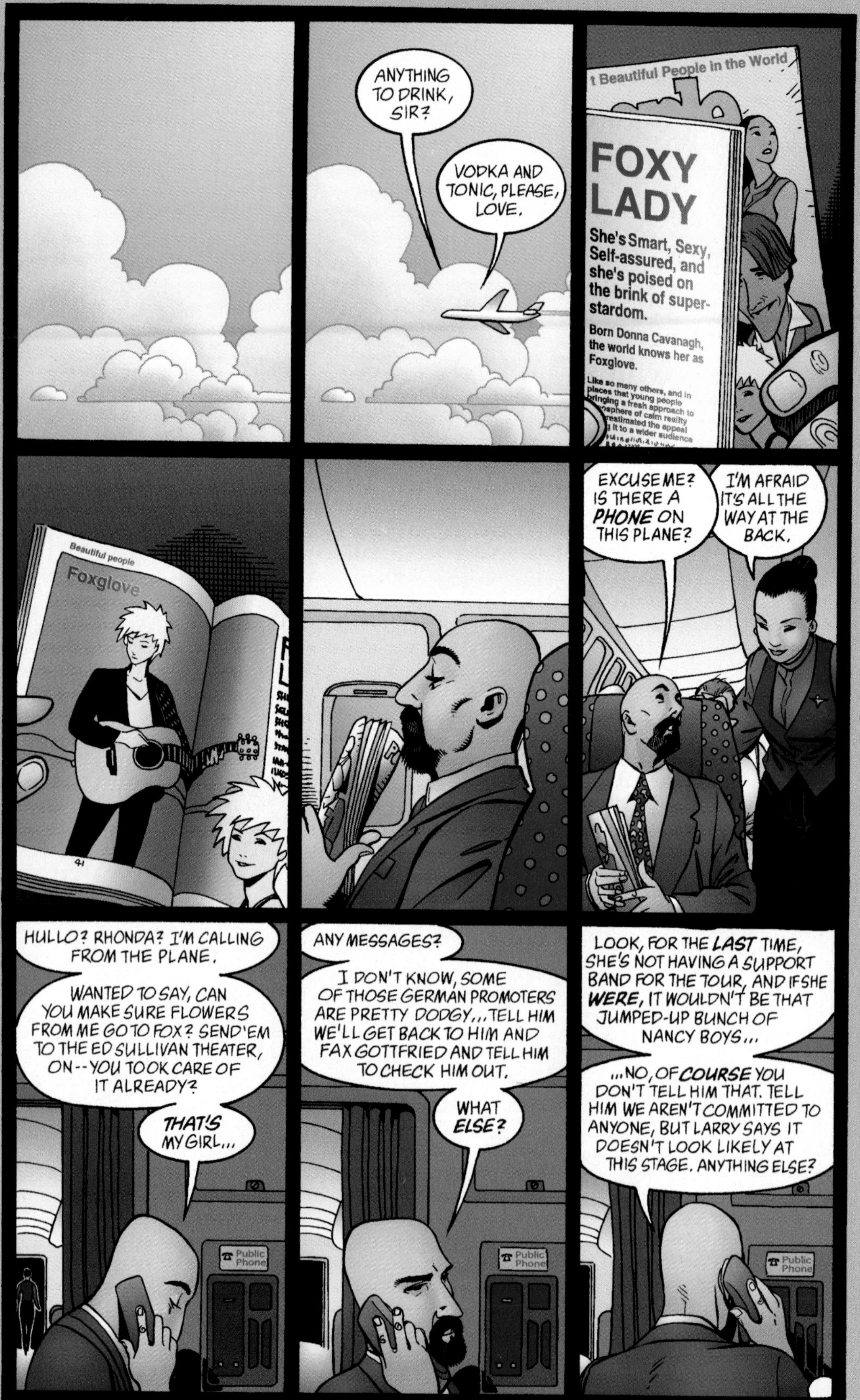

ANYTHING TO DRINK, SIR?
VODKA AND TONIC, PLEASE, LOVE.
t Beautiful People in the World
FOXY LADY
She's Smart, Sexy, Self-assured, and she's poised on the brink of super-stardom.
Born Donna Cavanagh, the world knows her as Foxglove.
Beautiful people
Foxglove
41
EXCUSE ME? IS THERE A *PHONE* ON THIS PLANE?
I'M AFRAID IT'S ALL THE WAY AT THE BACK.
HULLO? RHONDA? I'M CALLING FROM THE PLANE.
WANTED TO SAY, CAN YOU MAKE SURE FLOWERS FROM ME GO TO FOX? SEND 'EM TO THE ED SULLIVAN THEATER, ON-- YOU TOOK CARE OF IT ALREADY?
THAT'S MY GIRL...
Public Phone
ANY MESSAGES?
I DON'T KNOW, SOME OF THOSE GERMAN PROMOTERS ARE PRETTY DODGY... TELL HIM WE'LL GET BACK TO HIM AND FAX GOTTFRIED AND TELL HIM TO CHECK HIM OUT.
WHAT *ELSE*?
Public Phone
LOOK, FOR THE *LAST* TIME, SHE'S NOT HAVING A SUPPORT BAND FOR THE TOUR, AND IF SHE *WERE*, IT WOULDN'T BE THAT JUMPED-UP BUNCH OF NANCY BOYS...
...NO, OF *COURSE* YOU DON'T TELL HIM THAT. TELL HIM WE AREN'T COMMITTED TO ANYONE, BUT LARRY SAYS IT DOESN'T LOOK LIKELY AT THIS STAGE. ANYTHING ELSE?
Public Phone

NO,
I'M....

OW.

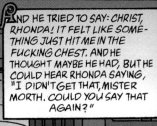

AND HE TRIED TO SAY: CHRIST, RHONDA! IT FELT LIKE SOMETHING JUST HIT ME IN THE FUCKING CHEST. AND HE THOUGHT MAYBE HE HAD, BUT HE COULD HEAR RHONDA SAYING, "I DIDN'T GET THAT, MISTER MORTH. COULD YOU SAY THAT AGAIN?"

AND THEN HE LET GO OF THE TELEPHONE AND SAT ON THE FLOOR, BECAUSE THAT WAS SUDDENLY THE ONLY SENSIBLE THING TO DO.

AND HE FOUND HIMSELF AMAZED BY HOW SOFT AND ENVELOPING THE FLOOR BY THE AEROPLANE TOILETS SEEMED TO BE.

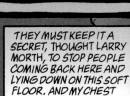

THEY MUST KEEP IT A SECRET, THOUGHT LARRY MORTH, TO STOP PEOPLE COMING BACK HERE AND LYING DOWN ON THIS SOFT FLOOR. AND MY CHEST STILL HURTS.

AND HE COULD HEAR A WOMAN SAYING, "IF THERE IS A MEDICAL DOCTOR ON BOARD THE PLANE, OR ANYONE WITH MEDICAL OR PARAMEDICAL EXPERIENCE, COULD THEY IDENTIFY THEMSELVES TO A MEMBER OF THE CABIN CREW?"

AND THE PAIN IN HIS CHEST WENT AWAY, SO, FOR A MOMENT, THERE WAS NOTHING BUT COMFORT AND WARMTH; AND THEN THERE WAS NOTHING AT ALL.

JUST A VOICE THAT SAID:

"LARRY?"

AND ANY WAY YOU LOOK YOU KNOW IT'S ON THE LEVEL

AND I DON'T CARE HOW IT APPEARS.

I'M NOT AFRAID OF THE WORLD, THE FLESH OR DEVIL

I'M JUST AFRAID OF NO MORE TEARS.

CAN YOU TURN MY MONITOR UP A BIT-- NO, THE GUITAR'S JUST FINE.

I NEVER THOUGHT THEY'D HAVE TO TEACH ME HOW TO WANT.

I THOUGHT THE PAIN WAS ALWAYS CLEAR.

I THOUGHT I'D BURN AND SCREAM AND NEVER BE FORGOTTEN.

I'VE LOST MY WAY AND FOUND MY FEAR.

WELL, YOU SLASH THROUGH THE CANVAS AND LITTLE SLITS OF LOVE SHINE THROUGH.

THAT'S WHAT GEORGE'S TONGUE SAID;

WELL YOU CAN DREAM IF YOU WANT BUT THE ONLY THING TO WAKE IS YOU.

THAT'S WHAT GEORGE'S TONGUE SAID.

I USED TO HATE THE WAY WE SHOUTED FOUGHT AND BICKERED,

NOW I'D BE GRATEFUL FOR A FIGHT.

YOU SAY NO WORDS AS THE TV BLUE LIGHT FLICKERED

AND TINY ACTORS SOB THEIR LINES INTO THE NIGHT.

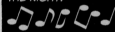

AND ANY WAY YOU LOOK YOU KNOW IT'S ON THE LEVEL,

AND I DON'T CARE HOW IT APPEARS.

I'M NOT AFRAID OF THE WORLD, THE FLESH OR DEVIL,

I'M JUST AFRAID OF NO MORE TEARS.

THAT'S WHAT GEORGE'S TONGUE SAID.

CLAP
CLAP
CLAP
CLAP

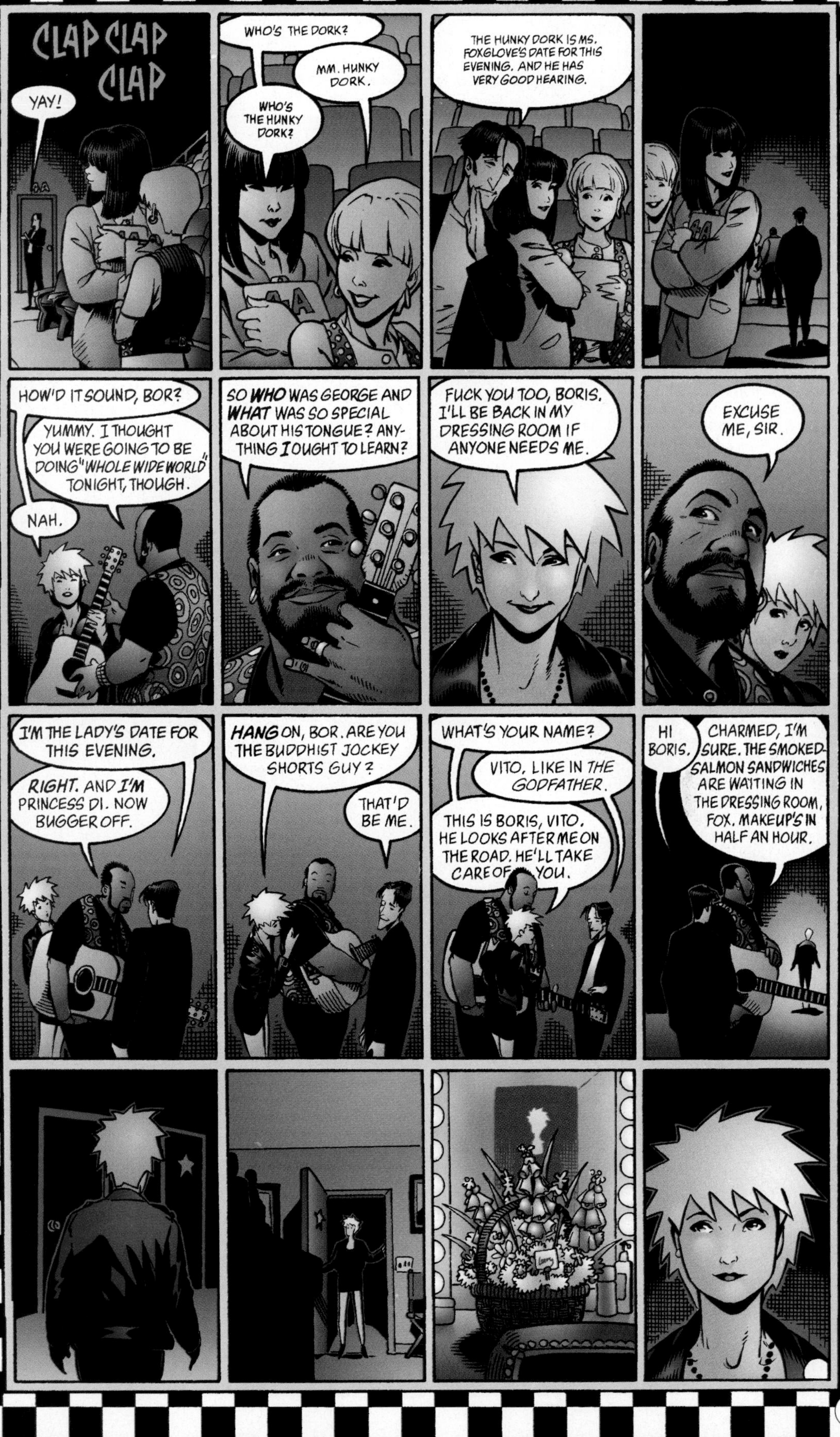
CLAP CLAP CLAP
YAY!
WHO'S THE DORK?
WHO'S THE HUNKY DORK?
MM. HUNKY DORK.
THE HUNKY DORK IS MS. FOXGLOVE'S DATE FOR THIS EVENING. AND HE HAS VERY GOOD HEARING.
HOW'D IT SOUND, BOR?
YUMMY. I THOUGHT YOU WERE GOING TO BE DOING "WHOLE WIDE WORLD" TONIGHT, THOUGH.
NAH.
SO WHO WAS GEORGE AND WHAT WAS SO SPECIAL ABOUT HIS TONGUE? ANYTHING I OUGHT TO LEARN?
FUCK YOU TOO, BORIS. I'LL BE BACK IN MY DRESSING ROOM IF ANYONE NEEDS ME.
EXCUSE ME, SIR.
I'M THE LADY'S DATE FOR THIS EVENING.
RIGHT. AND I'M PRINCESS DI. NOW BUGGER OFF.
HANG ON, BOR. ARE YOU THE BUDDHIST JOCKEY SHORTS GUY?
THAT'D BE ME.
WHAT'S YOUR NAME?
VITO. LIKE IN THE GODFATHER.
THIS IS BORIS, VITO. HE LOOKS AFTER ME ON THE ROAD. HE'LL TAKE CARE OF YOU.
HI BORIS.
CHARMED, I'M SURE. THE SMOKED-SALMON SANDWICHES ARE WAITING IN THE DRESSING ROOM, FOX. MAKEUP'S IN HALF AN HOUR.

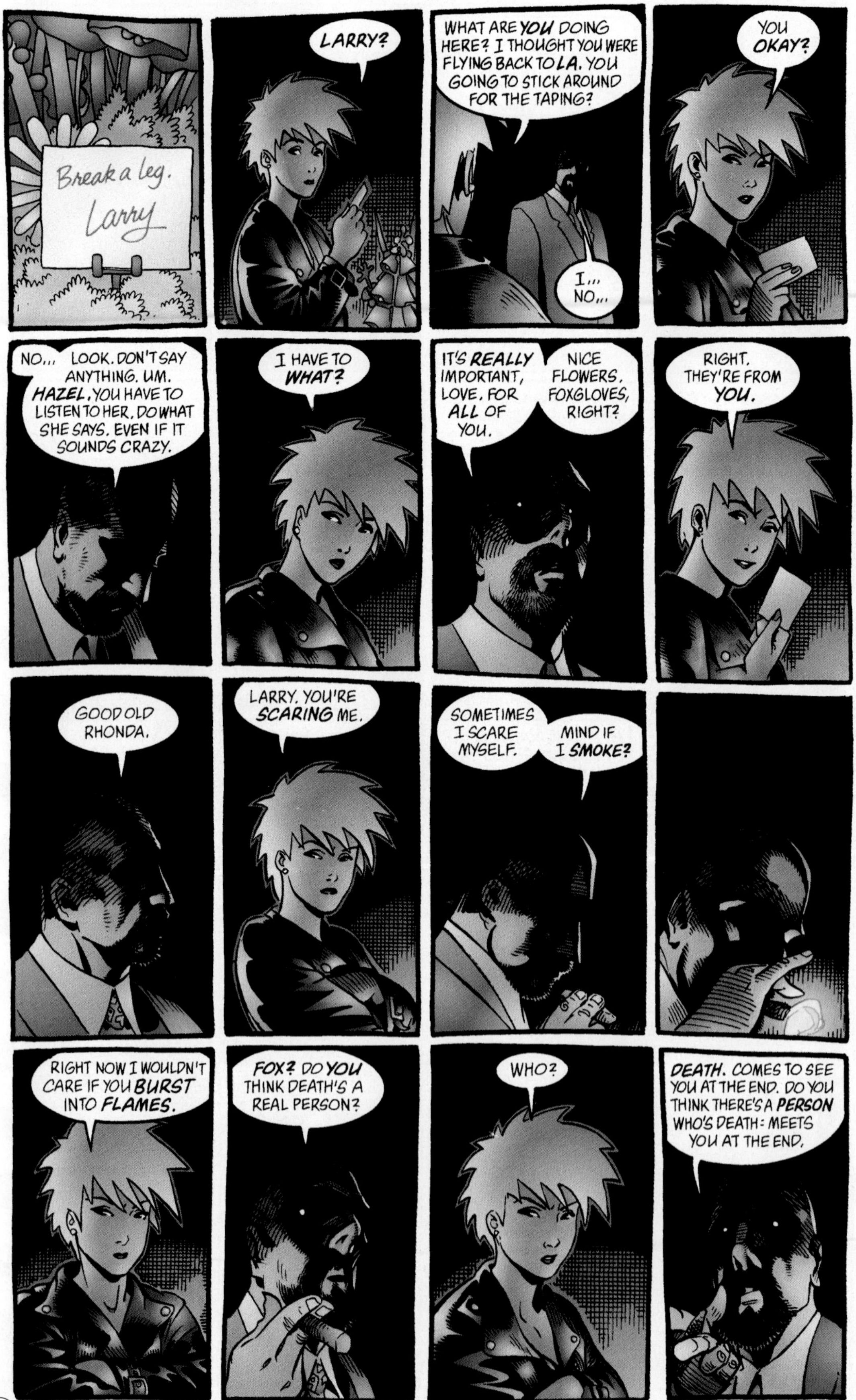
Break a leg.
Larry
LARRY?
WHAT ARE YOU DOING HERE? I THOUGHT YOU WERE FLYING BACK TO LA. YOU GOING TO STICK AROUND FOR THE TAPING?
I... NO...
YOU OKAY?
NO... LOOK. DON'T SAY ANYTHING. UM. HAZEL. YOU HAVE TO LISTEN TO HER, DO WHAT SHE SAYS. EVEN IF IT SOUNDS CRAZY.
I HAVE TO WHAT?
IT'S REALLY IMPORTANT, LOVE. FOR ALL OF YOU.
NICE FLOWERS. FOXGLOVES, RIGHT?
RIGHT. THEY'RE FROM YOU.
GOOD OLD RHONDA.
LARRY. YOU'RE SCARING ME.
SOMETIMES I SCARE MYSELF.
MIND IF I SMOKE?
RIGHT NOW I WOULDN'T CARE IF YOU BURST INTO FLAMES.
FOX? DO YOU THINK DEATH'S A REAL PERSON?
WHO?
DEATH. COMES TO SEE YOU AT THE END. DO YOU THINK THERE'S A PERSON WHO'S DEATH: MEETS YOU AT THE END.

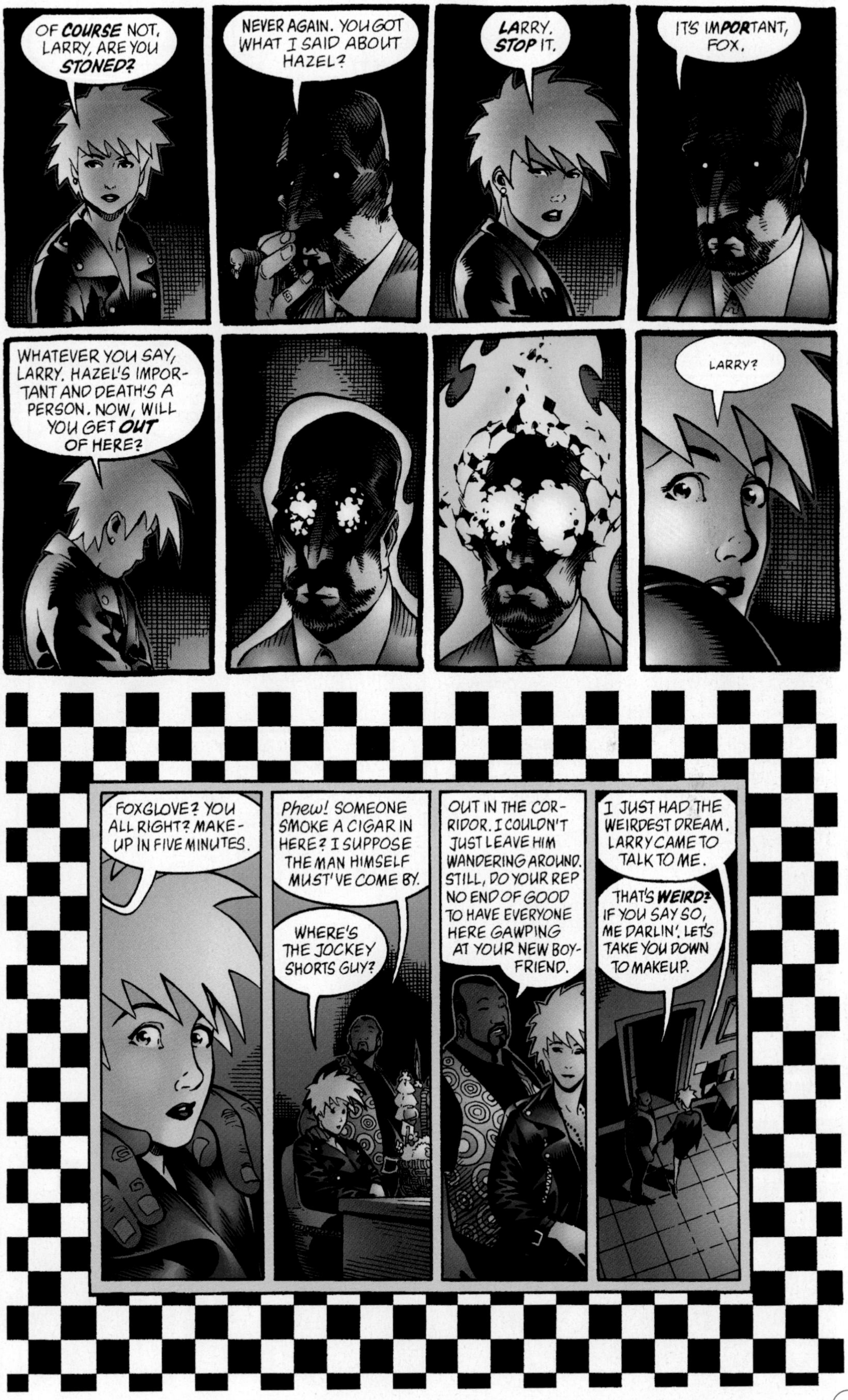

OF COURSE NOT. LARRY, ARE YOU STONED?
NEVER AGAIN. YOU GOT WHAT I SAID ABOUT HAZEL?
LARRY. STOP IT.
IT'S IMPORTANT, FOX.
WHATEVER YOU SAY, LARRY. HAZEL'S IMPORTANT AND DEATH'S A PERSON. NOW, WILL YOU GET OUT OF HERE?
LARRY?
FOXGLOVE? YOU ALL RIGHT? MAKE-UP IN FIVE MINUTES.
Phew! SOMEONE SMOKE A CIGAR IN HERE? I SUPPOSE THE MAN HIMSELF MUST'VE COME BY.
WHERE'S THE JOCKEY SHORTS GUY?
OUT IN THE CORRIDOR. I COULDN'T JUST LEAVE HIM WANDERING AROUND. STILL, DO YOUR REP NO END OF GOOD TO HAVE EVERYONE HERE GAWPING AT YOUR NEW BOYFRIEND.
I JUST HAD THE WEIRDEST DREAM. LARRY CAME TO TALK TO ME.
THAT'S WEIRD? IF YOU SAY SO, ME DARLIN'. LET'S TAKE YOU DOWN TO MAKEUP.

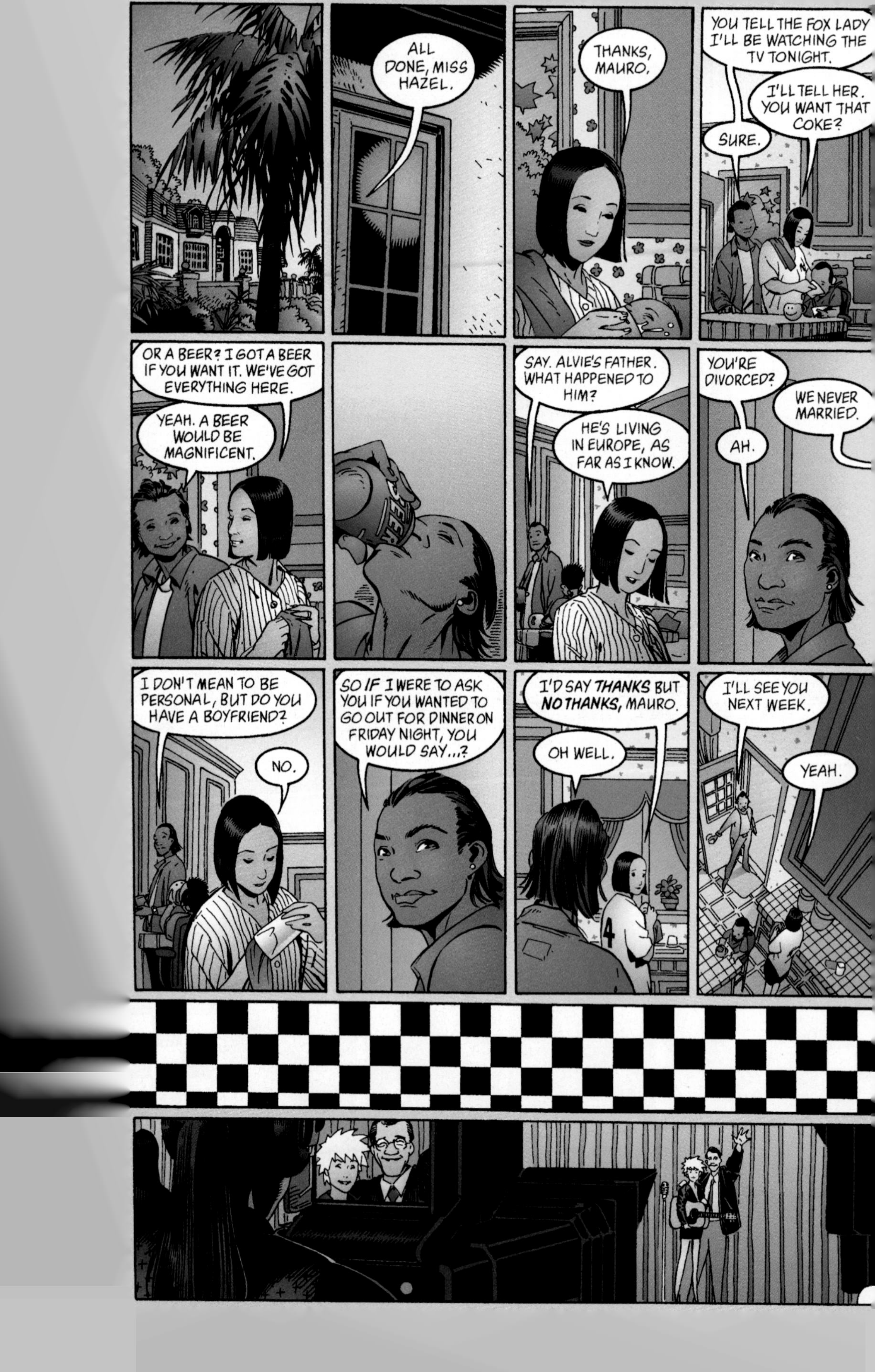
ALL DONE, MISS HAZEL.
THANKS, MAURO.
YOU TELL THE FOX LADY I'LL BE WATCHING THE TV TONIGHT.
I'LL TELL HER. YOU WANT THAT COKE?
SURE.
OR A BEER? I GOT A BEER IF YOU WANT IT. WE'VE GOT EVERYTHING HERE.
YEAH. A BEER WOULD BE MAGNIFICENT.
SAY. ALVIE'S FATHER. WHAT HAPPENED TO HIM?
HE'S LIVING IN EUROPE, AS FAR AS I KNOW.
YOU'RE DIVORCED?
WE NEVER MARRIED.
AH.
I DON'T MEAN TO BE PERSONAL, BUT DO YOU HAVE A BOYFRIEND?
NO.
SO IF I WERE TO ASK YOU IF YOU WANTED TO GO OUT FOR DINNER ON FRIDAY NIGHT, YOU WOULD SAY...?
I'D SAY THANKS BUT NO THANKS, MAURO.
OH WELL.
I'LL SEE YOU NEXT WEEK.
YEAH.

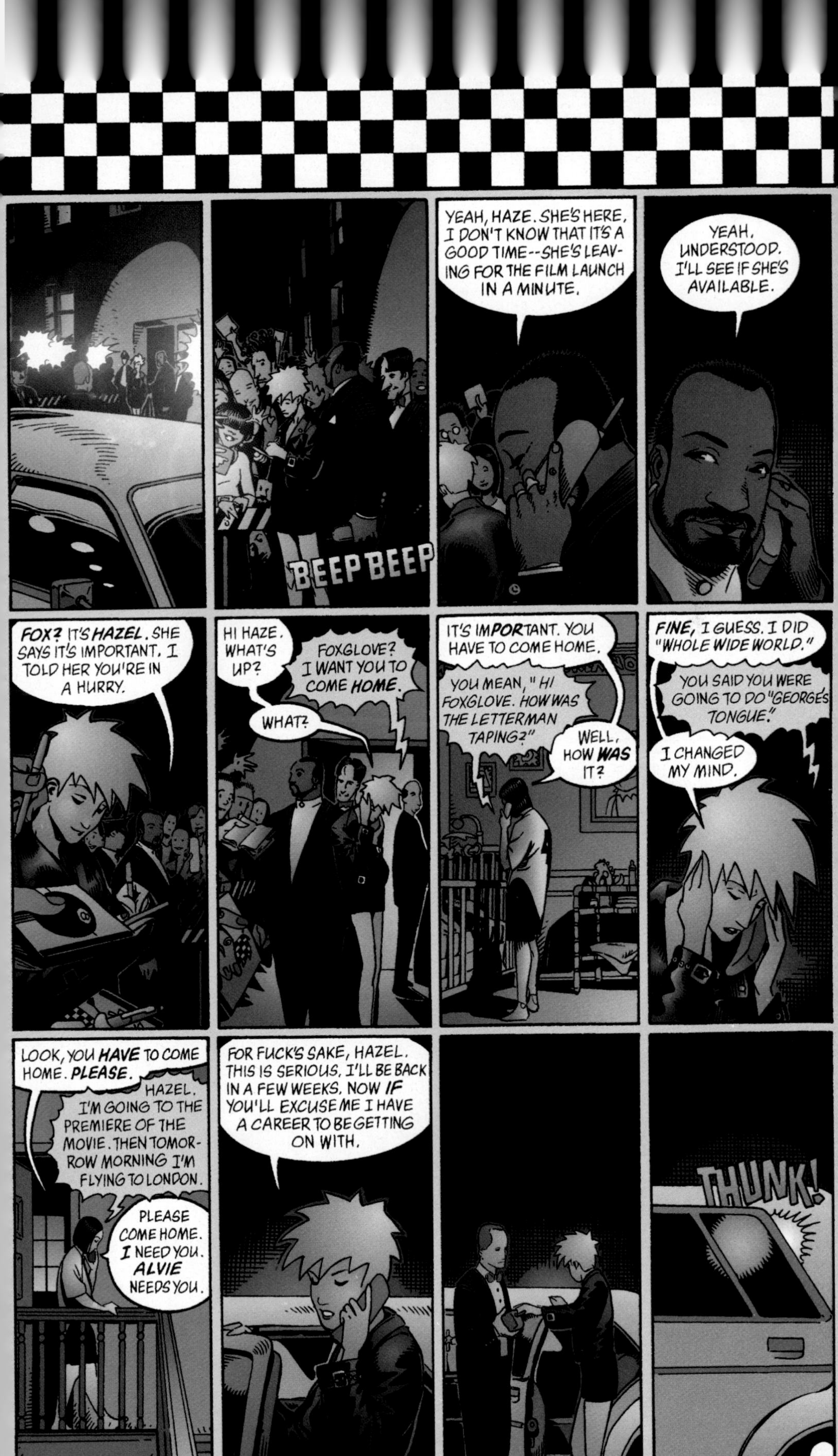
BEEP BEEP
YEAH, HAZE. SHE'S HERE, I DON'T KNOW THAT IT'S A GOOD TIME--SHE'S LEAVING FOR THE FILM LAUNCH IN A MINUTE.
YEAH, UNDERSTOOD. I'LL SEE IF SHE'S AVAILABLE.
FOX? IT'S HAZEL. SHE SAYS IT'S IMPORTANT. I TOLD HER YOU'RE IN A HURRY.
HI HAZE. WHAT'S UP?
FOXGLOVE? I WANT YOU TO COME HOME.
WHAT?
IT'S IMPORTANT. YOU HAVE TO COME HOME.
YOU MEAN, "HI FOXGLOVE. HOW WAS THE LETTERMAN TAPING?"
WELL, HOW WAS IT?
FINE, I GUESS. I DID "WHOLE WIDE WORLD."
YOU SAID YOU WERE GOING TO DO "GEORGE'S TONGUE."
I CHANGED MY MIND.
LOOK, YOU HAVE TO COME HOME. PLEASE.
HAZEL. I'M GOING TO THE PREMIERE OF THE MOVIE. THEN TOMORROW MORNING I'M FLYING TO LONDON.
PLEASE COME HOME. I NEED YOU. ALVIE NEEDS YOU.
FOR FUCK'S SAKE, HAZEL. THIS IS SERIOUS. I'LL BE BACK IN A FEW WEEKS. NOW IF YOU'LL EXCUSE ME I HAVE A CAREER TO BE GETTING ON WITH.
THUNK!

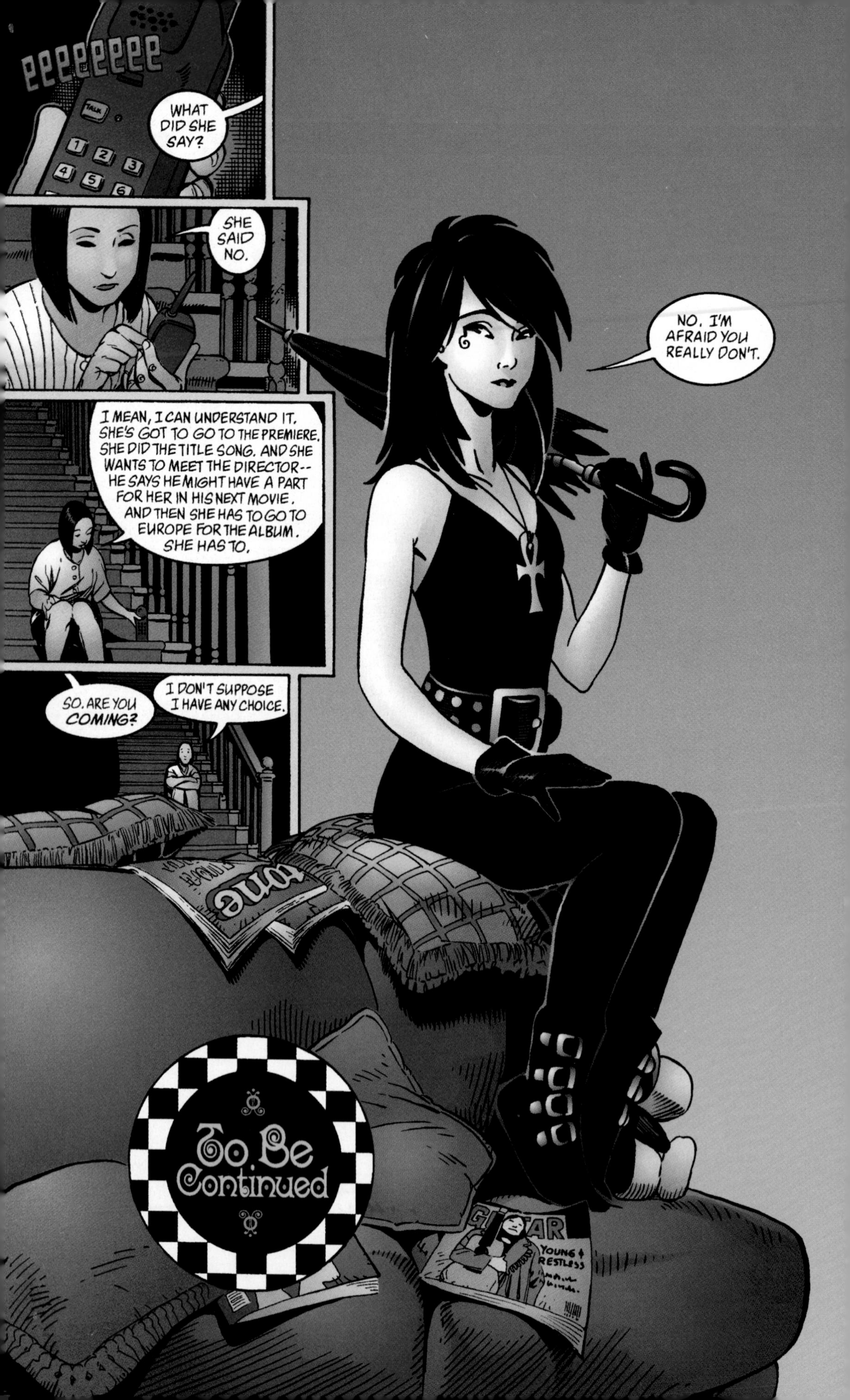
eeeeeeee
WHAT DID SHE SAY?
SHE SAID NO.
I MEAN, I CAN UNDERSTAND IT. SHE'S GOT TO GO TO THE PREMIERE. SHE DID THE TITLE SONG. AND SHE WANTS TO MEET THE DIRECTOR-- HE SAYS HE MIGHT HAVE A PART FOR HER IN HIS NEXT MOVIE. AND THEN SHE HAS TO GO TO EUROPE FOR THE ALBUM. SHE HAS TO.
SO. ARE YOU COMING?
I DON'T SUPPOSE I HAVE ANY CHOICE.
NO. I'M AFRAID YOU REALLY DON'T.
To Be Continued

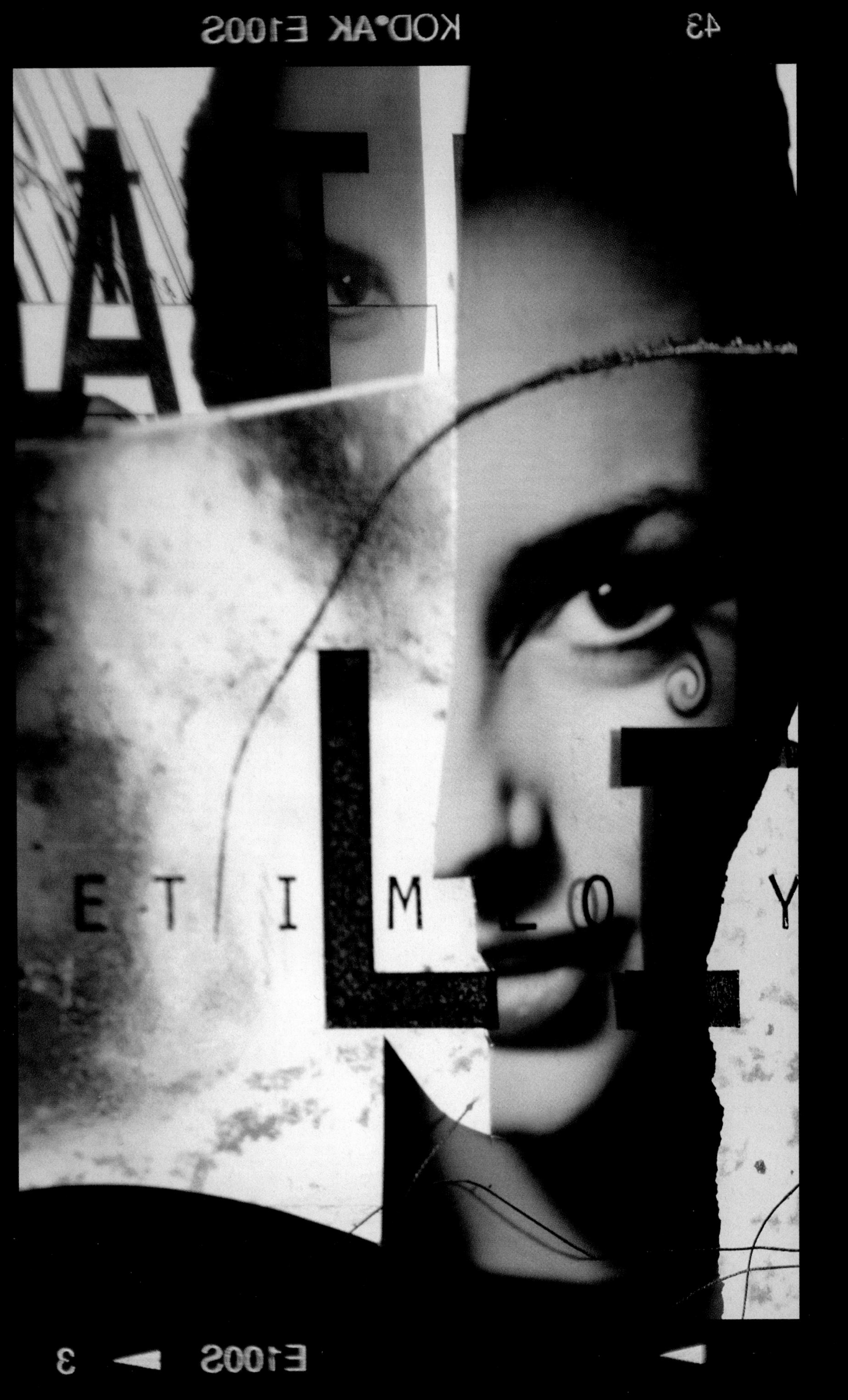

chapter two
imaginary solutions

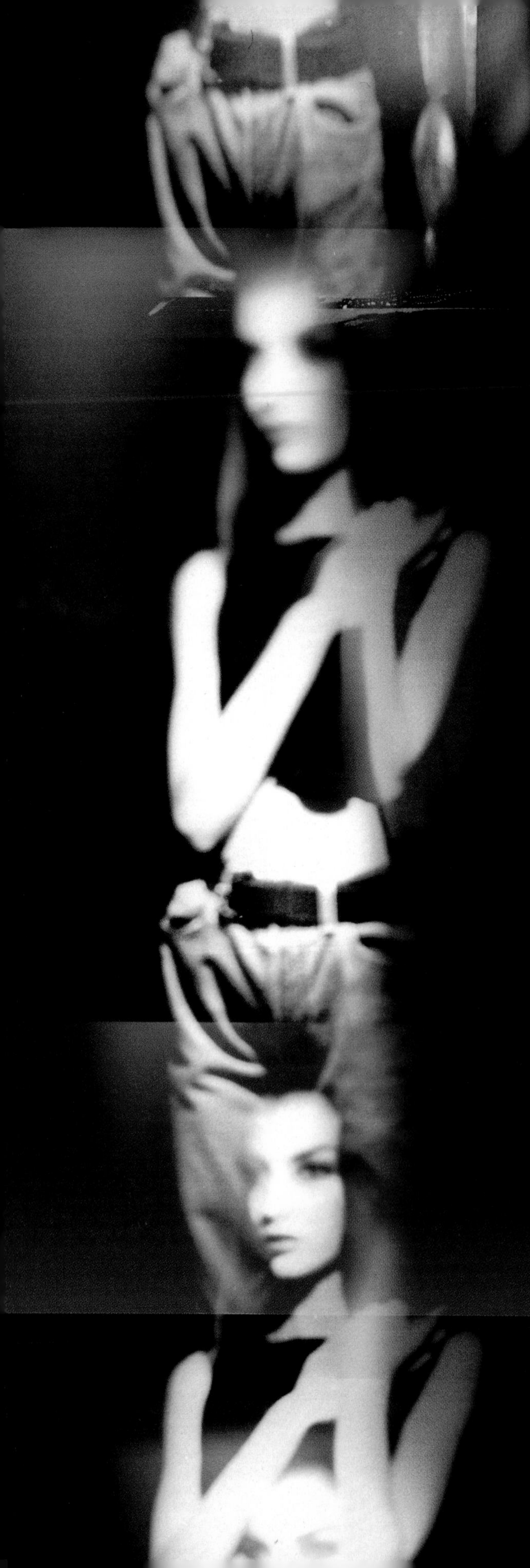

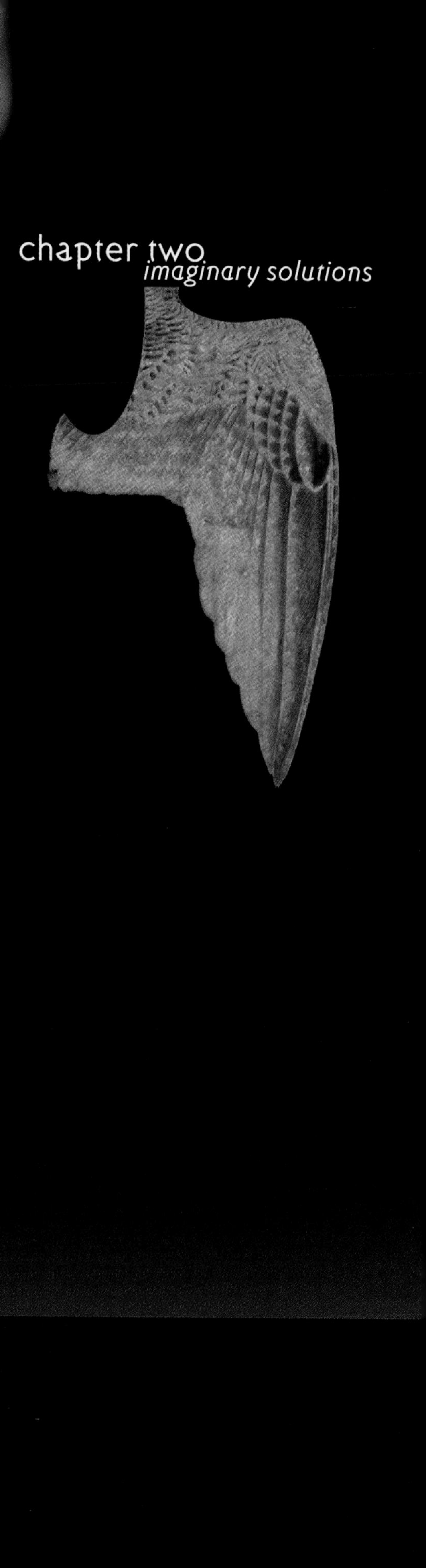

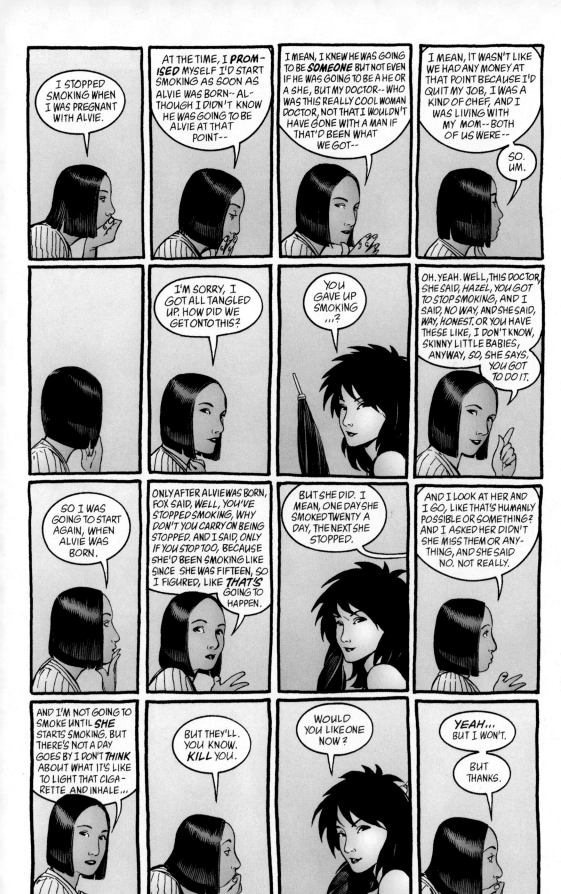

I STOPPED SMOKING WHEN I WAS PREGNANT WITH ALVIE.

AT THE TIME, I PROMISED MYSELF I'D START SMOKING AS SOON AS ALVIE WAS BORN-- ALTHOUGH I DIDN'T KNOW HE WAS GOING TO BE ALVIE AT THAT POINT--

I MEAN, I KNEW HE WAS GOING TO BE SOMEONE BUT NOT EVEN IF HE WAS GOING TO BE A HE OR A SHE, BUT MY DOCTOR-- WHO WAS THIS REALLY COOL WOMAN DOCTOR, NOT THAT I WOULDN'T HAVE GONE WITH A MAN IF THAT'D BEEN WHAT WE GOT--

I MEAN, IT WASN'T LIKE WE HAD ANY MONEY AT THAT POINT BECAUSE I'D QUIT MY JOB, I WAS A KIND OF CHEF, AND I WAS LIVING WITH MY MOM--BOTH OF US WERE--

SO. UM.

I'M SORRY, I GOT ALL TANGLED UP. HOW DID WE GET ONTO THIS?

YOU GAVE UP SMOKING ...?

OH. YEAH. WELL, THIS DOCTOR, SHE SAID, HAZEL, YOU GOT TO STOP SMOKING, AND I SAID, NO WAY, AND SHE SAID, WAY, HONEST. OR YOU HAVE THESE LIKE, I DON'T KNOW, SKINNY LITTLE BABIES, ANYWAY, SO, SHE SAYS, YOU GOT TO DO IT.

SO I WAS GOING TO START AGAIN, WHEN ALVIE WAS BORN.

ONLY AFTER ALVIE WAS BORN, FOX SAID, WELL, YOU'VE STOPPED SMOKING, WHY DON'T YOU CARRY ON BEING STOPPED. AND I SAID, ONLY IF YOU STOP TOO, BECAUSE SHE'D BEEN SMOKING LIKE SINCE SHE WAS FIFTEEN, SO I FIGURED, LIKE THAT'S GOING TO HAPPEN.

BUT SHE DID. I MEAN, ONE DAY SHE SMOKED TWENTY A DAY, THE NEXT SHE STOPPED.

AND I LOOK AT HER AND I GO, LIKE THAT'S HUMANLY POSSIBLE OR SOMETHING? AND I ASKED HER DIDN'T SHE MISS THEM OR ANYTHING, AND SHE SAID NO, NOT REALLY.

AND I'M NOT GOING TO SMOKE UNTIL SHE STARTS SMOKING, BUT THERE'S NOT A DAY GOES BY I DON'T THINK ABOUT WHAT IT'S LIKE TO LIGHT THAT CIGARETTE AND INHALE...

BUT THEY'LL. YOU KNOW. KILL YOU.

WOULD YOU LIKE ONE NOW?

YEAH... BUT I WON'T.

BUT THANKS.

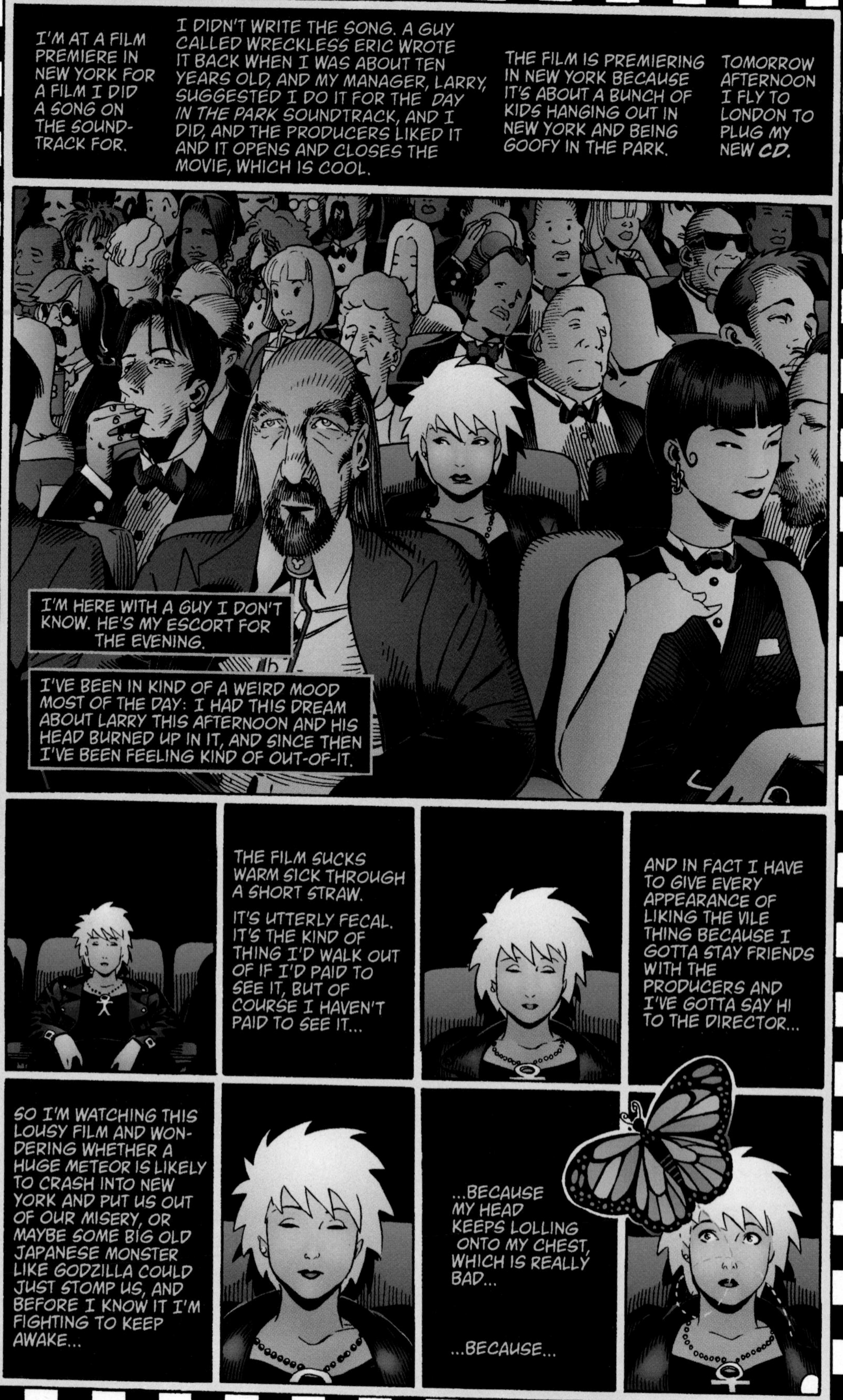
I'M AT A FILM PREMIERE IN NEW YORK FOR A FILM I DID A SONG ON THE SOUND-TRACK FOR.
I DIDN'T WRITE THE SONG. A GUY CALLED WRECKLESS ERIC WROTE IT BACK WHEN I WAS ABOUT TEN YEARS OLD, AND MY MANAGER, LARRY, SUGGESTED I DO IT FOR THE *DAY IN THE PARK* SOUNDTRACK, AND I DID, AND THE PRODUCERS LIKED IT AND IT OPENS AND CLOSES THE MOVIE, WHICH IS COOL.
THE FILM IS PREMIERING IN NEW YORK BECAUSE IT'S ABOUT A BUNCH OF KIDS HANGING OUT IN NEW YORK AND BEING GOOFY IN THE PARK.
TOMORROW AFTERNOON I FLY TO LONDON TO PLUG MY NEW **CD**.
I'M HERE WITH A GUY I DON'T KNOW. HE'S MY ESCORT FOR THE EVENING.
I'VE BEEN IN KIND OF A WEIRD MOOD MOST OF THE DAY: I HAD THIS DREAM ABOUT LARRY THIS AFTERNOON AND HIS HEAD BURNED UP IN IT, AND SINCE THEN I'VE BEEN FEELING KIND OF OUT-OF-IT.
THE FILM SUCKS WARM SICK THROUGH A SHORT STRAW.
IT'S UTTERLY FECAL. IT'S THE KIND OF THING I'D WALK OUT OF IF I'D PAID TO SEE IT, BUT OF COURSE I HAVEN'T PAID TO SEE IT...
AND IN FACT I HAVE TO GIVE EVERY APPEARANCE OF LIKING THE VILE THING BECAUSE I GOTTA STAY FRIENDS WITH THE PRODUCERS AND I'VE GOTTA SAY HI TO THE DIRECTOR...
SO I'M WATCHING THIS LOUSY FILM AND WON-DERING WHETHER A HUGE METEOR IS LIKELY TO CRASH INTO NEW YORK AND PUT US OUT OF OUR MISERY, OR MAYBE SOME BIG OLD JAPANESE MONSTER LIKE GODZILLA COULD JUST STOMP US, AND BEFORE I KNOW IT I'M FIGHTING TO KEEP AWAKE...
...BECAUSE MY HEAD KEEPS LOLLING ONTO MY CHEST, WHICH IS REALLY BAD...
...BECAUSE...

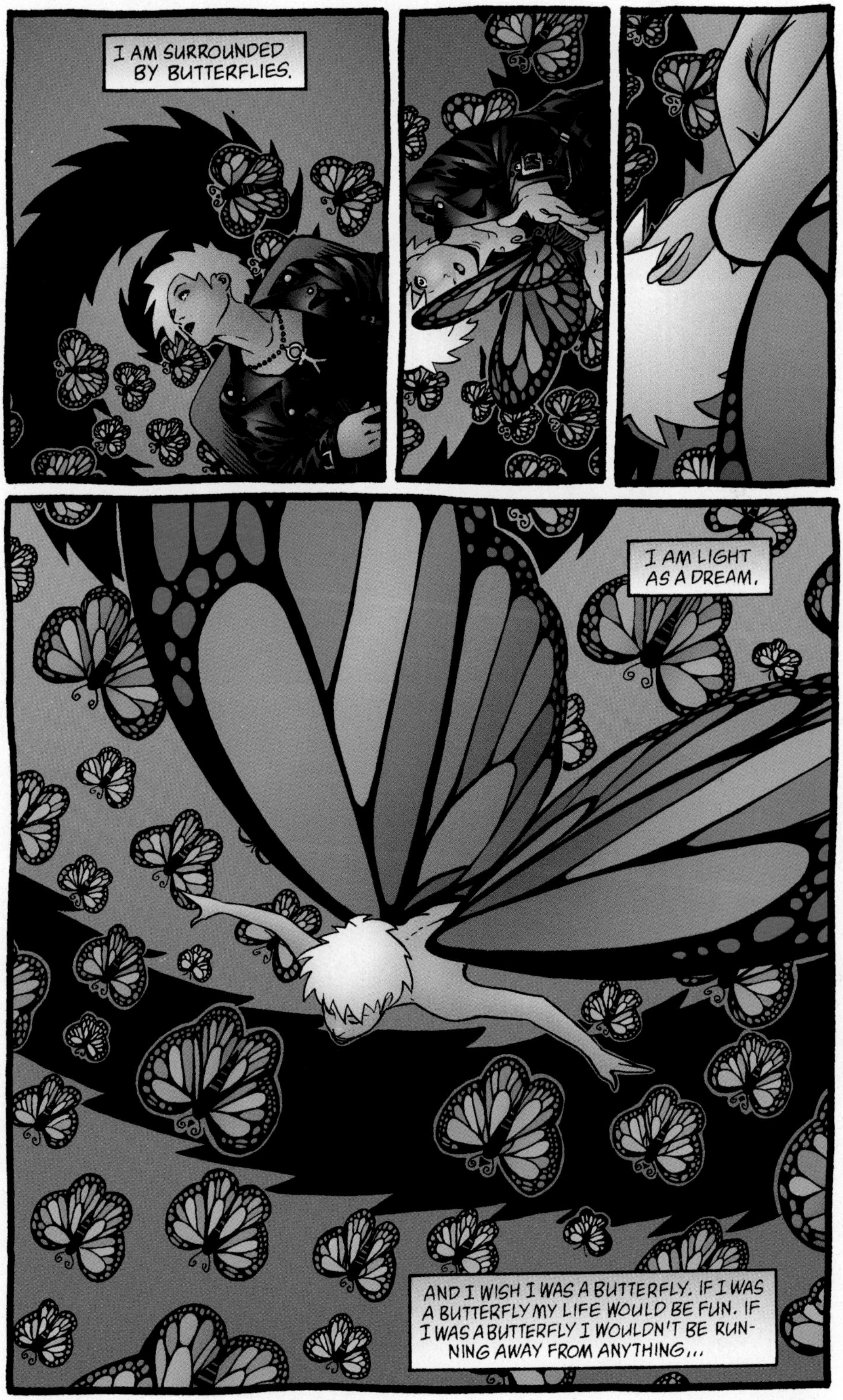
I AM SURROUNDED BY BUTTERFLIES.
I AM LIGHT AS A DREAM.
AND I WISH I WAS A BUTTERFLY. IF I WAS A BUTTERFLY MY LIFE WOULD BE FUN. IF I WAS A BUTTERFLY I WOULDN'T BE RUN-NING AWAY FROM ANYTHING...

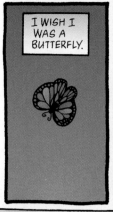

I WISH I WAS A BUTTERFLY.

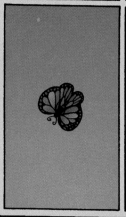

FOX? SOMETHING'S COME UP, LUV. IT'S A BIT URGENT.

WHUH--?

DEATH: THE TIME of your LIFE

CHAPTER TWO: Imaginary Solutions

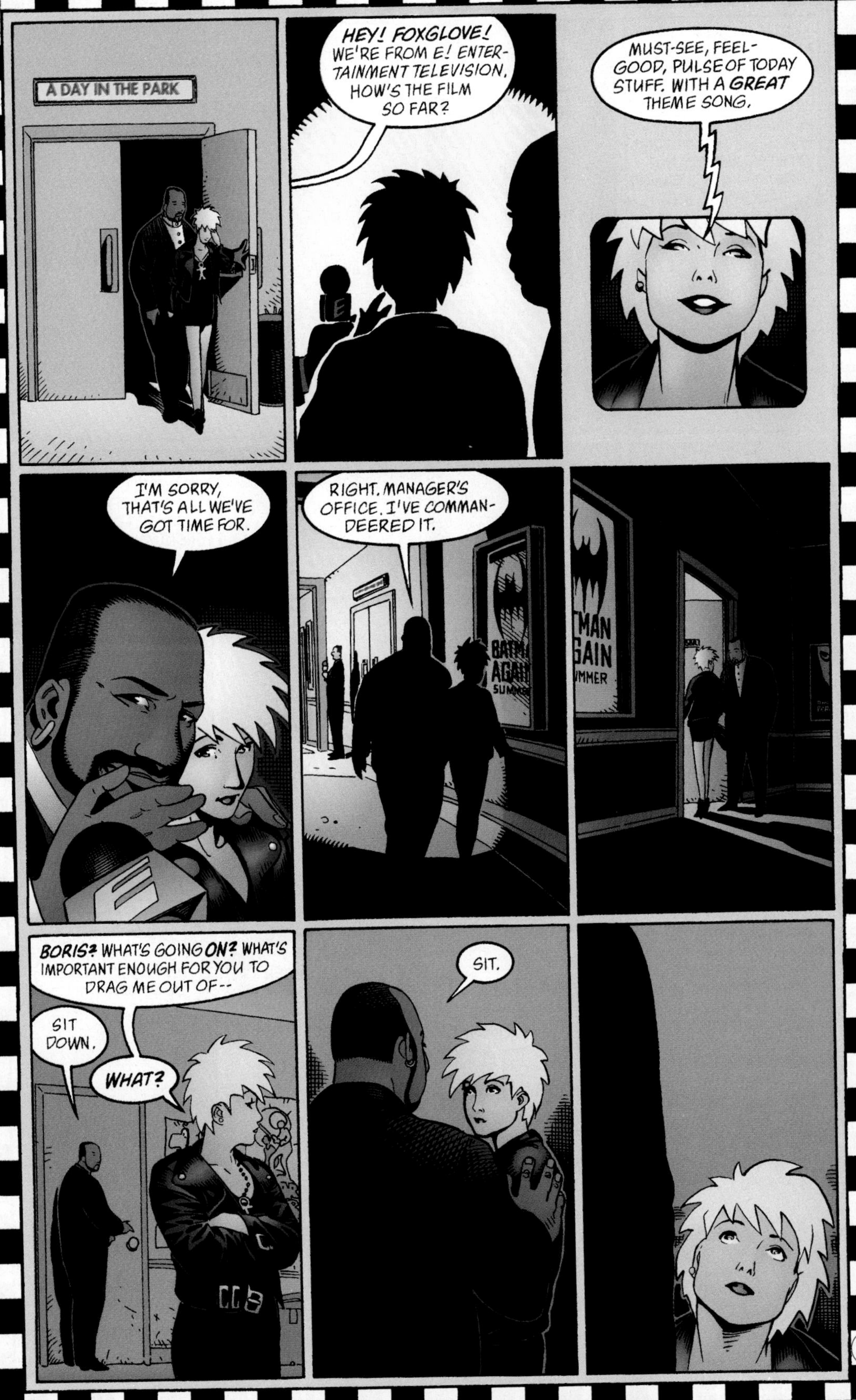
A DAY IN THE PARK
HEY! FOXGLOVE! WE'RE FROM E! ENTERTAINMENT TELEVISION. HOW'S THE FILM SO FAR?
MUST-SEE, FEEL-GOOD, PULSE OF TODAY STUFF. WITH A GREAT THEME SONG.
I'M SORRY, THAT'S ALL WE'VE GOT TIME FOR.
RIGHT. MANAGER'S OFFICE. I'VE COMMANDEERED IT.
BORIS? WHAT'S GOING ON? WHAT'S IMPORTANT ENOUGH FOR YOU TO DRAG ME OUT OF--
SIT DOWN.
WHAT?
SIT.

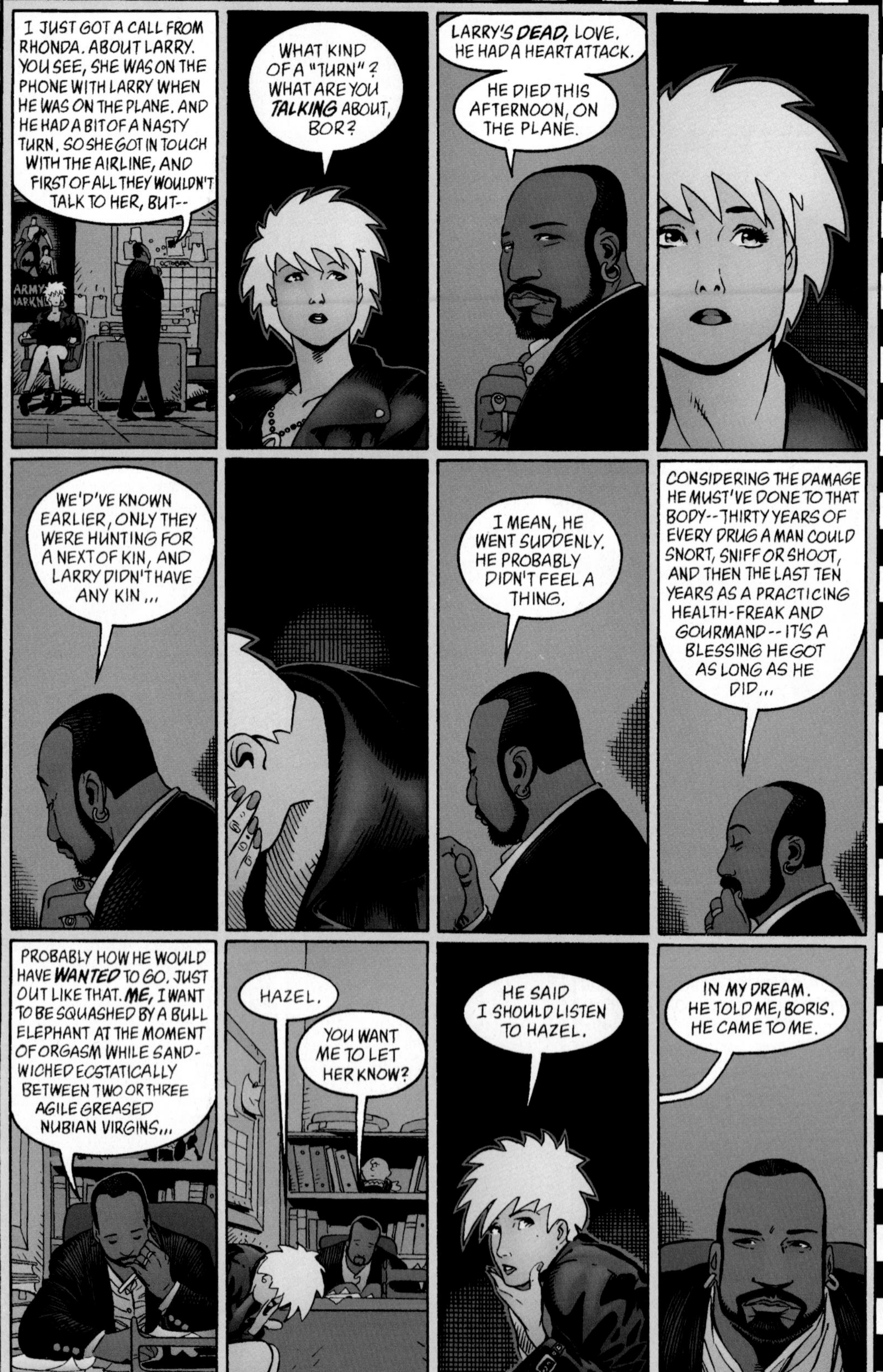
I JUST GOT A CALL FROM RHONDA. ABOUT LARRY. YOU SEE, SHE WAS ON THE PHONE WITH LARRY WHEN HE WAS ON THE PLANE. AND HE HAD A BIT OF A NASTY TURN, SO SHE GOT IN TOUCH WITH THE AIRLINE, AND FIRST OF ALL THEY WOULDN'T TALK TO HER, BUT--
WHAT KIND OF A "TURN"? WHAT ARE YOU TALKING ABOUT, BOR?
LARRY'S DEAD, LOVE. HE HAD A HEART ATTACK.
HE DIED THIS AFTERNOON, ON THE PLANE.
WE'D'VE KNOWN EARLIER, ONLY THEY WERE HUNTING FOR A NEXT OF KIN, AND LARRY DIDN'T HAVE ANY KIN...
I MEAN, HE WENT SUDDENLY. HE PROBABLY DIDN'T FEEL A THING.
CONSIDERING THE DAMAGE HE MUST'VE DONE TO THAT BODY--THIRTY YEARS OF EVERY DRUG A MAN COULD SNORT, SNIFF OR SHOOT, AND THEN THE LAST TEN YEARS AS A PRACTICING HEALTH-FREAK AND GOURMAND--IT'S A BLESSING HE GOT AS LONG AS HE DID...
PROBABLY HOW HE WOULD HAVE WANTED TO GO. JUST OUT LIKE THAT. ME, I WANT TO BE SQUASHED BY A BULL ELEPHANT AT THE MOMENT OF ORGASM WHILE SANDWICHED ECSTATICALLY BETWEEN TWO OR THREE AGILE GREASED NUBIAN VIRGINS...
HAZEL.
YOU WANT ME TO LET HER KNOW?
HE SAID I SHOULD LISTEN TO HAZEL.
IN MY DREAM. HE TOLD ME, BORIS. HE CAME TO ME.

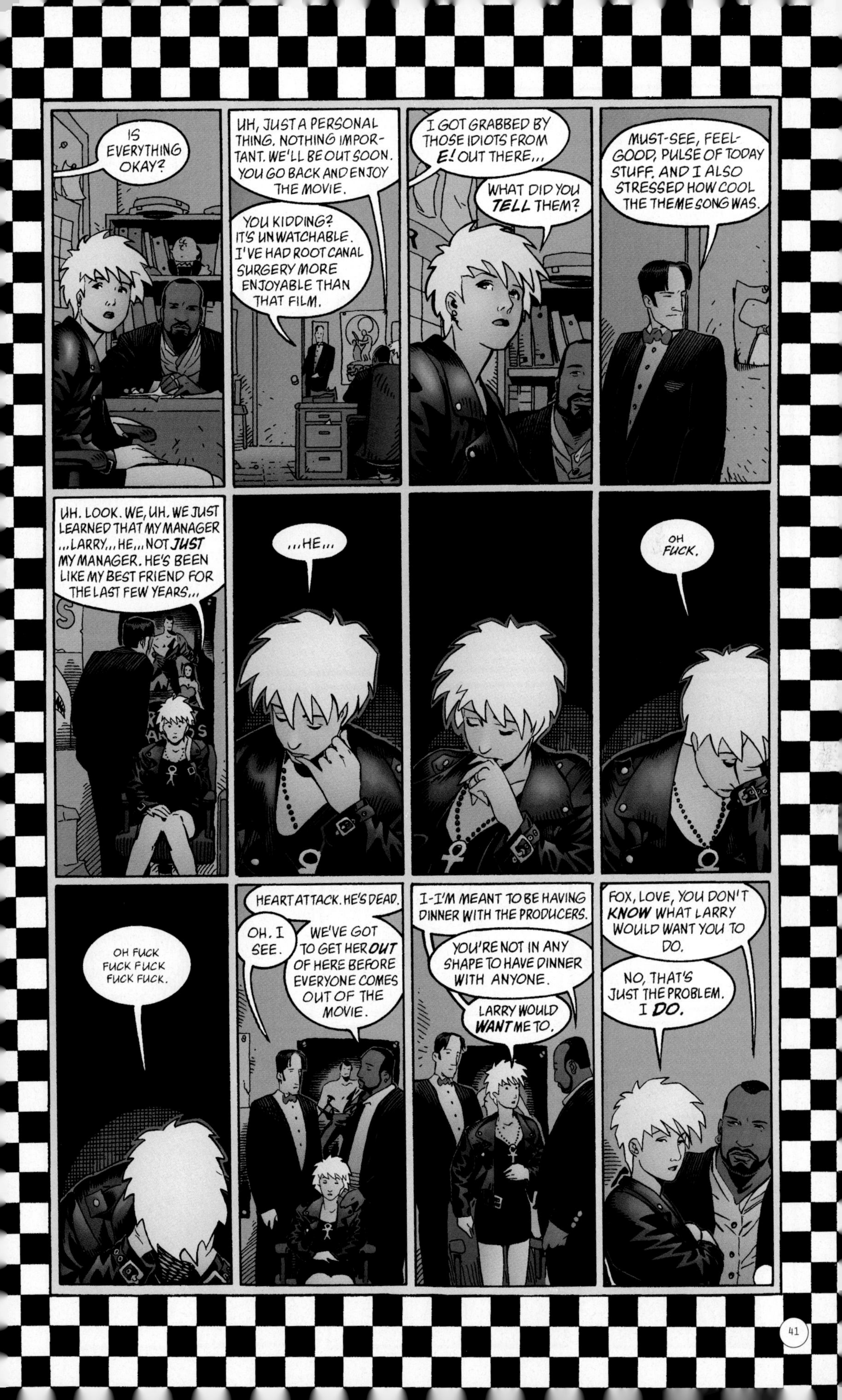

IS EVERYTHING OKAY?
UH, JUST A PERSONAL THING. NOTHING IMPORTANT. WE'LL BE OUT SOON. YOU GO BACK AND ENJOY THE MOVIE.
YOU KIDDING? IT'S UNWATCHABLE. I'VE HAD ROOT CANAL SURGERY MORE ENJOYABLE THAN THAT FILM.
I GOT GRABBED BY THOSE IDIOTS FROM *E!* OUT THERE...
WHAT DID YOU ***TELL*** THEM?
MUST-SEE, FEEL-GOOD, PULSE OF TODAY STUFF. AND I ALSO STRESSED HOW COOL THE THEME SONG WAS.
UH. LOOK. WE, UH. WE JUST LEARNED THAT MY MANAGER ...LARRY... HE... NOT ***JUST*** MY MANAGER. HE'S BEEN LIKE MY BEST FRIEND FOR THE LAST FEW YEARS...
...HE...
OH FUCK.
OH FUCK FUCK FUCK FUCK FUCK.
HEART ATTACK. HE'S DEAD.
OH. I SEE.
WE'VE GOT TO GET HER ***OUT*** OF HERE BEFORE EVERYONE COMES OUT OF THE MOVIE.
I-I'M MEANT TO BE HAVING DINNER WITH THE PRODUCERS.
YOU'RE NOT IN ANY SHAPE TO HAVE DINNER WITH ANYONE.
LARRY WOULD ***WANT*** ME TO.
FOX, LOVE, YOU DON'T ***KNOW*** WHAT LARRY WOULD WANT YOU TO DO.
NO, THAT'S JUST THE PROBLEM. I ***DO***.

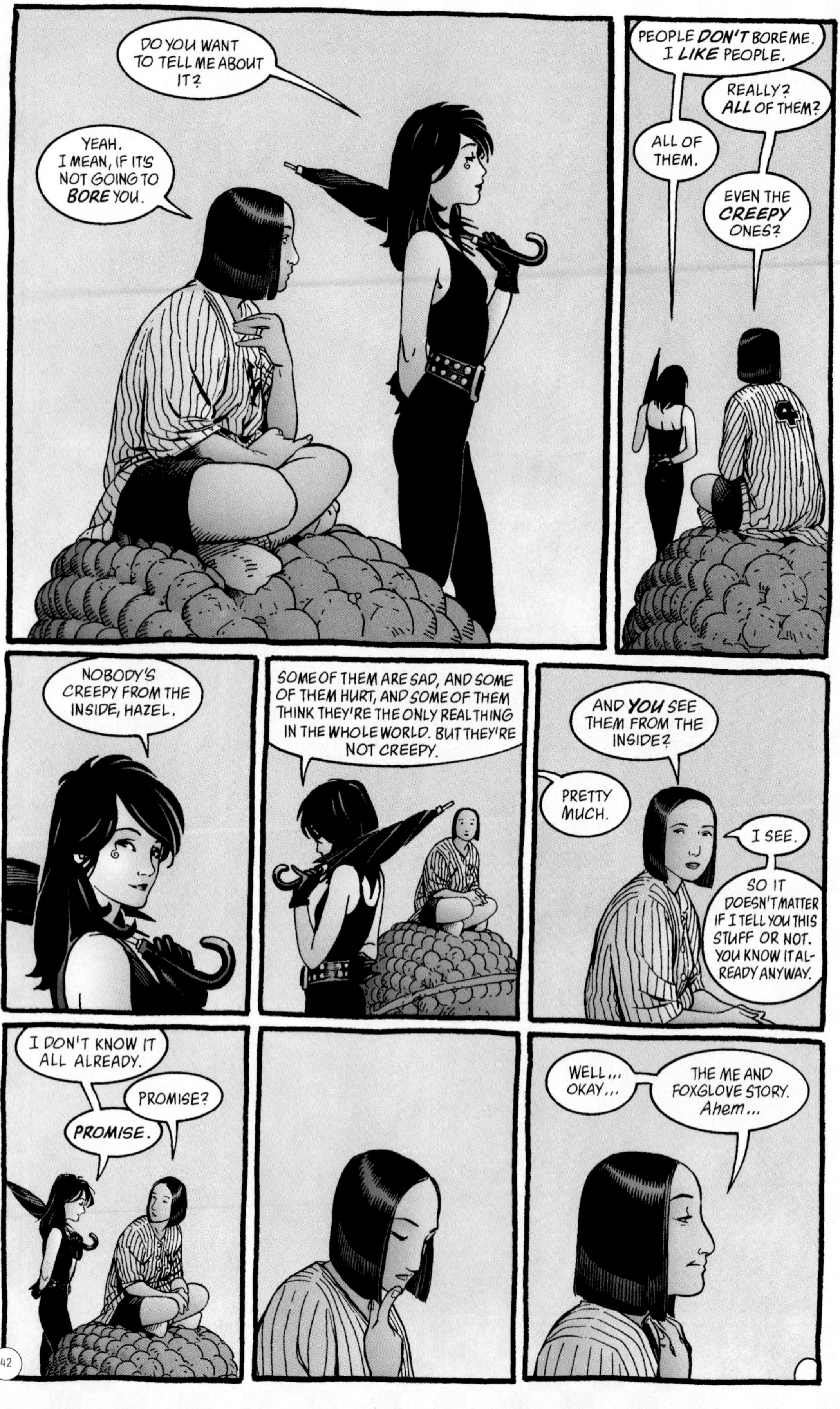

DO YOU WANT TO TELL ME ABOUT IT?
YEAH. I MEAN, IF IT'S NOT GOING TO BORE YOU.
PEOPLE DON'T BORE ME. I LIKE PEOPLE.
REALLY? ALL OF THEM?
ALL OF THEM.
EVEN THE CREEPY ONES?
NOBODY'S CREEPY FROM THE INSIDE, HAZEL.
SOME OF THEM ARE SAD, AND SOME OF THEM HURT, AND SOME OF THEM THINK THEY'RE THE ONLY REAL THING IN THE WHOLE WORLD. BUT THEY'RE NOT CREEPY.
AND YOU SEE THEM FROM THE INSIDE?
PRETTY MUCH.
I SEE.
SO IT DOESN'T MATTER IF I TELL YOU THIS STUFF OR NOT. YOU KNOW IT ALREADY ANYWAY.
I DON'T KNOW IT ALL ALREADY.
PROMISE?
PROMISE.
WELL... OKAY...
THE ME AND FOXGLOVE STORY. Ahem...

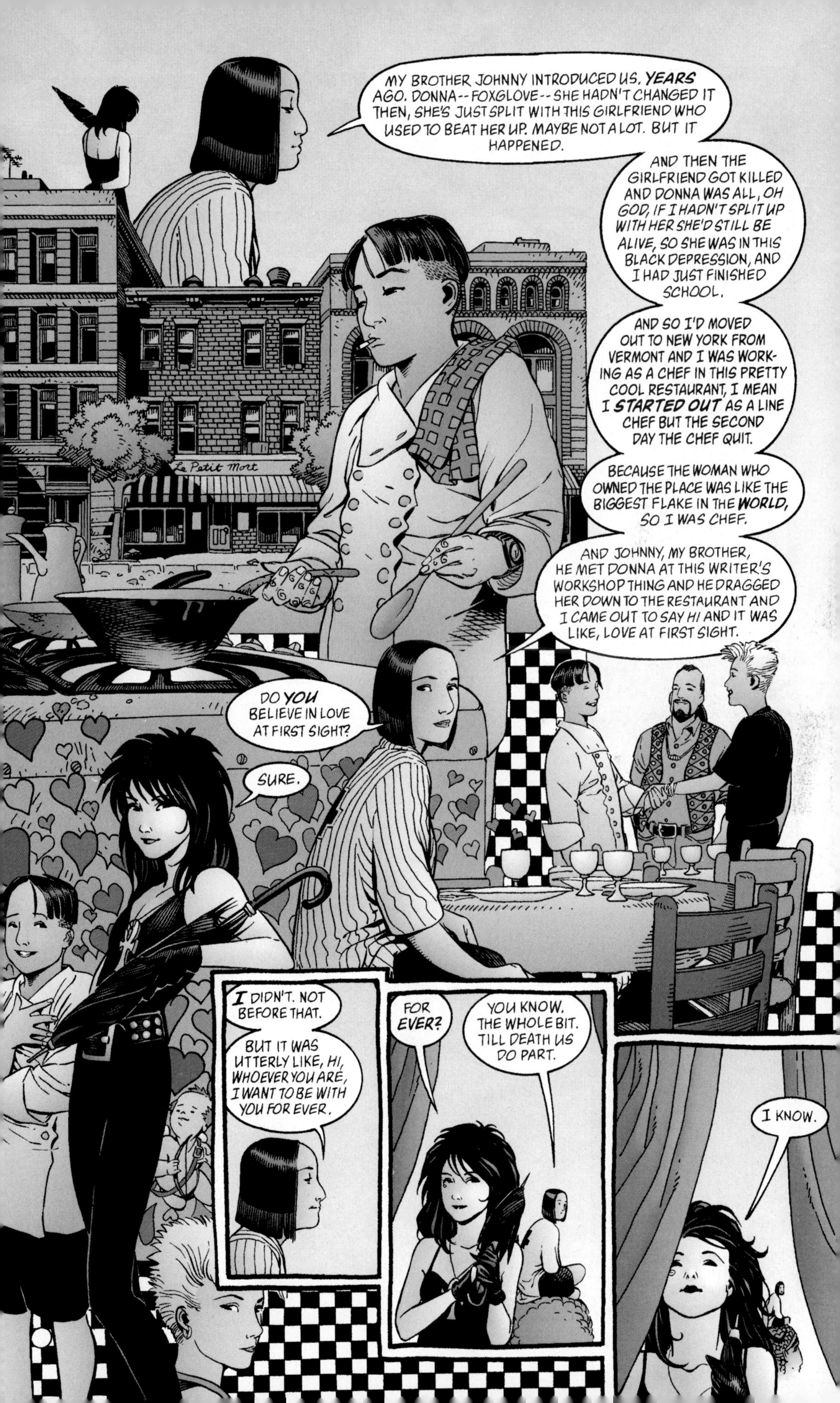
MY BROTHER JOHNNY INTRODUCED US, YEARS AGO. DONNA--FOXGLOVE--SHE HADN'T CHANGED IT THEN, SHE'S JUST SPLIT WITH THIS GIRLFRIEND WHO USED TO BEAT HER UP. MAYBE NOT A LOT. BUT IT HAPPENED.
AND THEN THE GIRLFRIEND GOT KILLED AND DONNA WAS ALL, OH GOD, IF I HADN'T SPLIT UP WITH HER SHE'D STILL BE ALIVE, SO SHE WAS IN THIS BLACK DEPRESSION, AND I HAD JUST FINISHED SCHOOL.
AND SO I'D MOVED OUT TO NEW YORK FROM VERMONT AND I WAS WORKING AS A CHEF IN THIS PRETTY COOL RESTAURANT, I MEAN I STARTED OUT AS A LINE CHEF BUT THE SECOND DAY THE CHEF QUIT.
BECAUSE THE WOMAN WHO OWNED THE PLACE WAS LIKE THE BIGGEST FLAKE IN THE WORLD, SO I WAS CHEF.
AND JOHNNY, MY BROTHER, HE MET DONNA AT THIS WRITER'S WORKSHOP THING AND HE DRAGGED HER DOWN TO THE RESTAURANT AND I CAME OUT TO SAY HI AND IT WAS LIKE, LOVE AT FIRST SIGHT.
Le Petit Mort
DO YOU BELIEVE IN LOVE AT FIRST SIGHT?
SURE.
I DIDN'T. NOT BEFORE THAT.
BUT IT WAS UTTERLY LIKE, HI, WHOEVER YOU ARE, I WANT TO BE WITH YOU FOR EVER.
FOR EVER?
YOU KNOW. THE WHOLE BIT. TILL DEATH US DO PART.
I KNOW.

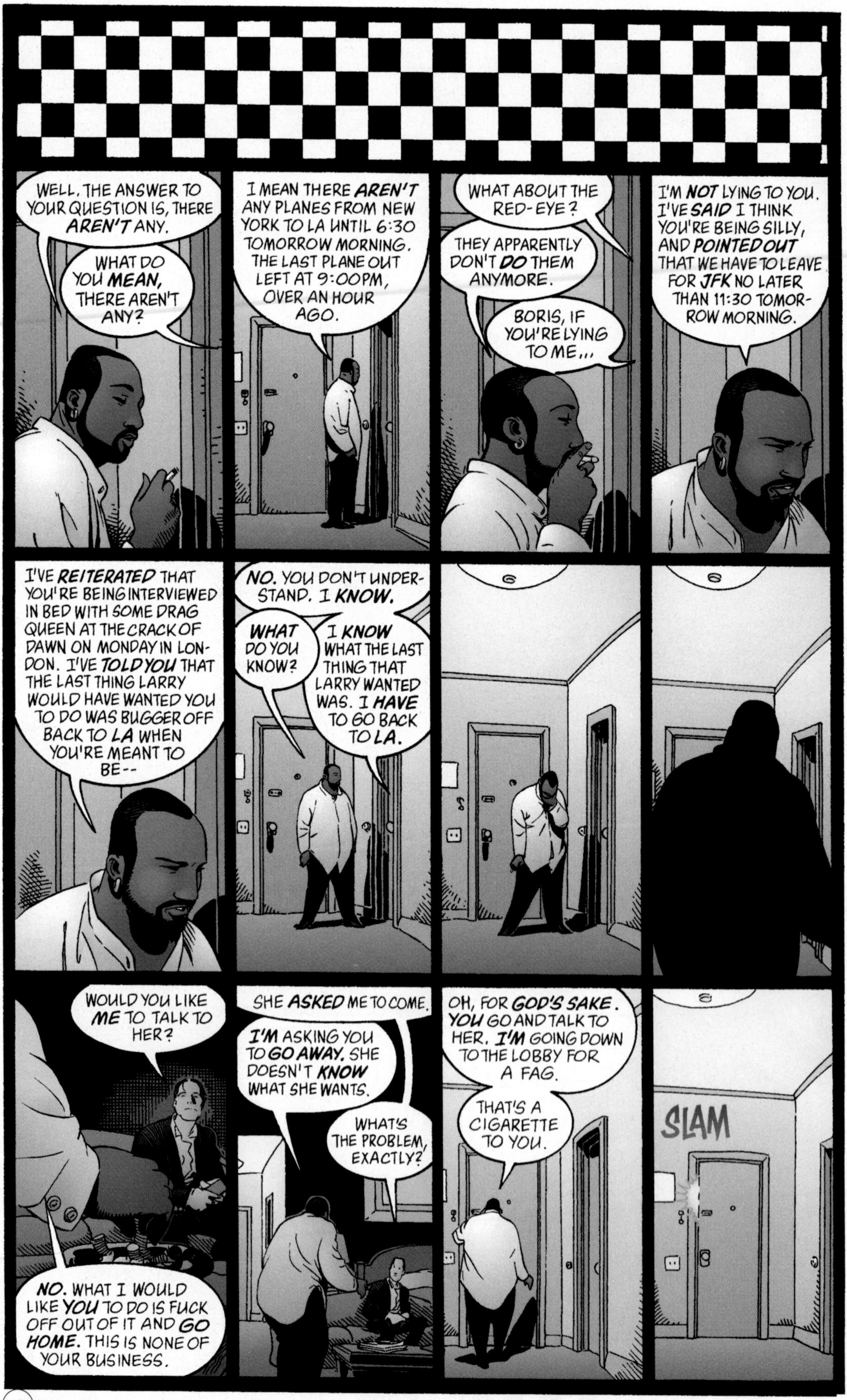
WELL, THE ANSWER TO YOUR QUESTION IS, THERE AREN'T ANY.
WHAT DO YOU MEAN, THERE AREN'T ANY?
I MEAN THERE AREN'T ANY PLANES FROM NEW YORK TO LA UNTIL 6:30 TOMORROW MORNING. THE LAST PLANE OUT LEFT AT 9:00PM, OVER AN HOUR AGO.
WHAT ABOUT THE RED-EYE?
THEY APPARENTLY DON'T DO THEM ANYMORE.
BORIS, IF YOU'RE LYING TO ME...
I'M NOT LYING TO YOU. I'VE SAID I THINK YOU'RE BEING SILLY, AND POINTED OUT THAT WE HAVE TO LEAVE FOR JFK NO LATER THAN 11:30 TOMORROW MORNING.
I'VE REITERATED THAT YOU'RE BEING INTERVIEWED IN BED WITH SOME DRAG QUEEN AT THE CRACK OF DAWN ON MONDAY IN LONDON. I'VE TOLD YOU THAT THE LAST THING LARRY WOULD HAVE WANTED YOU TO DO WAS BUGGER OFF BACK TO LA WHEN YOU'RE MEANT TO BE--
NO. YOU DON'T UNDERSTAND. I KNOW.
WHAT DO YOU KNOW?
I KNOW WHAT THE LAST THING THAT LARRY WANTED WAS. I HAVE TO GO BACK TO LA.
WOULD YOU LIKE ME TO TALK TO HER?
NO. WHAT I WOULD LIKE YOU TO DO IS FUCK OFF OUT OF IT AND GO HOME. THIS IS NONE OF YOUR BUSINESS.
SHE ASKED ME TO COME.
I'M ASKING YOU TO GO AWAY. SHE DOESN'T KNOW WHAT SHE WANTS.
WHAT'S THE PROBLEM, EXACTLY?
OH, FOR GOD'S SAKE. YOU GO AND TALK TO HER. I'M GOING DOWN TO THE LOBBY FOR A FAG.
THAT'S A CIGARETTE TO YOU.
SLAM

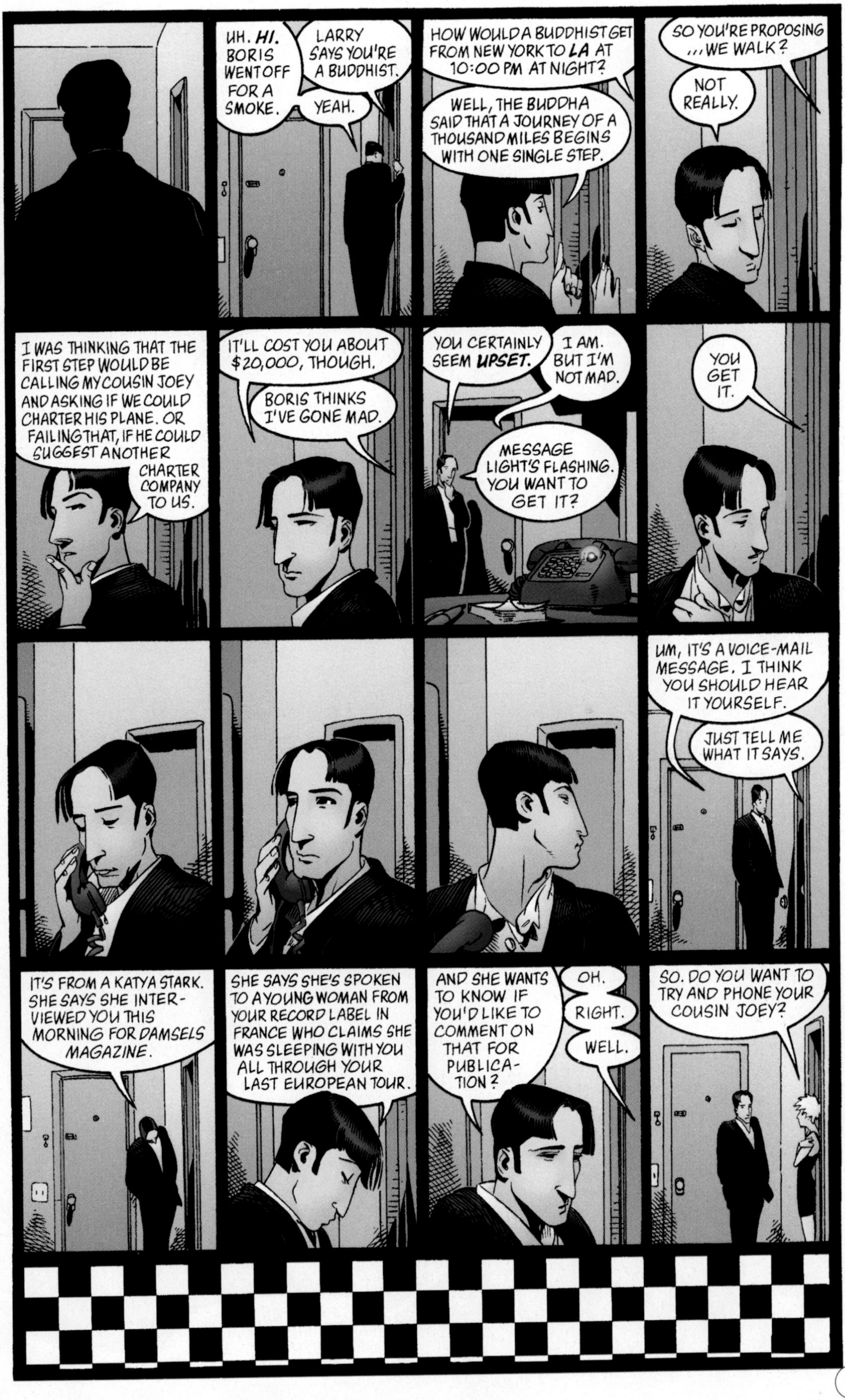
UH. HI. BORIS WENT OFF FOR A SMOKE.
LARRY SAYS YOU'RE A BUDDHIST.
YEAH.
HOW WOULD A BUDDHIST GET FROM NEW YORK TO LA AT 10:00 PM AT NIGHT?
WELL, THE BUDDHA SAID THAT A JOURNEY OF A THOUSAND MILES BEGINS WITH ONE SINGLE STEP.
SO YOU'RE PROPOSING ...WE WALK?
NOT REALLY.
I WAS THINKING THAT THE FIRST STEP WOULD BE CALLING MY COUSIN JOEY AND ASKING IF WE COULD CHARTER HIS PLANE. OR FAILING THAT, IF HE COULD SUGGEST ANOTHER CHARTER COMPANY TO US.
IT'LL COST YOU ABOUT $20,000, THOUGH.
BORIS THINKS I'VE GONE MAD.
YOU CERTAINLY SEEM UPSET.
I AM. BUT I'M NOT MAD.
MESSAGE LIGHT'S FLASHING. YOU WANT TO GET IT?
YOU GET IT.
UM, IT'S A VOICE-MAIL MESSAGE. I THINK YOU SHOULD HEAR IT YOURSELF.
JUST TELL ME WHAT IT SAYS.
IT'S FROM A KATYA STARK. SHE SAYS SHE INTER-VIEWED YOU THIS MORNING FOR DAMSELS MAGAZINE.
SHE SAYS SHE'S SPOKEN TO A YOUNG WOMAN FROM YOUR RECORD LABEL IN FRANCE WHO CLAIMS SHE WAS SLEEPING WITH YOU ALL THROUGH YOUR LAST EUROPEAN TOUR.
AND SHE WANTS TO KNOW IF YOU'D LIKE TO COMMENT ON THAT FOR PUBLICA-TION?
OH.
RIGHT.
WELL.
SO. DO YOU WANT TO TRY AND PHONE YOUR COUSIN JOEY?

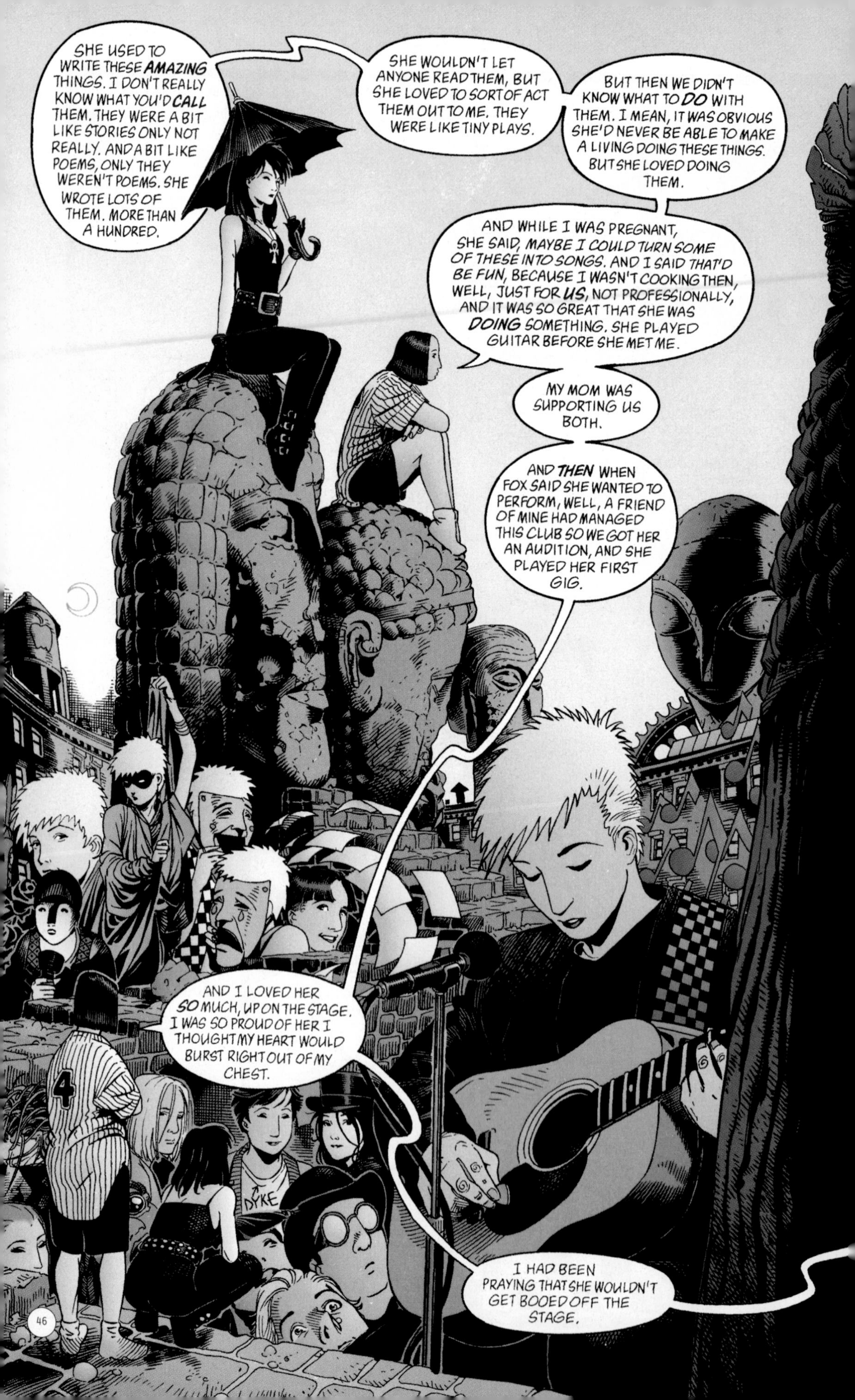
SHE USED TO WRITE THESE AMAZING THINGS. I DON'T REALLY KNOW WHAT YOU'D CALL THEM. THEY WERE A BIT LIKE STORIES ONLY NOT REALLY. AND A BIT LIKE POEMS, ONLY THEY WEREN'T POEMS. SHE WROTE LOTS OF THEM. MORE THAN A HUNDRED.
SHE WOULDN'T LET ANYONE READ THEM, BUT SHE LOVED TO SORT OF ACT THEM OUT TO ME. THEY WERE LIKE TINY PLAYS.
BUT THEN WE DIDN'T KNOW WHAT TO DO WITH THEM. I MEAN, IT WAS OBVIOUS SHE'D NEVER BE ABLE TO MAKE A LIVING DOING THESE THINGS. BUT SHE LOVED DOING THEM.
AND WHILE I WAS PREGNANT, SHE SAID, MAYBE I COULD TURN SOME OF THESE INTO SONGS. AND I SAID THAT'D BE FUN, BECAUSE I WASN'T COOKING THEN, WELL, JUST FOR US, NOT PROFESSIONALLY, AND IT WAS SO GREAT THAT SHE WAS DOING SOMETHING. SHE PLAYED GUITAR BEFORE SHE MET ME.
MY MOM WAS SUPPORTING US BOTH.
AND THEN WHEN FOX SAID SHE WANTED TO PERFORM, WELL, A FRIEND OF MINE HAD MANAGED THIS CLUB SO WE GOT HER AN AUDITION, AND SHE PLAYED HER FIRST GIG.
AND I LOVED HER SO MUCH, UP ON THE STAGE. I WAS SO PROUD OF HER I THOUGHT MY HEART WOULD BURST RIGHT OUT OF MY CHEST.
I HAD BEEN PRAYING THAT SHE WOULDN'T GET BOOED OFF THE STAGE.
DYKE
4

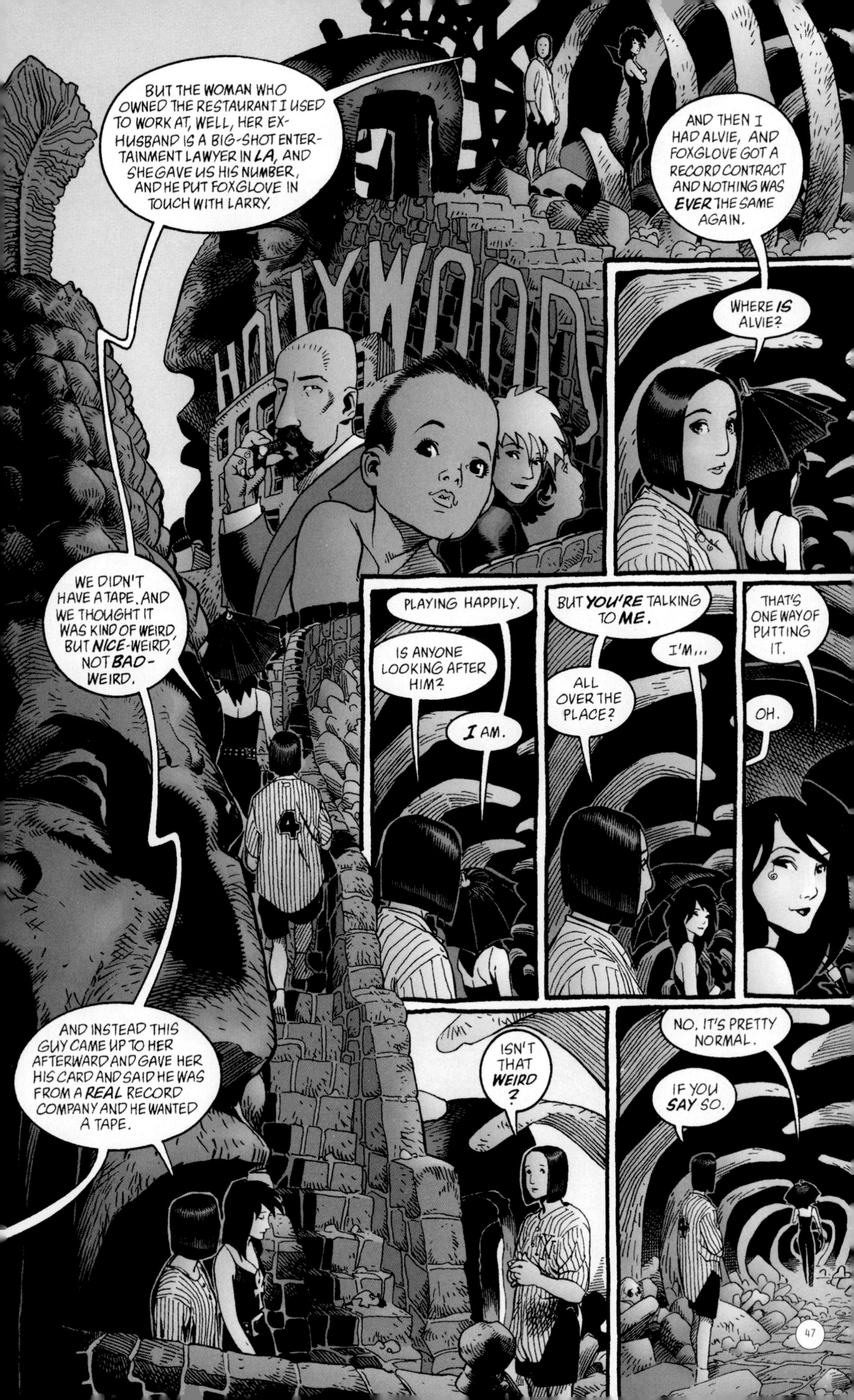

BUT THE WOMAN WHO OWNED THE RESTAURANT I USED TO WORK AT, WELL, HER EX-HUSBAND IS A BIG-SHOT ENTERTAINMENT LAWYER IN LA, AND SHE GAVE US HIS NUMBER, AND HE PUT FOXGLOVE IN TOUCH WITH LARRY.
WE DIDN'T HAVE A TAPE, AND WE THOUGHT IT WAS KIND OF WEIRD, BUT NICE-WEIRD, NOT BAD-WEIRD.
AND INSTEAD THIS GUY CAME UP TO HER AFTERWARD AND GAVE HER HIS CARD AND SAID HE WAS FROM A REAL RECORD COMPANY AND HE WANTED A TAPE.
AND THEN I HAD ALVIE, AND FOXGLOVE GOT A RECORD CONTRACT AND NOTHING WAS EVER THE SAME AGAIN.
HOLLYWOOD
WHERE IS ALVIE?
PLAYING HAPPILY.
IS ANYONE LOOKING AFTER HIM?
I AM.
BUT YOU'RE TALKING TO ME.
I'M...
ALL OVER THE PLACE?
THAT'S ONE WAY OF PUTTING IT.
OH.
ISN'T THAT WEIRD?
NO. IT'S PRETTY NORMAL.
IF YOU SAY SO.

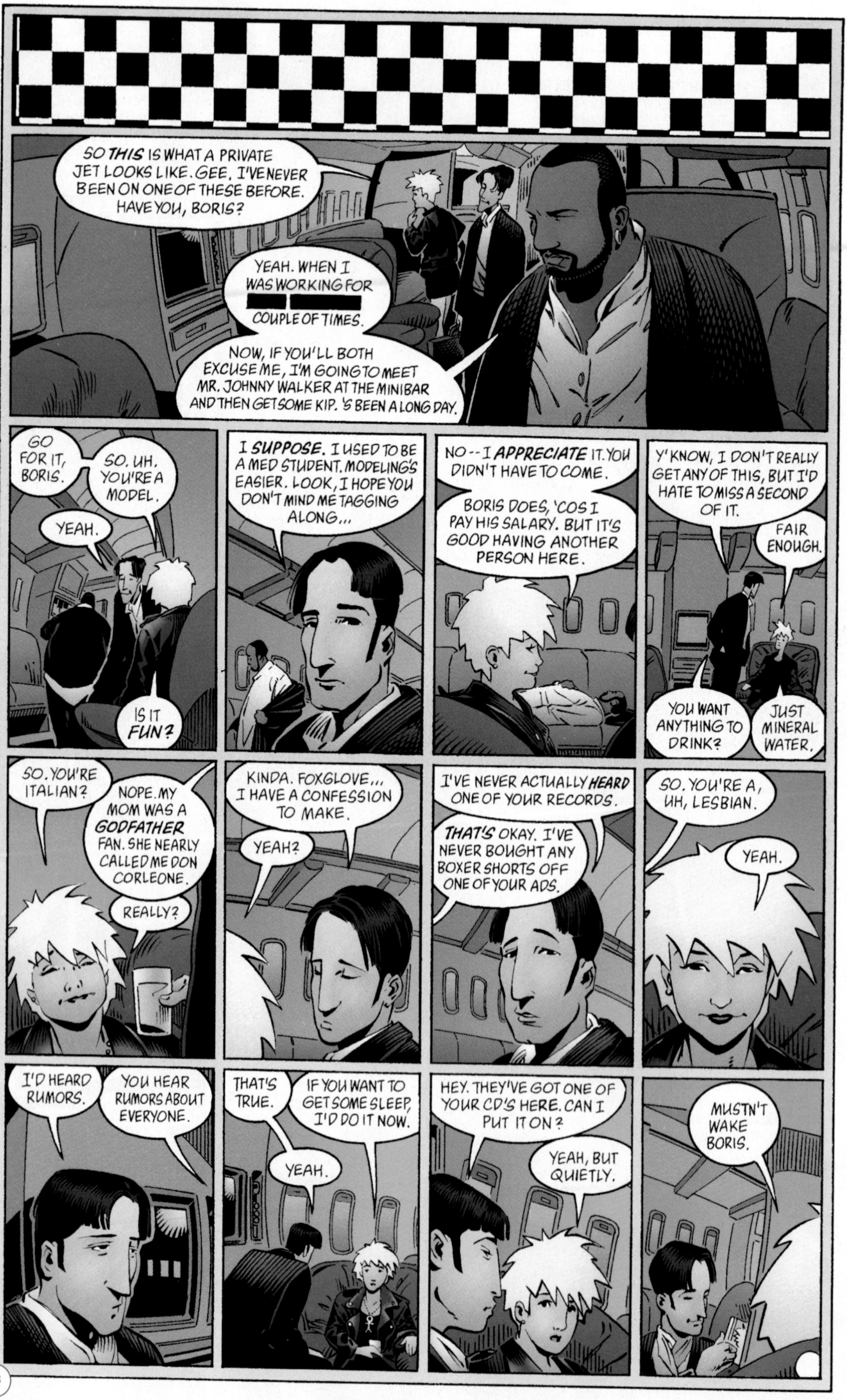
SO THIS IS WHAT A PRIVATE JET LOOKS LIKE. GEE, I'VE NEVER BEEN ON ONE OF THESE BEFORE. HAVE YOU, BORIS?
YEAH. WHEN I WAS WORKING FOR [redacted] COUPLE OF TIMES.
NOW, IF YOU'LL BOTH EXCUSE ME, I'M GOING TO MEET MR. JOHNNY WALKER AT THE MINIBAR AND THEN GET SOME KIP. 'S BEEN A LONG DAY.
GO FOR IT, BORIS.
SO, UH, YOU'RE A MODEL.
YEAH.
IS IT FUN?
I SUPPOSE. I USED TO BE A MED STUDENT. MODELING'S EASIER. LOOK, I HOPE YOU DON'T MIND ME TAGGING ALONG...
NO -- I APPRECIATE IT. YOU DIDN'T HAVE TO COME.
BORIS DOES, 'COS I PAY HIS SALARY. BUT IT'S GOOD HAVING ANOTHER PERSON HERE.
Y'KNOW, I DON'T REALLY GET ANY OF THIS, BUT I'D HATE TO MISS A SECOND OF IT.
FAIR ENOUGH.
YOU WANT ANYTHING TO DRINK?
JUST MINERAL WATER.
SO. YOU'RE ITALIAN?
NOPE. MY MOM WAS A GODFATHER FAN. SHE NEARLY CALLED ME DON CORLEONE.
REALLY?
KINDA. FOXGLOVE... I HAVE A CONFESSION TO MAKE.
YEAH?
I'VE NEVER ACTUALLY HEARD ONE OF YOUR RECORDS.
THAT'S OKAY. I'VE NEVER BOUGHT ANY BOXER SHORTS OFF ONE OF YOUR ADS.
SO. YOU'RE A, UH, LESBIAN.
YEAH.
I'D HEARD RUMORS.
YOU HEAR RUMORS ABOUT EVERYONE.
THAT'S TRUE.
IF YOU WANT TO GET SOME SLEEP, I'D DO IT NOW.
YEAH.
HEY. THEY'VE GOT ONE OF YOUR CD'S HERE. CAN I PUT IT ON?
YEAH, BUT QUIETLY.
MUSTN'T WAKE BORIS.

 **O**UTSIDE MY WINDOW IT'S DARK.

WHEN I WAS YOUNGER I USED TO WRITE LITTLE STORIES.

 I'M KIND OF FREAKED OUT ABOUT THE COST OF HIRING THIS PLANE.

I'M KIND OF FREAKED OUT ABOUT THE COST OF EVERY-THING. AT LAST ACCOUNTING I WAS ABOUT $1.3 MILLION IN DEBT TO THE RECORD COMPANY.

 I'VE GOT A FEW HUNDRED THOUSAND TUCKED AWAY IN A PUBLISHING ACCOUNT, AND I'VE GOT THE HOUSE IN BEVERLY HILLS, AND THAT TAKES CARE OF HAZEL AND ALVIE AND SOMEWHERE TO STAY WHEN I'M HOME...

AND TAXES...

BUT I HAVEN'T BEEN HOME VERY MUCH IN THE LAST YEAR OR SO, HAVE I?

 FOR THE HUNDREDTH TIME TONIGHT I PICK UP THE PHONE AND I CALL HOME. I CALL THE HOUSE NUMBER AND THE PRIVATE NUMBER AND THE SECRET NUMBER THAT ONLY LARRY HAD...

NO REPLY...

AND MY HEAD IS FILLED WITH NOISES AND VOICES AND MY CHEST FEELS EMPTY AND MY MIND FEELS NUMB.

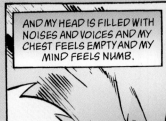

I FIND MYSELF REMEMBER-ING THAT NIGHT IN HAMBURG, WITH VÉRONIQUE, STUMBLING BACK FROM THE GIG ALL SWEATY AND GIGGLY--

--AND DANCING AROUND THE ROOM AND JUST PULLING HER TO ME AND KISSING HER BEFORE I HAD A CHANCE TO THINK ABOUT WHAT I WAS DOING--

--BECAUSE I WAS SO FAR FROM HOME--

--STUTTERING MY LUST INTO THE NIGHT--

--WAVING GOODBYE TO VÉRONIQUE IN AMSTERDAM AIRPORT AT THE END OF THE TOUR, AND PROMISING TO KEEP IN TOUCH, AND KNOWING I NEVER WOULD--

--HER HEAD BETWEEN MY LEGS--

--KNOWING SOMEWHERE DOWN DEEP THAT I COULD TAKE WHATEVER I WANTED, BUT THAT ONE DAY IT WOULD ALL HAVE TO BE PAID FOR--

-- SHIVERING NOW, MY FINGERS AND MY BODY ARE CHILLED. I WISH I WAS ASLEEP. BORIS SNUFFLES AND GRUNTS IN HIS SLEEP LIKE AN OLD BEAR HIBERNATING. WONDERING WHERE HAZEL COULD BE, IF ALVIE'S OKAY...

AND AN AIRPLANE IS SUCH A PERFECT MACHINE. IF IT CRASHES IT'S NOT YOUR FAULT. A FAST FIREBALL TRIP INTO NOTHING...

THAT ISN'T SUICIDE. IS IT?

THE THOUGHT COMFORTS ME. OUTSIDE MY WINDOW THE SKY IS TURNING A COLD PRE-DAWN GRAY. THE DESERT BENEATH US LOOKS LIKE A SLICE OF NOWHERE.

AND I REALIZE I'VE FORGOTTEN THE NAME OF THE BUDDHIST JOCKEY SHORTS GUY ALREADY

AND

WE'LL BE LANDING IN

UNDER AN HOUR

SO THERE'S NO

POINT

IN

FALLING

ASLEEP...

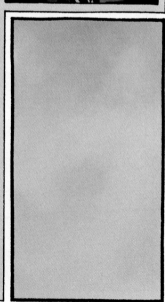

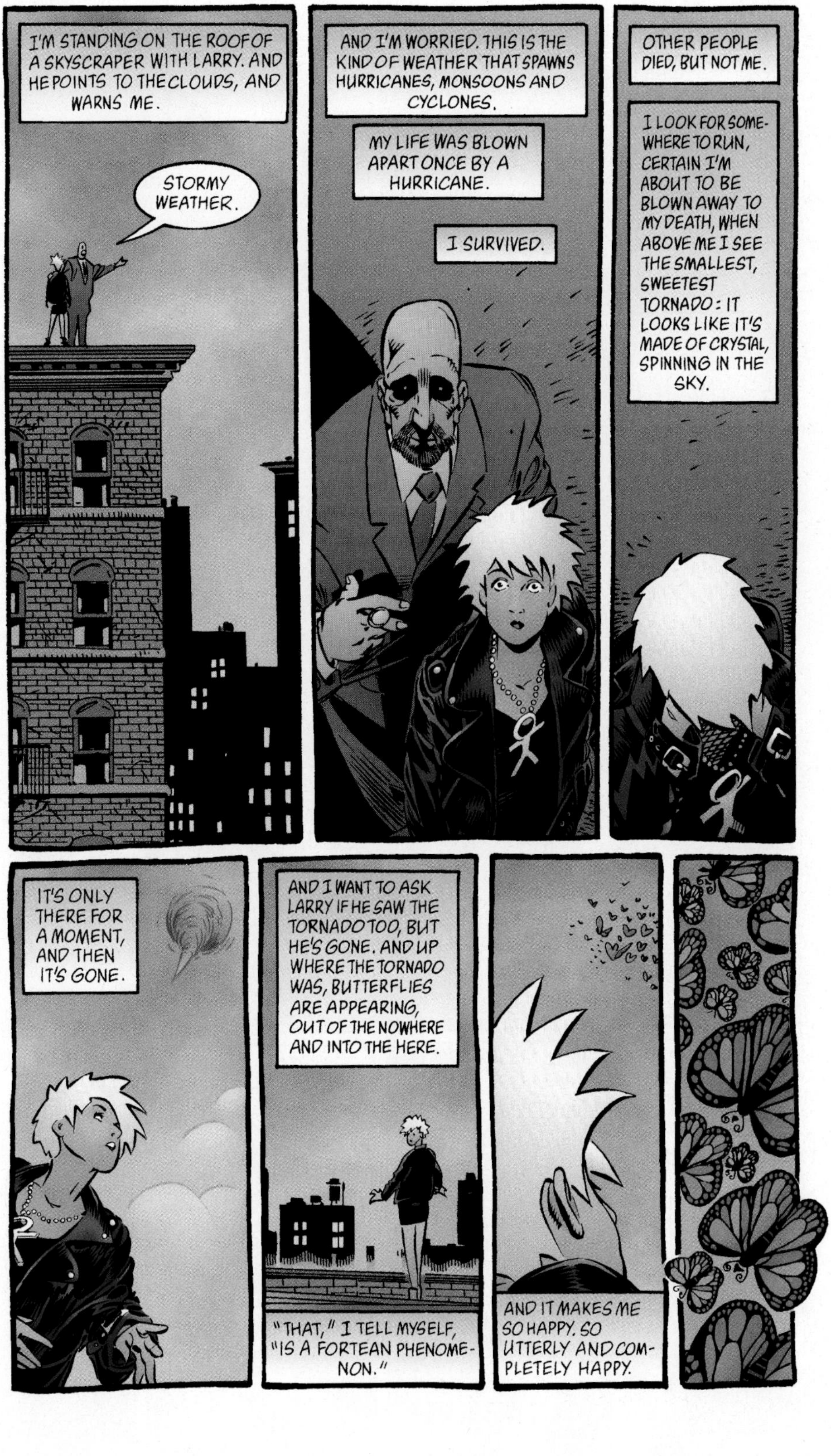
I'M STANDING ON THE ROOF OF A SKYSCRAPER WITH LARRY. AND HE POINTS TO THE CLOUDS, AND WARNS ME.
STORMY WEATHER.
AND I'M WORRIED. THIS IS THE KIND OF WEATHER THAT SPAWNS HURRICANES, MONSOONS AND CYCLONES.
MY LIFE WAS BLOWN APART ONCE BY A HURRICANE.
I SURVIVED.
OTHER PEOPLE DIED, BUT NOT ME.
I LOOK FOR SOME-WHERE TO RUN, CERTAIN I'M ABOUT TO BE BLOWN AWAY TO MY DEATH, WHEN ABOVE ME I SEE THE SMALLEST, SWEETEST TORNADO: IT LOOKS LIKE IT'S MADE OF CRYSTAL, SPINNING IN THE SKY.
IT'S ONLY THERE FOR A MOMENT, AND THEN IT'S GONE.
AND I WANT TO ASK LARRY IF HE SAW THE TORNADO TOO, BUT HE'S GONE. AND UP WHERE THE TORNADO WAS, BUTTERFLIES ARE APPEARING, OUT OF THE NOWHERE AND INTO THE HERE.
"THAT," I TELL MYSELF, "IS A FORTEAN PHENOME-NON."
AND IT MAKES ME SO HAPPY. SO UTTERLY AND COM-PLETELY HAPPY.

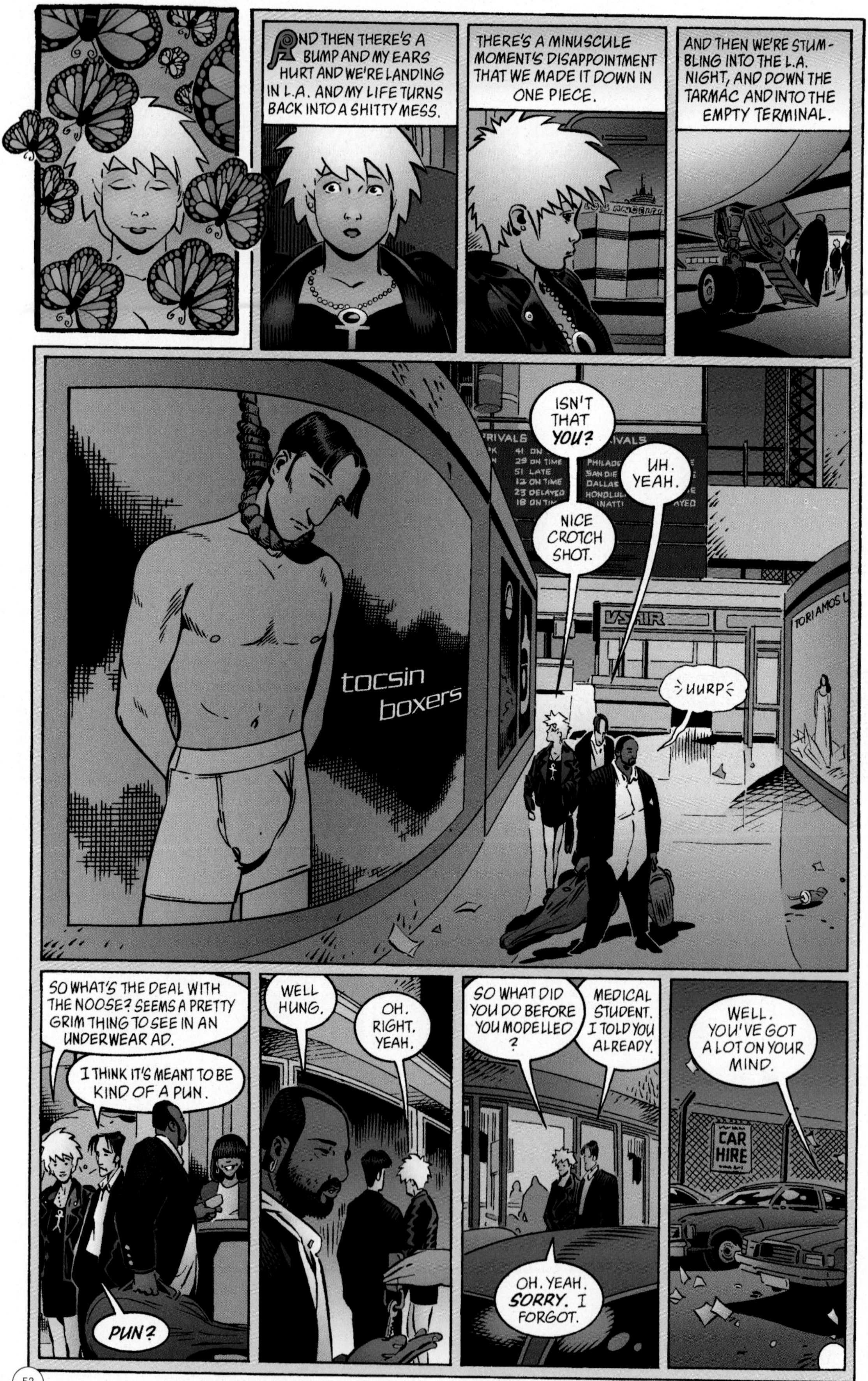
AND THEN THERE'S A BUMP AND MY EARS HURT AND WE'RE LANDING IN L.A. AND MY LIFE TURNS BACK INTO A SHITTY MESS.
THERE'S A MINUSCULE MOMENT'S DISAPPOINTMENT THAT WE MADE IT DOWN IN ONE PIECE.
AND THEN WE'RE STUMBLING INTO THE L.A. NIGHT, AND DOWN THE TARMAC AND INTO THE EMPTY TERMINAL.
tocsin boxers
ISN'T THAT YOU?
UH. YEAH.
NICE CROTCH SHOT.
USAIR
TORI AMOS
UURP
SO WHAT'S THE DEAL WITH THE NOOSE? SEEMS A PRETTY GRIM THING TO SEE IN AN UNDERWEAR AD.
I THINK IT'S MEANT TO BE KIND OF A PUN.
PUN?
WELL HUNG.
OH. RIGHT. YEAH.
SO WHAT DID YOU DO BEFORE YOU MODELLED?
MEDICAL STUDENT. I TOLD YOU ALREADY.
OH. YEAH. SORRY. I FORGOT.
WELL. YOU'VE GOT A LOT ON YOUR MIND.
CAR HIRE

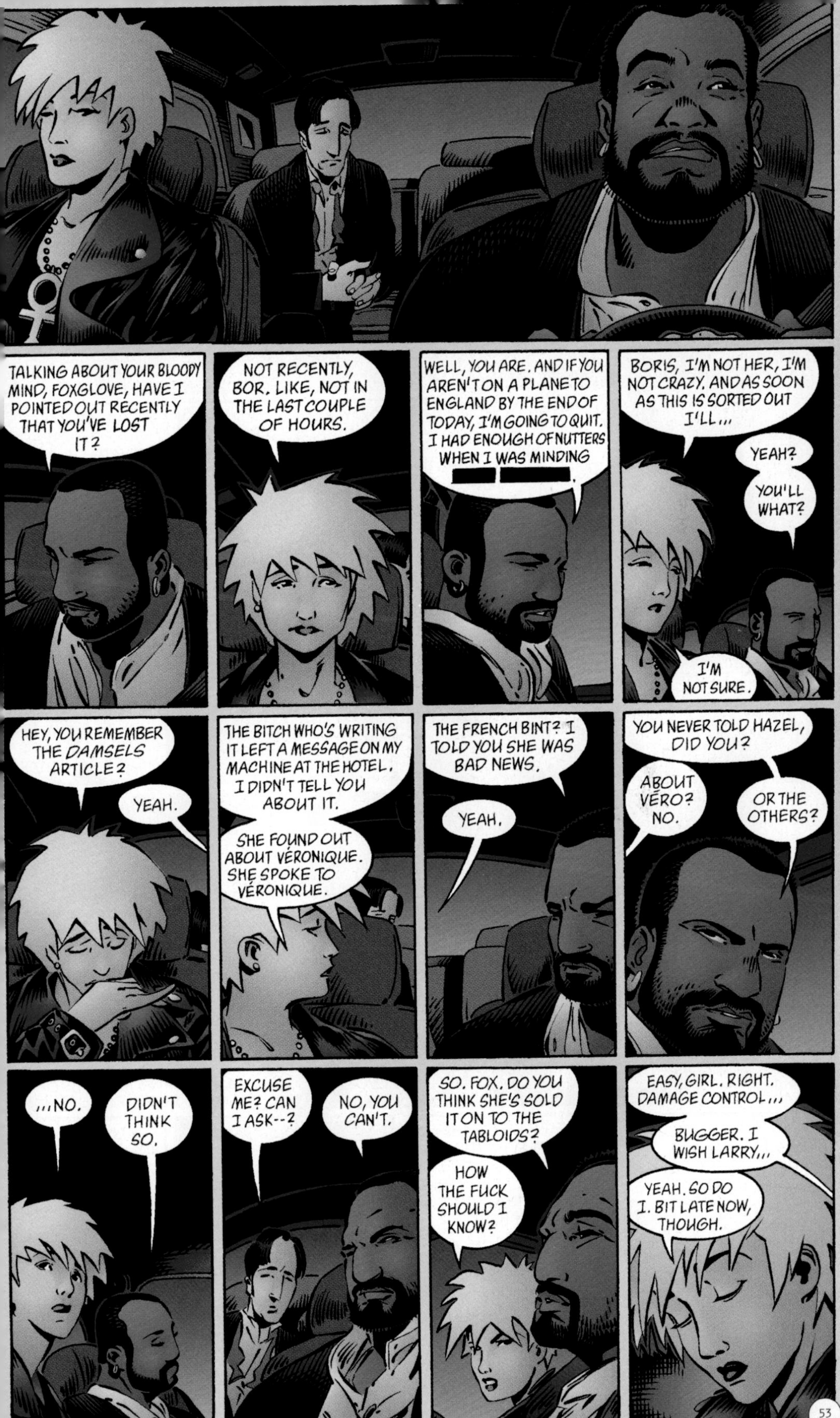
TALKING ABOUT YOUR BLOODY MIND, FOXGLOVE, HAVE I POINTED OUT RECENTLY THAT YOU'VE LOST IT?
NOT RECENTLY, BOR. LIKE, NOT IN THE LAST COUPLE OF HOURS.
WELL, YOU ARE. AND IF YOU AREN'T ON A PLANE TO ENGLAND BY THE END OF TODAY, I'M GOING TO QUIT. I HAD ENOUGH OF NUTTERS WHEN I WAS MINDING [redacted].
BORIS, I'M NOT HER, I'M NOT CRAZY. AND AS SOON AS THIS IS SORTED OUT I'LL...
YEAH?
YOU'LL WHAT?
I'M NOT SURE.
HEY, YOU REMEMBER THE *DAMSELS* ARTICLE?
YEAH.
THE BITCH WHO'S WRITING IT LEFT A MESSAGE ON MY MACHINE AT THE HOTEL. I DIDN'T TELL YOU ABOUT IT.
SHE FOUND OUT ABOUT VÉRONIQUE. SHE SPOKE TO VÉRONIQUE.
THE FRENCH BINT? I TOLD YOU SHE WAS BAD NEWS.
YEAH.
YOU NEVER TOLD HAZEL, DID YOU?
ABOUT VÉRO? NO.
OR THE OTHERS?
...NO.
DIDN'T THINK SO.
EXCUSE ME? CAN I ASK--?
NO, YOU CAN'T.
SO. FOX. DO YOU THINK SHE'S SOLD IT ON TO THE TABLOIDS?
HOW THE FUCK SHOULD I KNOW?
EASY, GIRL. RIGHT. DAMAGE CONTROL...
BUGGER. I WISH LARRY...
YEAH. SO DO I. BIT LATE NOW, THOUGH.

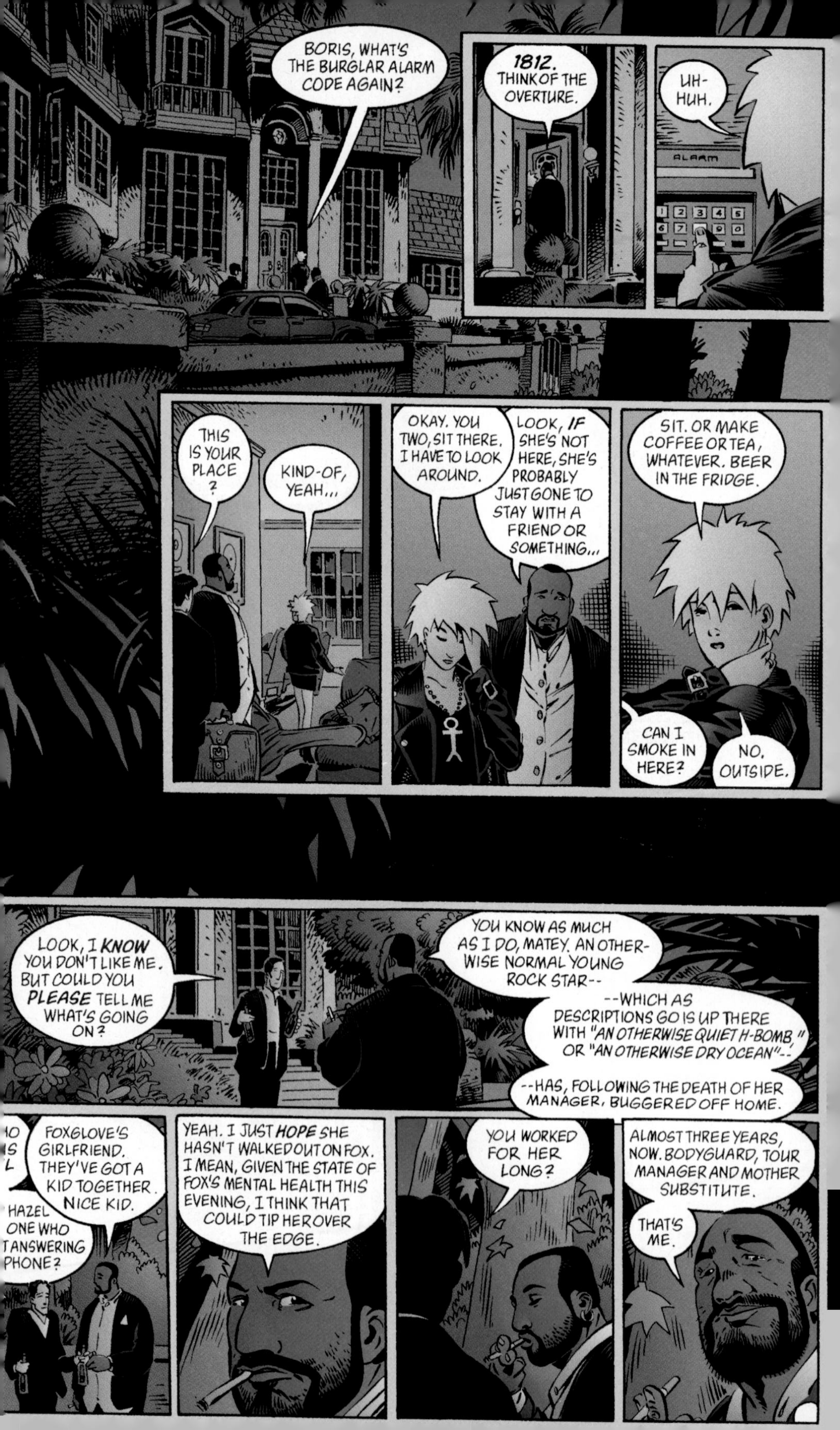

BORIS, WHAT'S THE BURGLAR ALARM CODE AGAIN?
1812. THINK OF THE OVERTURE.
UH-HUH.
ALARM
THIS IS YOUR PLACE?
KIND-OF, YEAH...
OKAY. YOU TWO, SIT THERE. I HAVE TO LOOK AROUND.
LOOK, IF SHE'S NOT HERE, SHE'S PROBABLY JUST GONE TO STAY WITH A FRIEND OR SOMETHING...
SIT. OR MAKE COFFEE OR TEA, WHATEVER. BEER IN THE FRIDGE.
CAN I SMOKE IN HERE?
NO. OUTSIDE.
LOOK, I KNOW YOU DON'T LIKE ME. BUT COULD YOU PLEASE TELL ME WHAT'S GOING ON?
YOU KNOW AS MUCH AS I DO, MATEY. AN OTHERWISE NORMAL YOUNG ROCK STAR--
--WHICH AS DESCRIPTIONS GO IS UP THERE WITH "AN OTHERWISE QUIET H-BOMB," OR "AN OTHERWISE DRY OCEAN"--
--HAS, FOLLOWING THE DEATH OF HER MANAGER, BUGGERED OFF HOME.
HAZEL ONE WHO ANSWERING PHONE?
FOXGLOVE'S GIRLFRIEND. THEY'VE GOT A KID TOGETHER. NICE KID.
YEAH. I JUST HOPE SHE HASN'T WALKED OUT ON FOX. I MEAN, GIVEN THE STATE OF FOX'S MENTAL HEALTH THIS EVENING, I THINK THAT COULD TIP HER OVER THE EDGE.
YOU WORKED FOR HER LONG?
ALMOST THREE YEARS, NOW. BODYGUARD, TOUR MANAGER AND MOTHER SUBSTITUTE.
THAT'S ME.

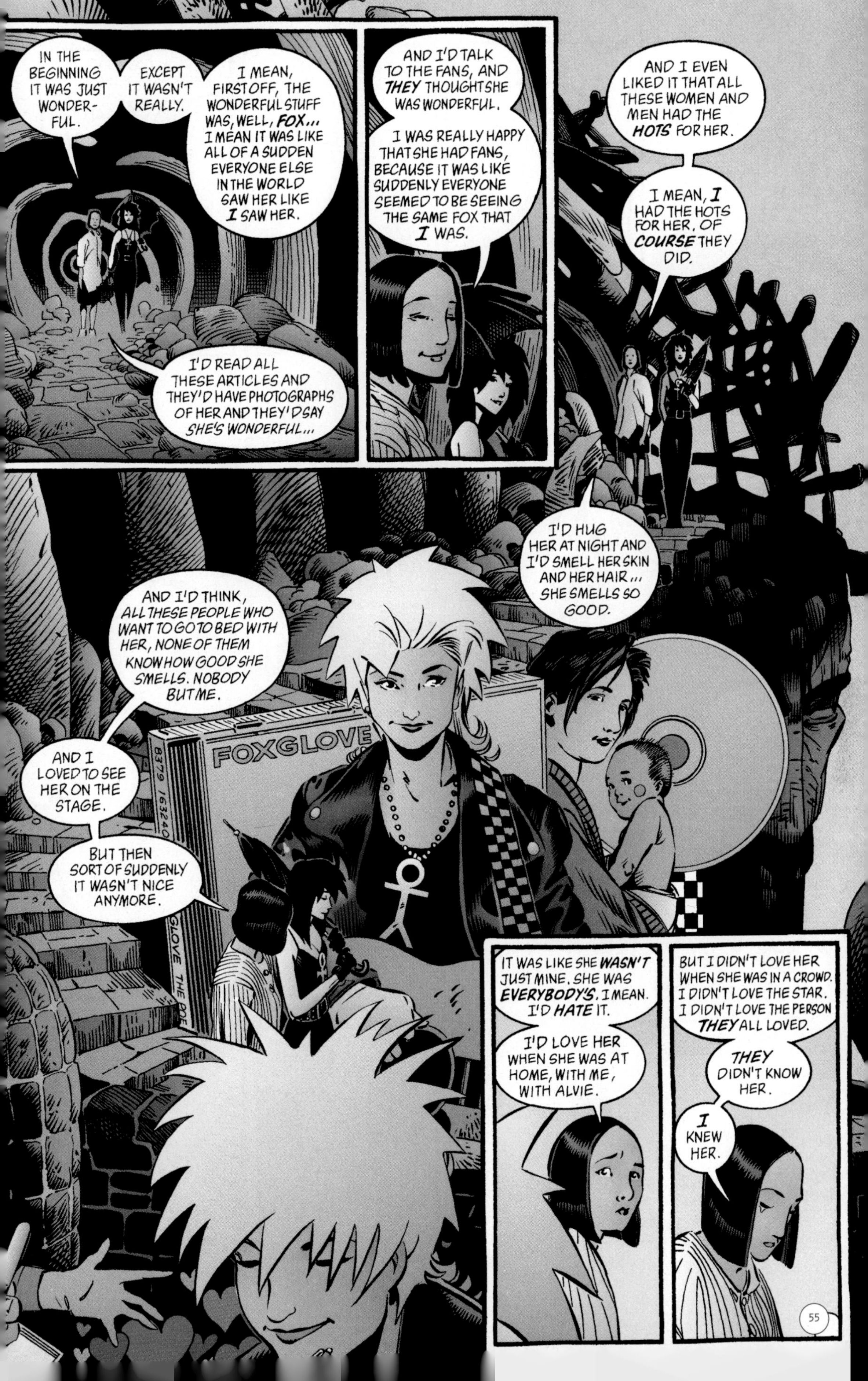
IN THE BEGINNING IT WAS JUST WONDERFUL.
EXCEPT IT WASN'T REALLY.
I MEAN, FIRST OFF, THE WONDERFUL STUFF WAS, WELL, FOX... I MEAN IT WAS LIKE ALL OF A SUDDEN EVERYONE ELSE IN THE WORLD SAW HER LIKE I SAW HER.
I'D READ ALL THESE ARTICLES AND THEY'D HAVE PHOTOGRAPHS OF HER AND THEY'D SAY SHE'S WONDERFUL...
AND I'D TALK TO THE FANS, AND THEY THOUGHT SHE WAS WONDERFUL.
I WAS REALLY HAPPY THAT SHE HAD FANS, BECAUSE IT WAS LIKE SUDDENLY EVERYONE SEEMED TO BE SEEING THE SAME FOX THAT I WAS.
AND I EVEN LIKED IT THAT ALL THESE WOMEN AND MEN HAD THE HOTS FOR HER.
I MEAN, I HAD THE HOTS FOR HER, OF COURSE THEY DID.
I'D HUG HER AT NIGHT AND I'D SMELL HER SKIN AND HER HAIR... SHE SMELLS SO GOOD.
AND I'D THINK, ALL THESE PEOPLE WHO WANT TO GO TO BED WITH HER, NONE OF THEM KNOW HOW GOOD SHE SMELLS. NOBODY BUT ME.
FOXGLOVE
8379 16324
AND I LOVED TO SEE HER ON THE STAGE.
BUT THEN SORT OF SUDDENLY IT WASN'T NICE ANYMORE.
IT WAS LIKE SHE WASN'T JUST MINE. SHE WAS EVERYBODY'S, I MEAN. I'D HATE IT.
I'D LOVE HER WHEN SHE WAS AT HOME, WITH ME, WITH ALVIE.
BUT I DIDN'T LOVE HER WHEN SHE WAS IN A CROWD. I DIDN'T LOVE THE STAR. I DIDN'T LOVE THE PERSON THEY ALL LOVED.
THEY DIDN'T KNOW HER.
I KNEW HER.

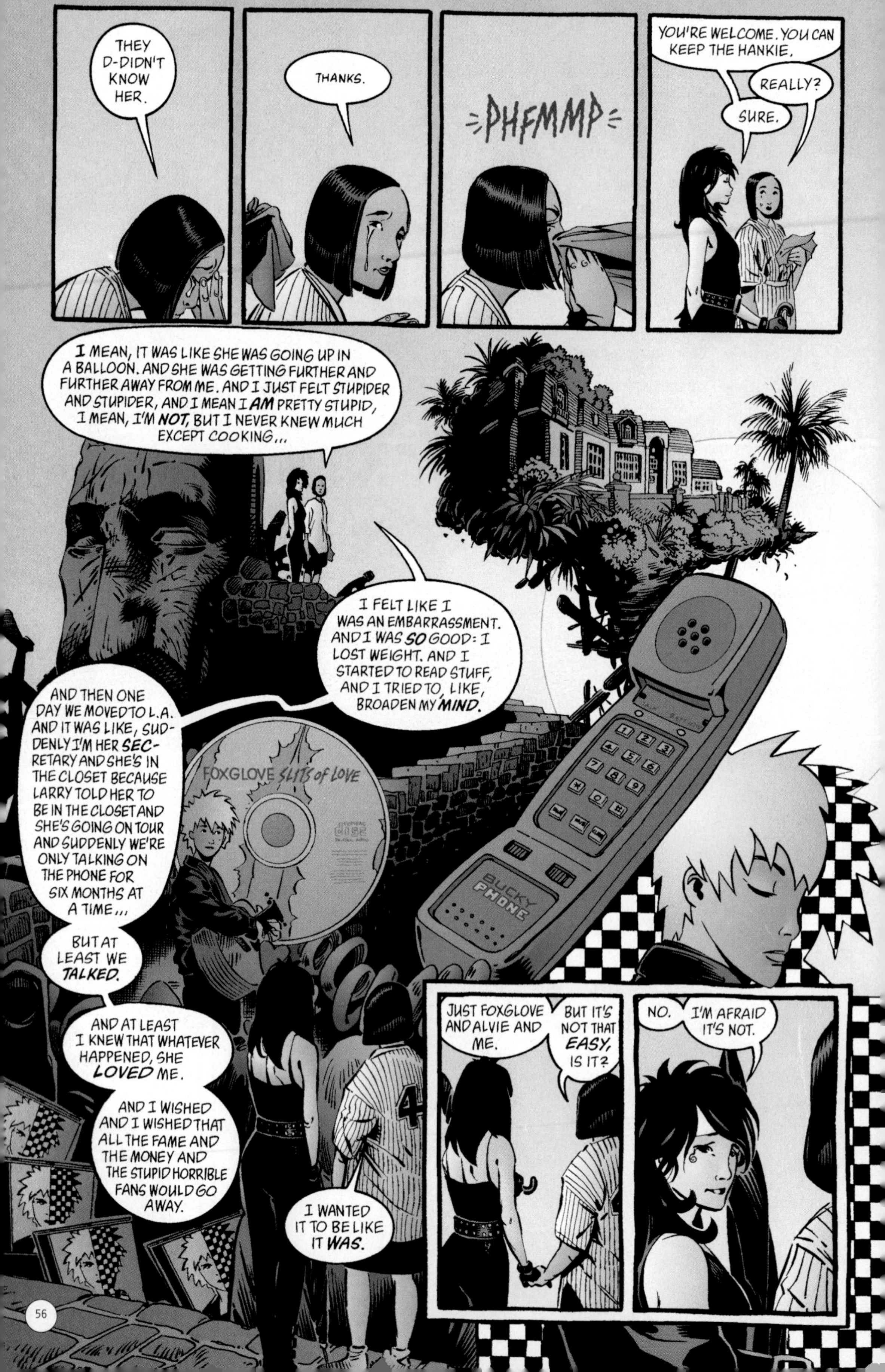
THEY D-DIDN'T KNOW HER.
THANKS.
PHFMMP
YOU'RE WELCOME. YOU CAN KEEP THE HANKIE.
REALLY?
SURE.
I MEAN, IT WAS LIKE SHE WAS GOING UP IN A BALLOON. AND SHE WAS GETTING FURTHER AND FURTHER AWAY FROM ME. AND I JUST FELT STUPIDER AND STUPIDER, AND I MEAN I AM PRETTY STUPID, I MEAN, I'M NOT, BUT I NEVER KNEW MUCH EXCEPT COOKING...
I FELT LIKE I WAS AN EMBARRASSMENT. AND I WAS SO GOOD: I LOST WEIGHT. AND I STARTED TO READ STUFF, AND I TRIED TO, LIKE, BROADEN MY MIND.
AND THEN ONE DAY WE MOVED TO L.A. AND IT WAS LIKE, SUDDENLY I'M HER SECRETARY AND SHE'S IN THE CLOSET BECAUSE LARRY TOLD HER TO BE IN THE CLOSET AND SHE'S GOING ON TOUR AND SUDDENLY WE'RE ONLY TALKING ON THE PHONE FOR SIX MONTHS AT A TIME...
FOXGLOVE SLITS of LOVE
BUCKY PHONE
BUT AT LEAST WE TALKED.
AND AT LEAST I KNEW THAT WHATEVER HAPPENED, SHE LOVED ME.
AND I WISHED AND I WISHED THAT ALL THE FAME AND THE MONEY AND THE STUPID HORRIBLE FANS WOULD GO AWAY.
I WANTED IT TO BE LIKE IT WAS.
JUST FOXGLOVE AND ALVIE AND ME.
BUT IT'S NOT THAT EASY, IS IT?
NO.
I'M AFRAID IT'S NOT.

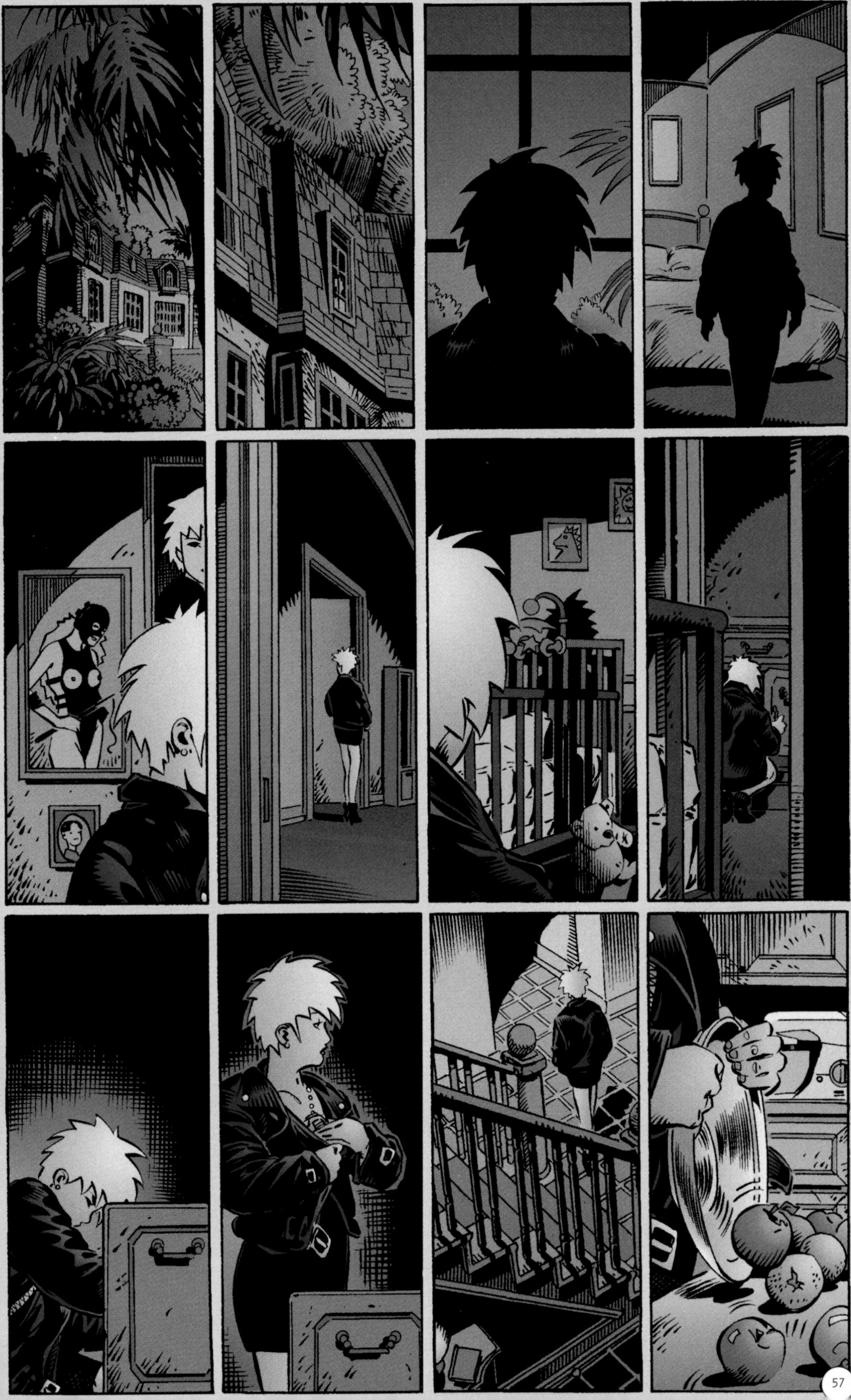

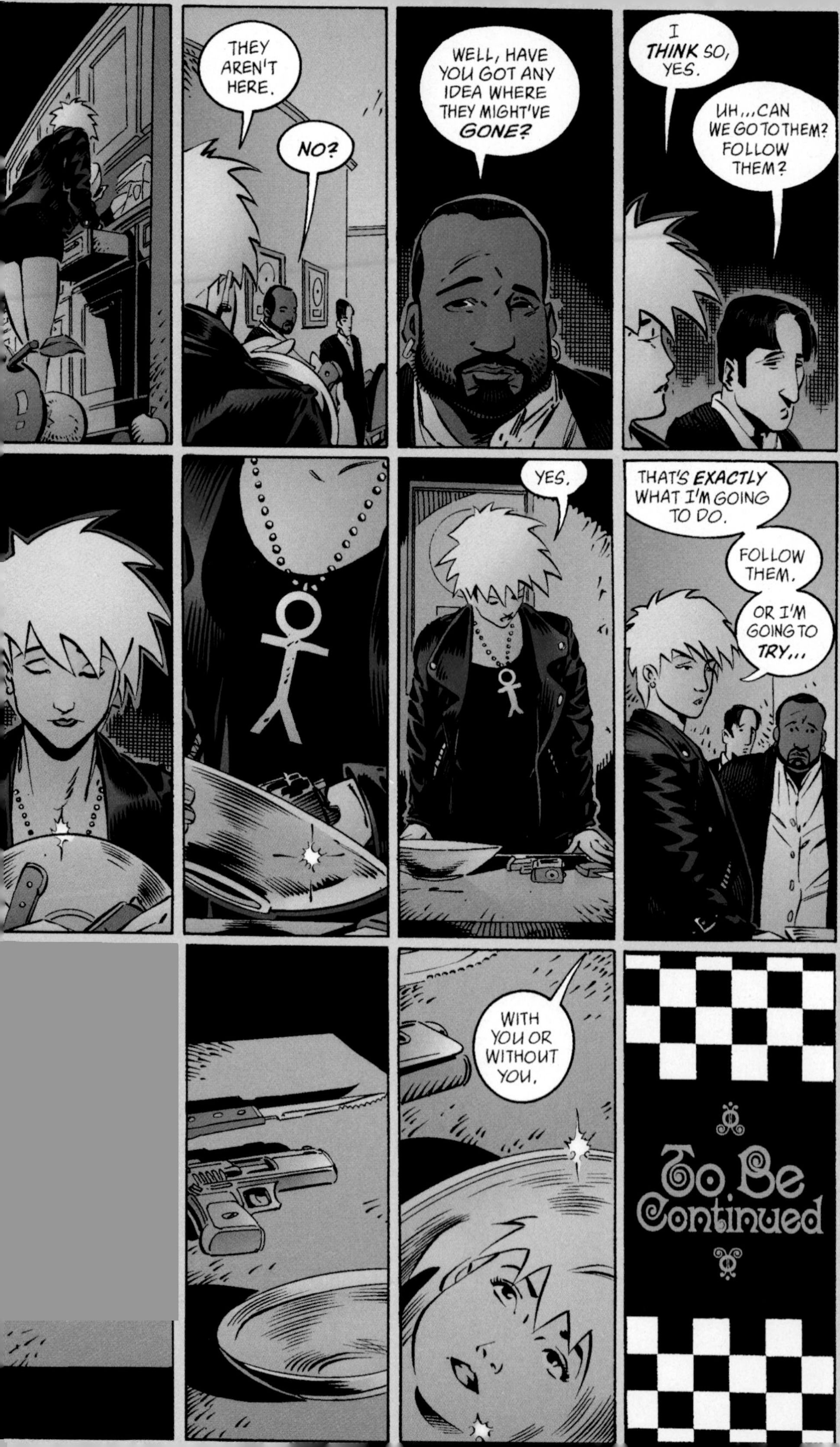
THEY AREN'T HERE.
NO?
WELL, HAVE YOU GOT ANY IDEA WHERE THEY MIGHT'VE GONE?
I THINK SO, YES.
UH...CAN WE GO TO THEM? FOLLOW THEM?
YES.
THAT'S EXACTLY WHAT I'M GOING TO DO.
FOLLOW THEM.
OR I'M GOING TO TRY...
WITH YOU OR WITHOUT YOU.
To Be Continued

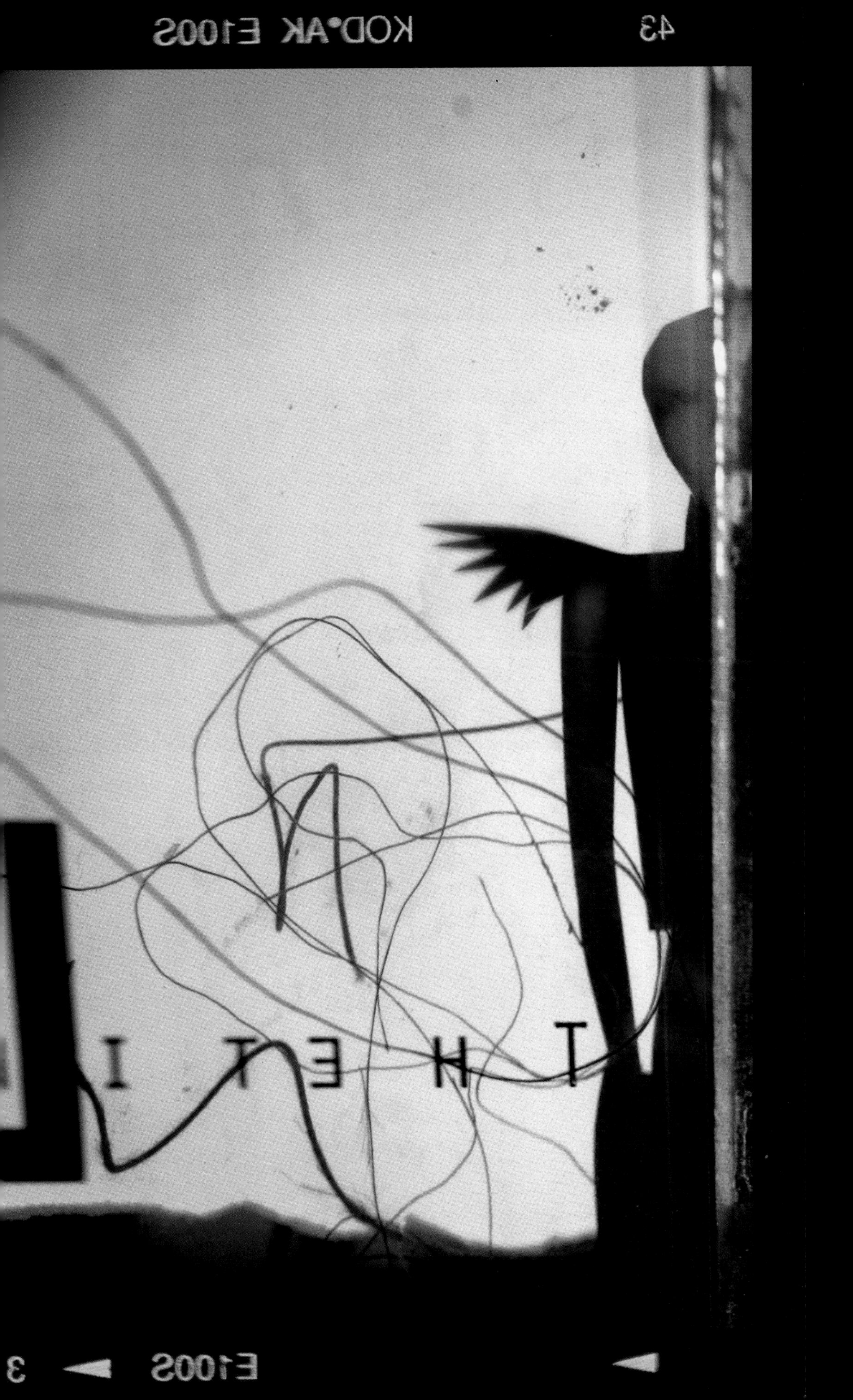
KOD•AK E100S
43
E100S
3

chapter three
the time of your life

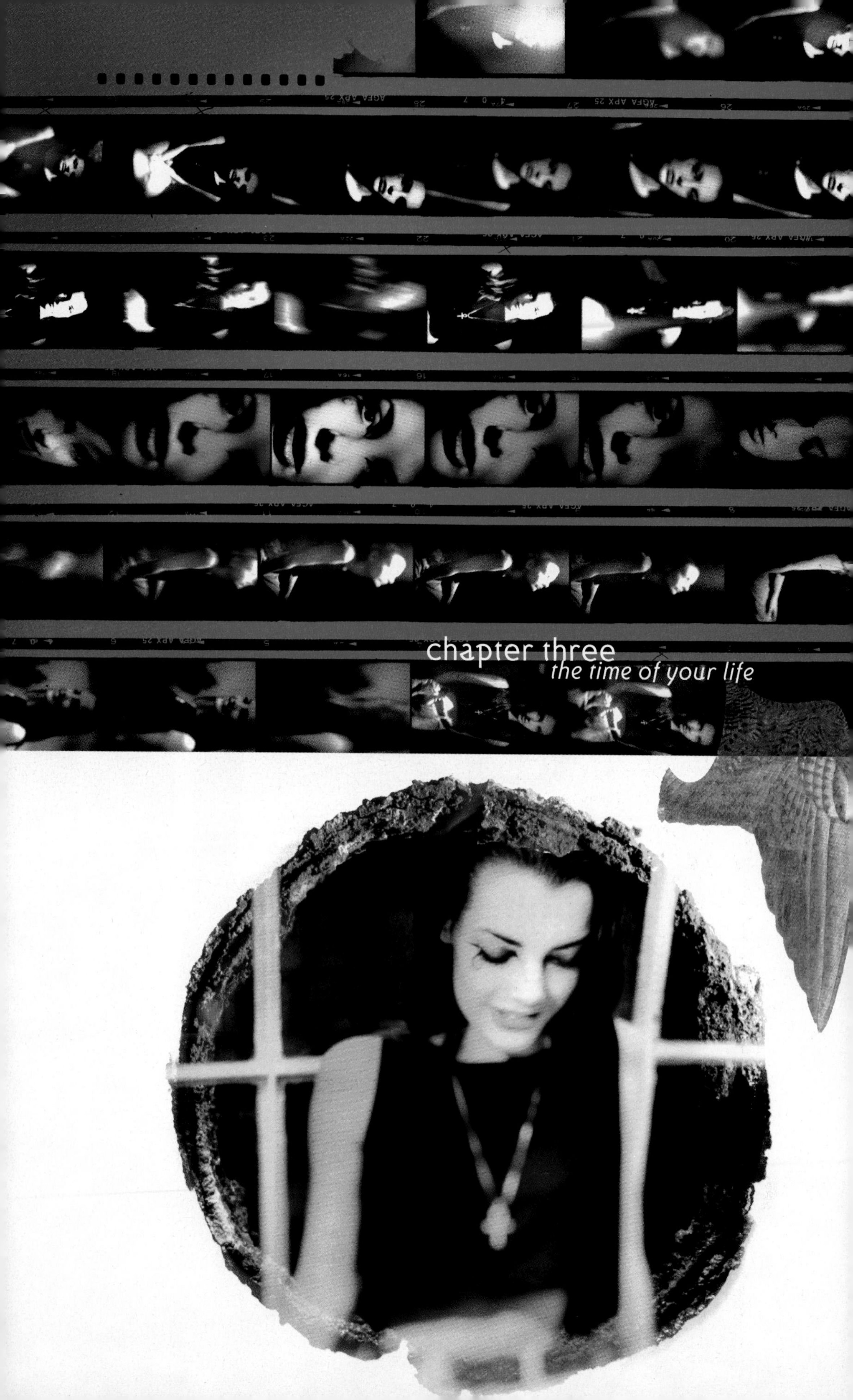

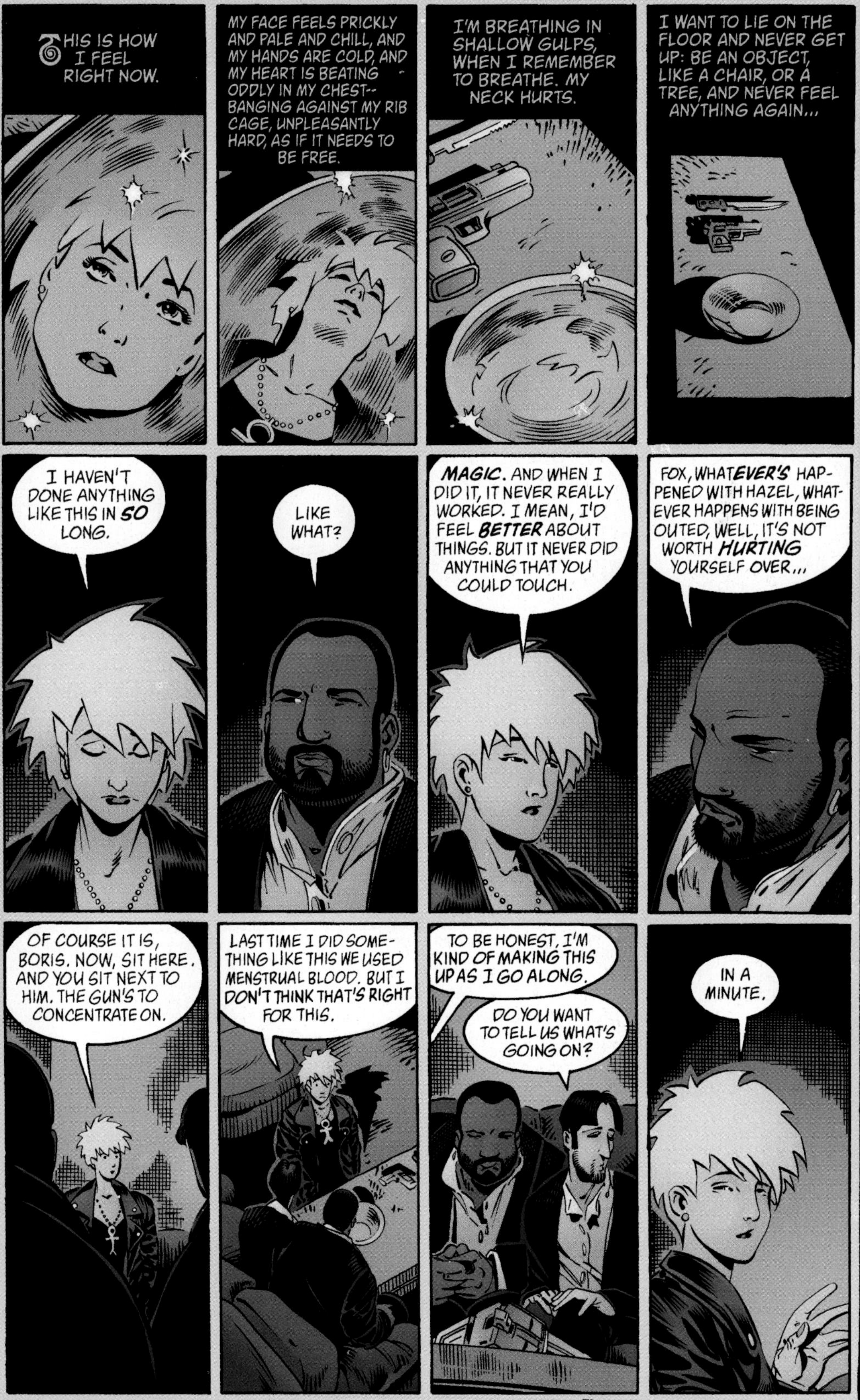
THIS IS HOW I FEEL RIGHT NOW.
MY FACE FEELS PRICKLY AND PALE AND CHILL, AND MY HANDS ARE COLD, AND MY HEART IS BEATING ODDLY IN MY CHEST-- BANGING AGAINST MY RIB CAGE, UNPLEASANTLY HARD, AS IF IT NEEDS TO BE FREE.
I'M BREATHING IN SHALLOW GULPS, WHEN I REMEMBER TO BREATHE. MY NECK HURTS.
I WANT TO LIE ON THE FLOOR AND NEVER GET UP: BE AN OBJECT, LIKE A CHAIR, OR A TREE, AND NEVER FEEL ANYTHING AGAIN...
I HAVEN'T DONE ANYTHING LIKE THIS IN SO LONG.
LIKE WHAT?
MAGIC. AND WHEN I DID IT, IT NEVER REALLY WORKED. I MEAN, I'D FEEL BETTER ABOUT THINGS. BUT IT NEVER DID ANYTHING THAT YOU COULD TOUCH.
FOX, WHATEVER'S HAPPENED WITH HAZEL, WHATEVER HAPPENS WITH BEING OUTED, WELL, IT'S NOT WORTH HURTING YOURSELF OVER...
OF COURSE IT IS, BORIS. NOW, SIT HERE. AND YOU SIT NEXT TO HIM. THE GUN'S TO CONCENTRATE ON.
LAST TIME I DID SOMETHING LIKE THIS WE USED MENSTRUAL BLOOD. BUT I DON'T THINK THAT'S RIGHT FOR THIS.
TO BE HONEST, I'M KIND OF MAKING THIS UP AS I GO ALONG.
DO YOU WANT TO TELL US WHAT'S GOING ON?
IN A MINUTE.

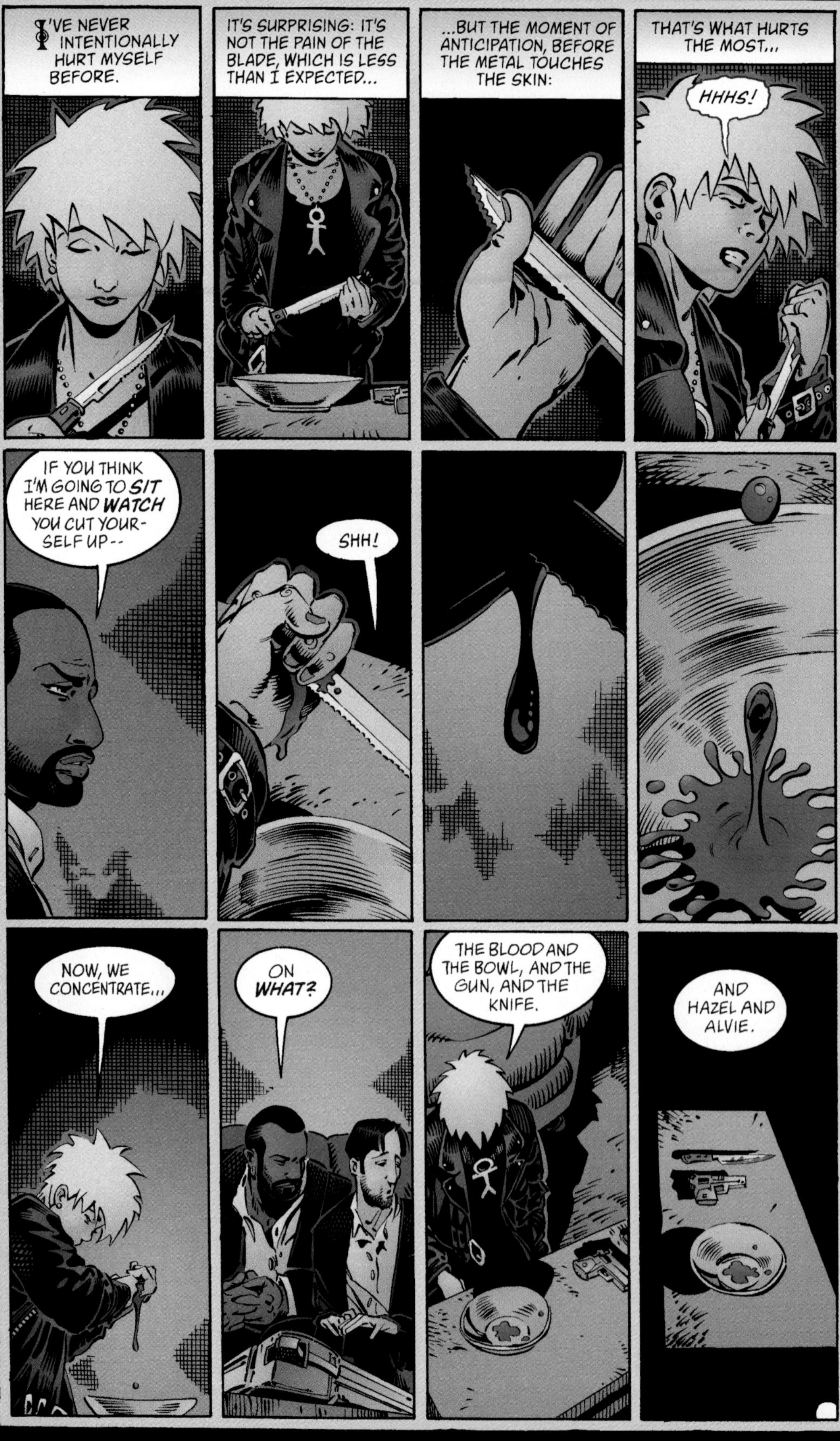
I'VE NEVER INTENTIONALLY HURT MYSELF BEFORE.
IT'S SURPRISING: IT'S NOT THE PAIN OF THE BLADE, WHICH IS LESS THAN I EXPECTED...
...BUT THE MOMENT OF ANTICIPATION, BEFORE THE METAL TOUCHES THE SKIN:
THAT'S WHAT HURTS THE MOST...
HHHS!
IF YOU THINK I'M GOING TO SIT HERE AND WATCH YOU CUT YOURSELF UP--
SHH!
NOW, WE CONCENTRATE...
ON WHAT?
THE BLOOD AND THE BOWL, AND THE GUN, AND THE KNIFE.
AND HAZEL AND ALVIE.

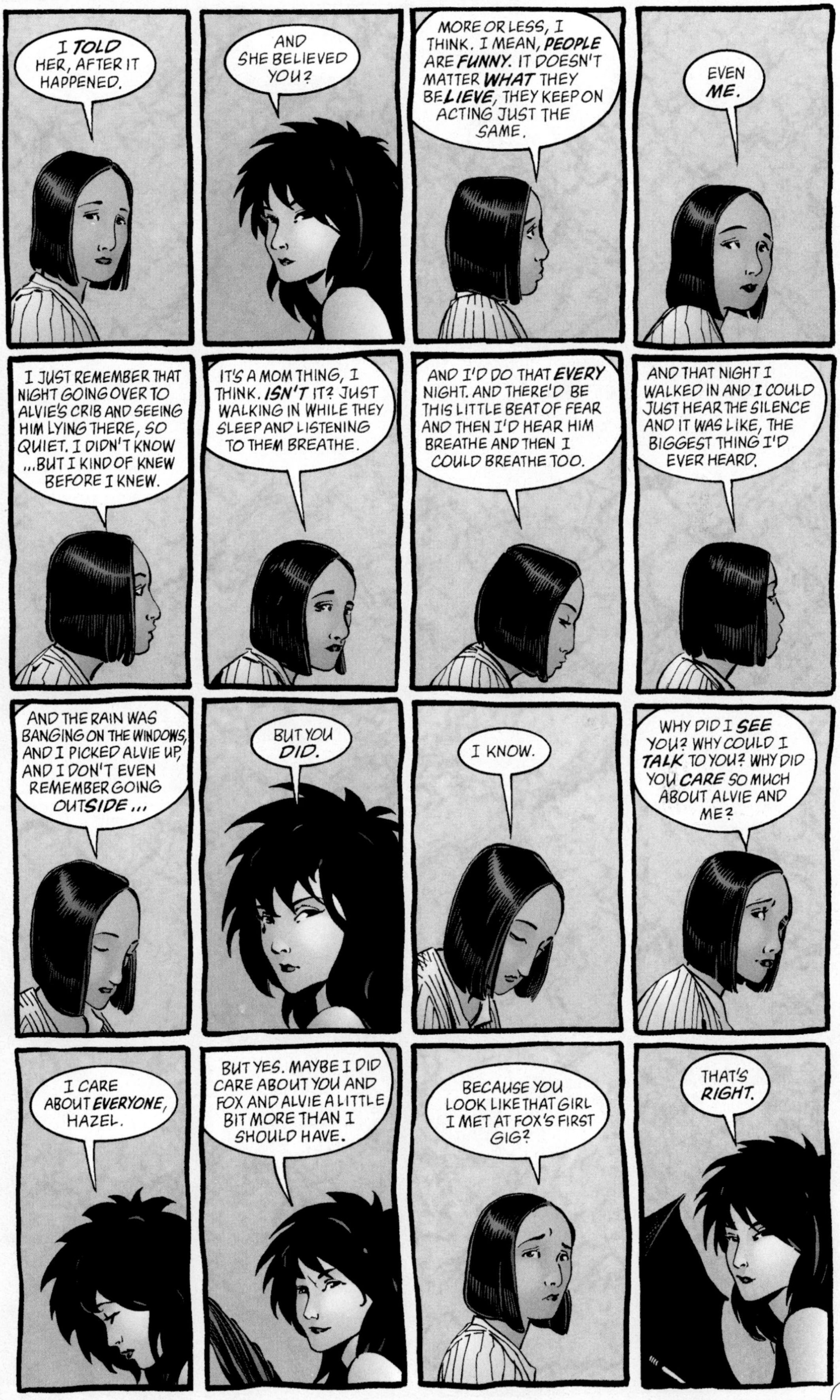
I TOLD HER, AFTER IT HAPPENED.
AND SHE BELIEVED YOU?
MORE OR LESS, I THINK. I MEAN, PEOPLE ARE FUNNY. IT DOESN'T MATTER WHAT THEY BELIEVE, THEY KEEP ON ACTING JUST THE SAME.
EVEN ME.
I JUST REMEMBER THAT NIGHT GOING OVER TO ALVIE'S CRIB AND SEEING HIM LYING THERE, SO QUIET. I DIDN'T KNOW ...BUT I KIND OF KNEW BEFORE I KNEW.
IT'S A MOM THING, I THINK. ISN'T IT? JUST WALKING IN WHILE THEY SLEEP AND LISTENING TO THEM BREATHE.
AND I'D DO THAT EVERY NIGHT. AND THERE'D BE THIS LITTLE BEAT OF FEAR AND THEN I'D HEAR HIM BREATHE AND THEN I COULD BREATHE TOO.
AND THAT NIGHT I WALKED IN AND I COULD JUST HEAR THE SILENCE AND IT WAS LIKE, THE BIGGEST THING I'D EVER HEARD.
AND THE RAIN WAS BANGING ON THE WINDOWS, AND I PICKED ALVIE UP, AND I DON'T EVEN REMEMBER GOING OUTSIDE ...
BUT YOU DID.
I KNOW.
WHY DID I SEE YOU? WHY COULD I TALK TO YOU? WHY DID YOU CARE SO MUCH ABOUT ALVIE AND ME?
I CARE ABOUT EVERYONE, HAZEL.
BUT YES. MAYBE I DID CARE ABOUT YOU AND FOX AND ALVIE A LITTLE BIT MORE THAN I SHOULD HAVE.
BECAUSE YOU LOOK LIKE THAT GIRL I MET AT FOX'S FIRST GIG?
THAT'S RIGHT.

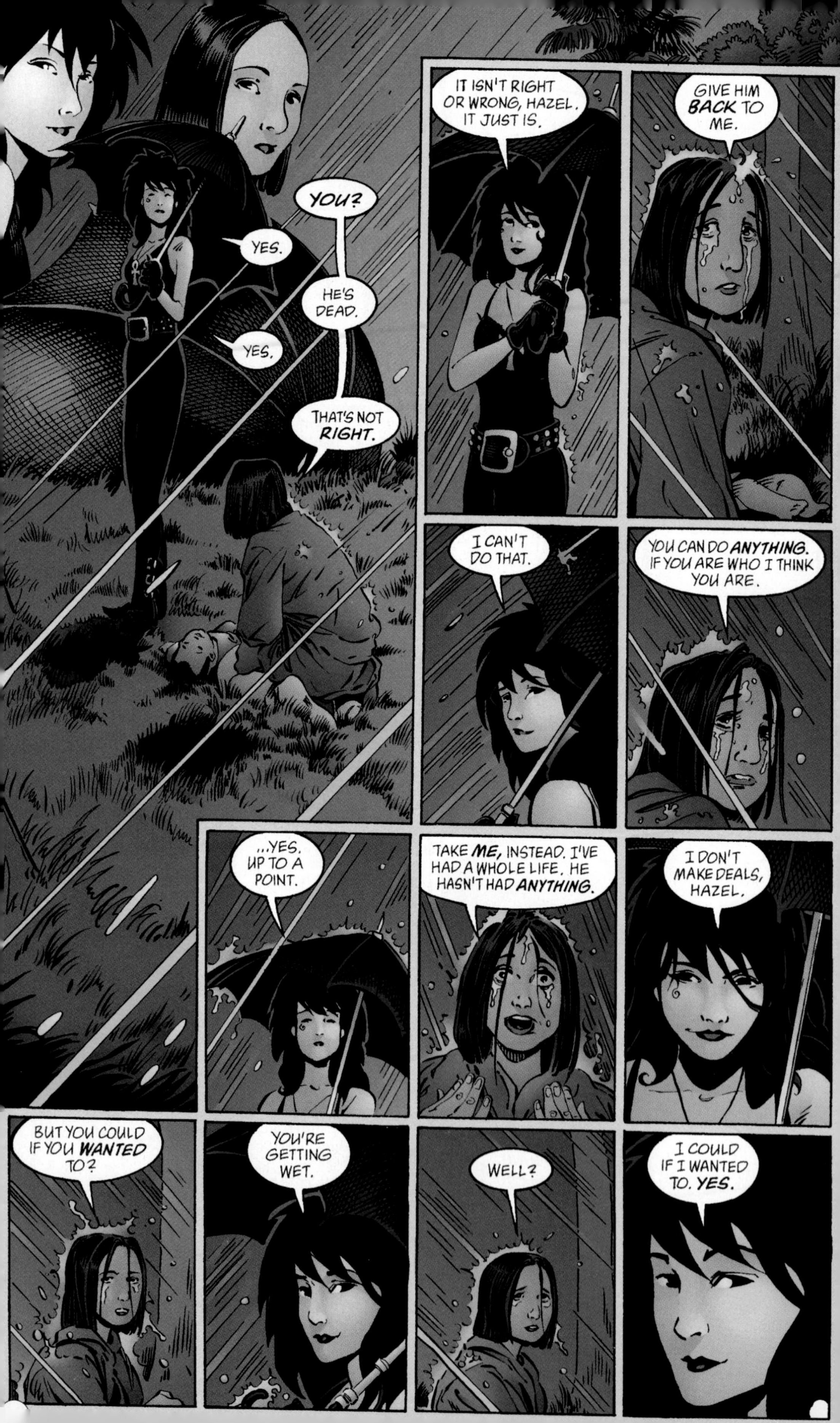
YOU?
YES.
HE'S DEAD.
YES.
THAT'S NOT RIGHT.
IT ISN'T RIGHT OR WRONG, HAZEL. IT JUST IS.
GIVE HIM BACK TO ME.
I CAN'T DO THAT.
YOU CAN DO ANYTHING. IF YOU ARE WHO I THINK YOU ARE.
...YES. UP TO A POINT.
TAKE ME, INSTEAD. I'VE HAD A WHOLE LIFE. HE HASN'T HAD ANYTHING.
I DON'T MAKE DEALS, HAZEL.
BUT YOU COULD IF YOU WANTED TO?
YOU'RE GETTING WET.
WELL?
I COULD IF I WANTED TO. YES.

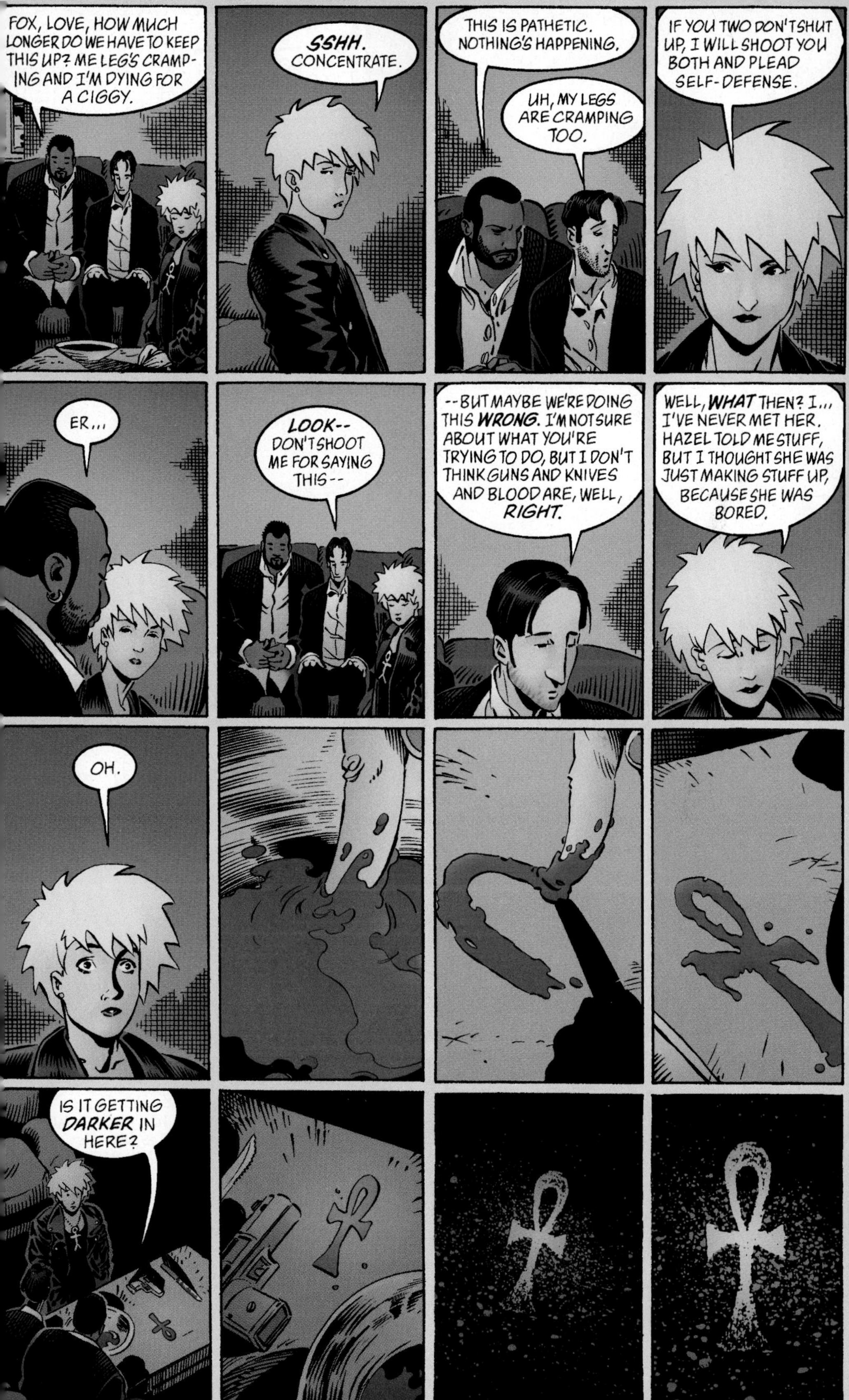
FOX, LOVE, HOW MUCH LONGER DO WE HAVE TO KEEP THIS UP? ME LEG'S CRAMPING AND I'M DYING FOR A CIGGY.
SSHH. CONCENTRATE.
THIS IS PATHETIC. NOTHING'S HAPPENING.
UH, MY LEGS ARE CRAMPING TOO.
IF YOU TWO DON'T SHUT UP, I WILL SHOOT YOU BOTH AND PLEAD SELF-DEFENSE.
ER...
LOOK-- DON'T SHOOT ME FOR SAYING THIS--
--BUT MAYBE WE'RE DOING THIS WRONG. I'M NOT SURE ABOUT WHAT YOU'RE TRYING TO DO, BUT I DON'T THINK GUNS AND KNIVES AND BLOOD ARE, WELL, RIGHT.
WELL, WHAT THEN? I... I'VE NEVER MET HER. HAZEL TOLD ME STUFF, BUT I THOUGHT SHE WAS JUST MAKING STUFF UP, BECAUSE SHE WAS BORED.
OH.
IS IT GETTING DARKER IN HERE?

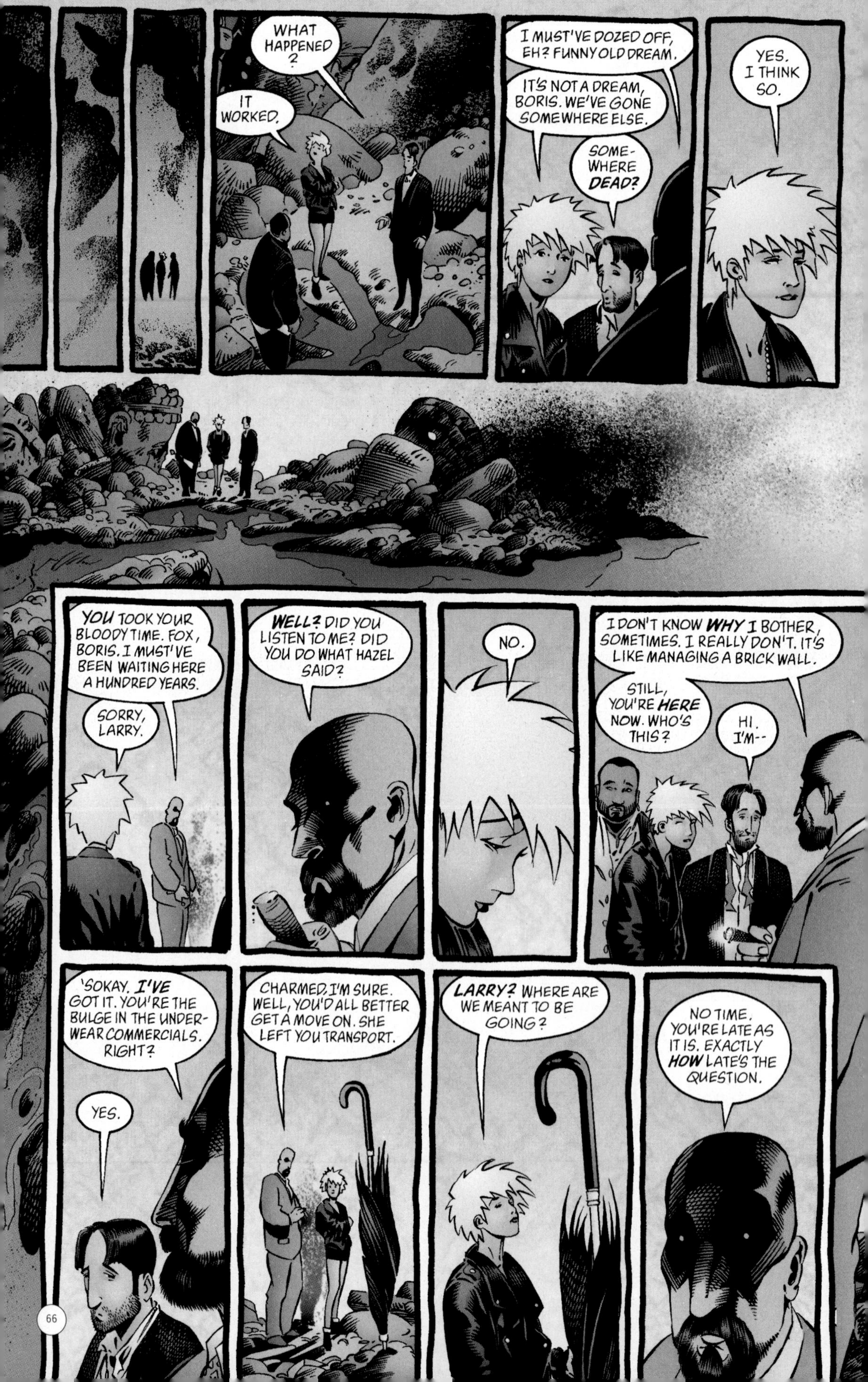
WHAT HAPPENED?
IT WORKED.
I MUST'VE DOZED OFF, EH? FUNNY OLD DREAM.
IT'S NOT A DREAM, BORIS. WE'VE GONE SOMEWHERE ELSE.
SOME-WHERE DEAD?
YES. I THINK SO.
YOU TOOK YOUR BLOODY TIME. FOX, BORIS. I MUST'VE BEEN WAITING HERE A HUNDRED YEARS.
SORRY, LARRY.
WELL? DID YOU LISTEN TO ME? DID YOU DO WHAT HAZEL SAID?
NO.
I DON'T KNOW WHY I BOTHER, SOMETIMES. I REALLY DON'T. IT'S LIKE MANAGING A BRICK WALL.
STILL, YOU'RE HERE NOW. WHO'S THIS?
HI. I'M--
'SOKAY. I'VE GOT IT. YOU'RE THE BULGE IN THE UNDER-WEAR COMMERCIALS. RIGHT?
YES.
CHARMED, I'M SURE. WELL, YOU'D ALL BETTER GET A MOVE ON. SHE LEFT YOU TRANSPORT.
LARRY? WHERE ARE WE MEANT TO BE GOING?
NO TIME. YOU'RE LATE AS IT IS. EXACTLY HOW LATE'S THE QUESTION.

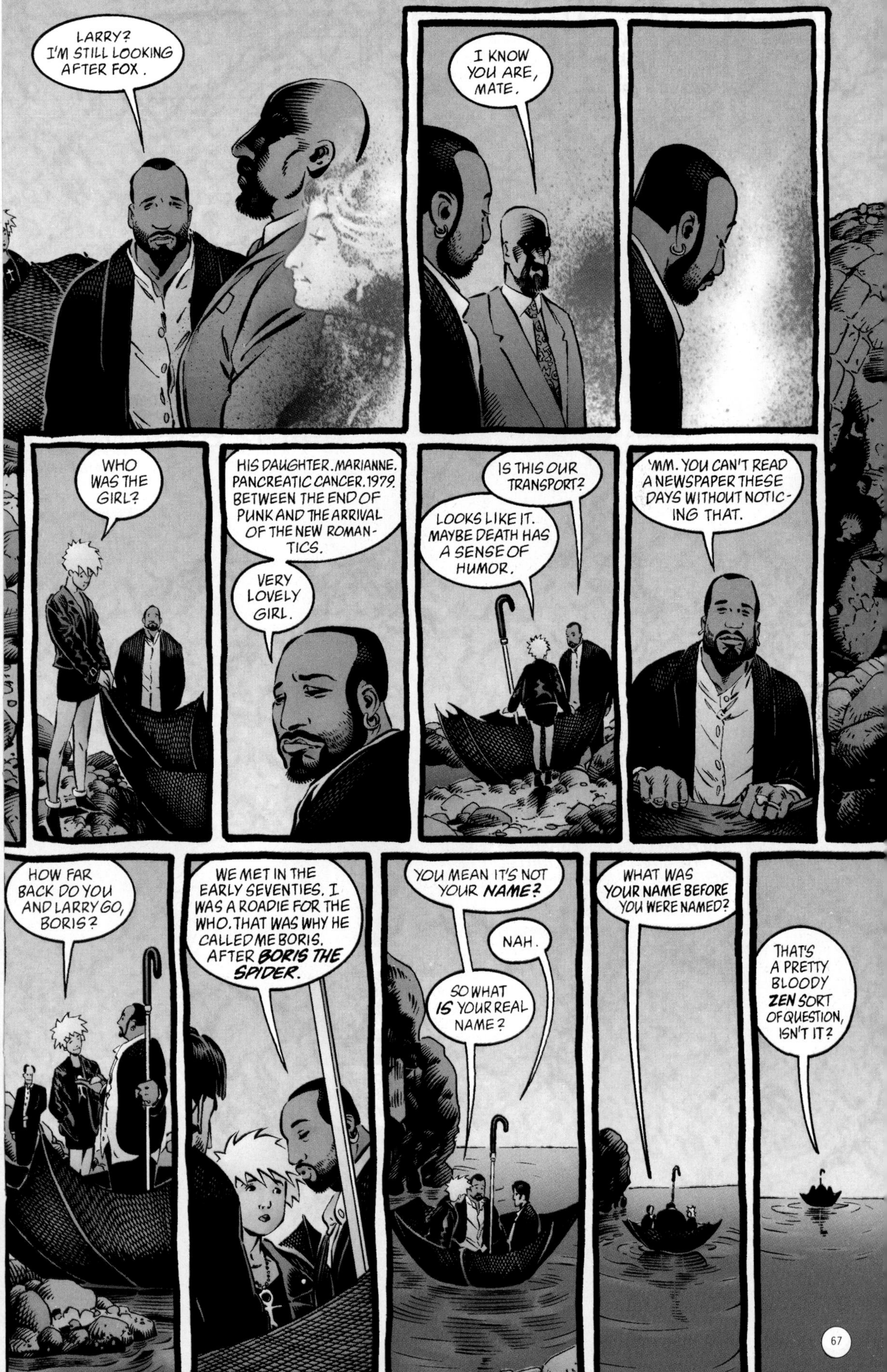
LARRY? I'M STILL LOOKING AFTER FOX.
I KNOW YOU ARE, MATE.
WHO WAS THE GIRL?
HIS DAUGHTER. MARIANNE. PANCREATIC CANCER. 1979. BETWEEN THE END OF PUNK AND THE ARRIVAL OF THE NEW ROMAN-TICS.
VERY LOVELY GIRL.
IS THIS OUR TRANSPORT?
LOOKS LIKE IT. MAYBE DEATH HAS A SENSE OF HUMOR.
'MM. YOU CAN'T READ A NEWSPAPER THESE DAYS WITHOUT NOTIC-ING THAT.
HOW FAR BACK DO YOU AND LARRY GO, BORIS?
WE MET IN THE EARLY SEVENTIES. I WAS A ROADIE FOR THE WHO. THAT WAS WHY HE CALLED ME BORIS. AFTER BORIS THE SPIDER.
YOU MEAN IT'S NOT YOUR NAME?
NAH.
SO WHAT IS YOUR REAL NAME?
WHAT WAS YOUR NAME BEFORE YOU WERE NAMED?
THAT'S A PRETTY BLOODY ZEN SORT OF QUESTION, ISN'T IT?

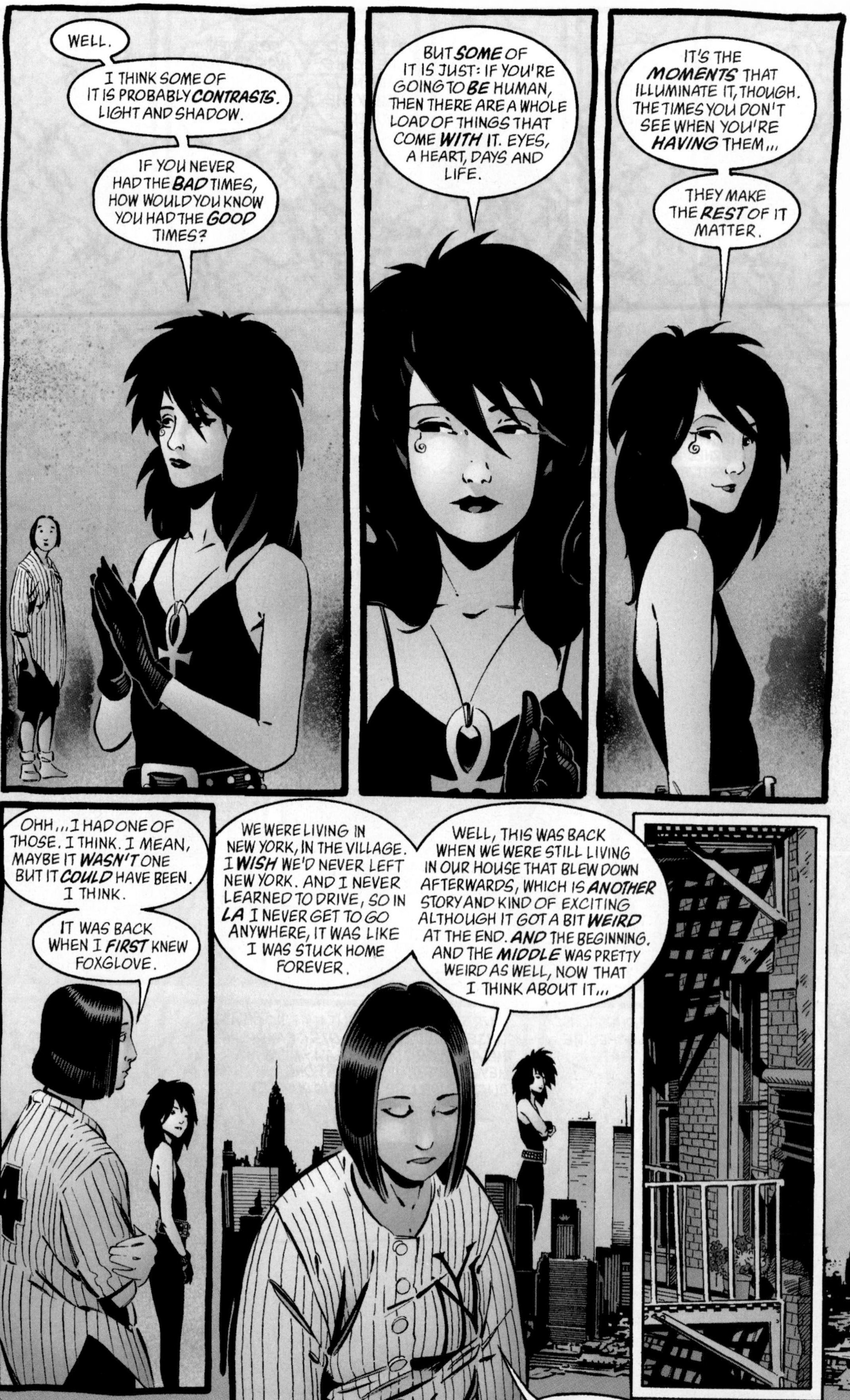
WELL.
I THINK SOME OF IT IS PROBABLY CONTRASTS. LIGHT AND SHADOW.
IF YOU NEVER HAD THE BAD TIMES, HOW WOULD YOU KNOW YOU HAD THE GOOD TIMES?
BUT SOME OF IT IS JUST: IF YOU'RE GOING TO BE HUMAN, THEN THERE ARE A WHOLE LOAD OF THINGS THAT COME WITH IT. EYES, A HEART, DAYS AND LIFE.
IT'S THE MOMENTS THAT ILLUMINATE IT, THOUGH. THE TIMES YOU DON'T SEE WHEN YOU'RE HAVING THEM...
THEY MAKE THE REST OF IT MATTER.
OHH...I HAD ONE OF THOSE. I THINK. I MEAN, MAYBE IT WASN'T ONE BUT IT COULD HAVE BEEN. I THINK.
IT WAS BACK WHEN I FIRST KNEW FOXGLOVE.
WE WERE LIVING IN NEW YORK, IN THE VILLAGE. I WISH WE'D NEVER LEFT NEW YORK. AND I NEVER LEARNED TO DRIVE, SO IN LA I NEVER GET TO GO ANYWHERE, IT WAS LIKE I WAS STUCK HOME FOREVER.
WELL, THIS WAS BACK WHEN WE WERE STILL LIVING IN OUR HOUSE THAT BLEW DOWN AFTERWARDS, WHICH IS ANOTHER STORY AND KIND OF EXCITING ALTHOUGH IT GOT A BIT WEIRD AT THE END. AND THE BEGINNING. AND THE MIDDLE WAS PRETTY WEIRD AS WELL, NOW THAT I THINK ABOUT IT...
ANYWAY...

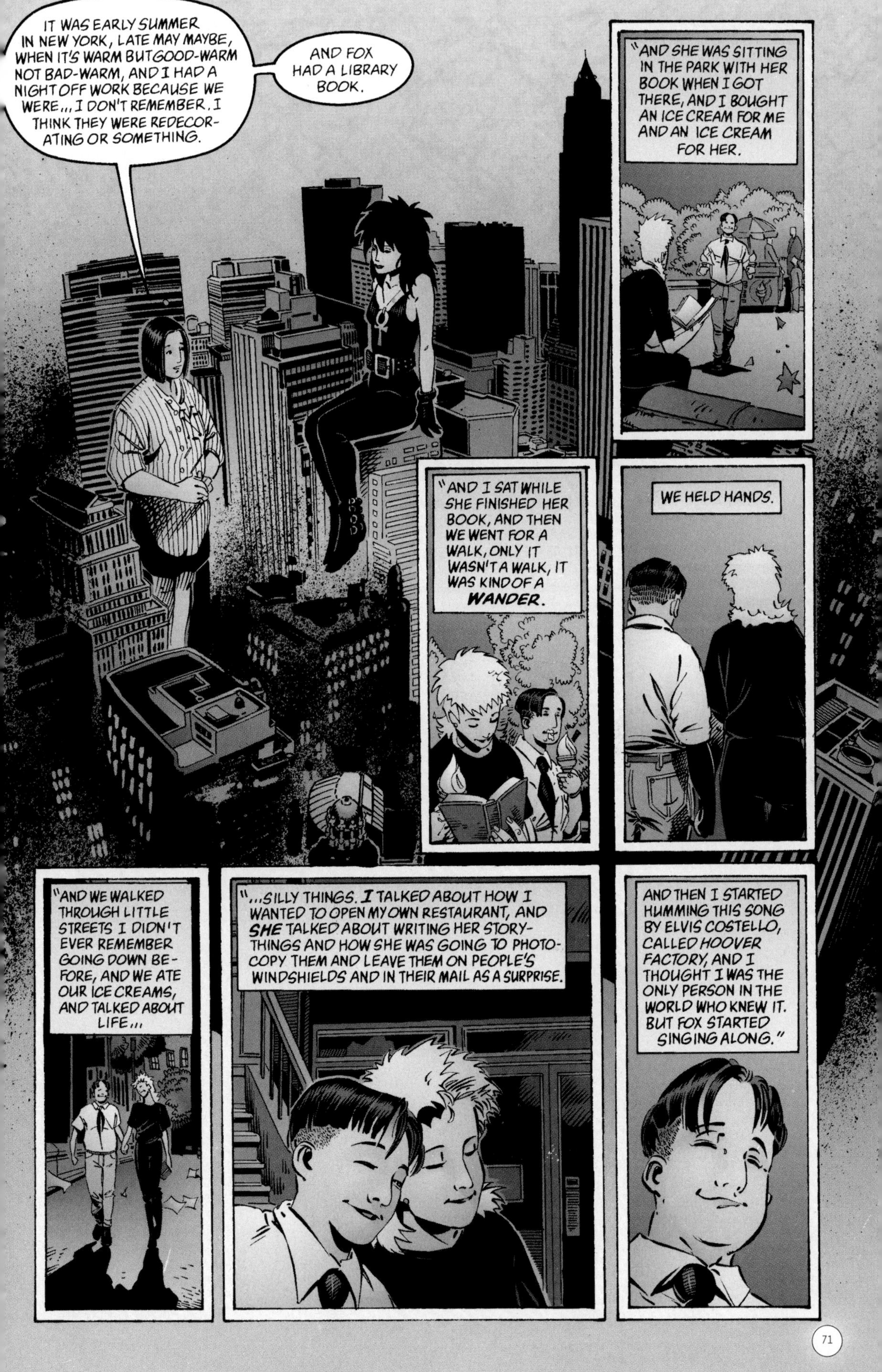

IT WAS EARLY SUMMER IN NEW YORK, LATE MAY MAYBE, WHEN IT'S WARM BUT GOOD-WARM NOT BAD-WARM, AND I HAD A NIGHT OFF WORK BECAUSE WE WERE... I DON'T REMEMBER. I THINK THEY WERE REDECORATING OR SOMETHING.
AND FOX HAD A LIBRARY BOOK.
"AND SHE WAS SITTING IN THE PARK WITH HER BOOK WHEN I GOT THERE, AND I BOUGHT AN ICE CREAM FOR ME AND AN ICE CREAM FOR HER.
"AND I SAT WHILE SHE FINISHED HER BOOK, AND THEN WE WENT FOR A WALK, ONLY IT WASN'T A WALK, IT WAS KIND OF A WANDER.
WE HELD HANDS.
"AND WE WALKED THROUGH LITTLE STREETS I DIDN'T EVER REMEMBER GOING DOWN BEFORE, AND WE ATE OUR ICE CREAMS, AND TALKED ABOUT LIFE...
"...SILLY THINGS. I TALKED ABOUT HOW I WANTED TO OPEN MY OWN RESTAURANT, AND SHE TALKED ABOUT WRITING HER STORY-THINGS AND HOW SHE WAS GOING TO PHOTOCOPY THEM AND LEAVE THEM ON PEOPLE'S WINDSHIELDS AND IN THEIR MAIL AS A SURPRISE.
AND THEN I STARTED HUMMING THIS SONG BY ELVIS COSTELLO, CALLED HOOVER FACTORY, AND I THOUGHT I WAS THE ONLY PERSON IN THE WORLD WHO KNEW IT. BUT FOX STARTED SINGING ALONG."

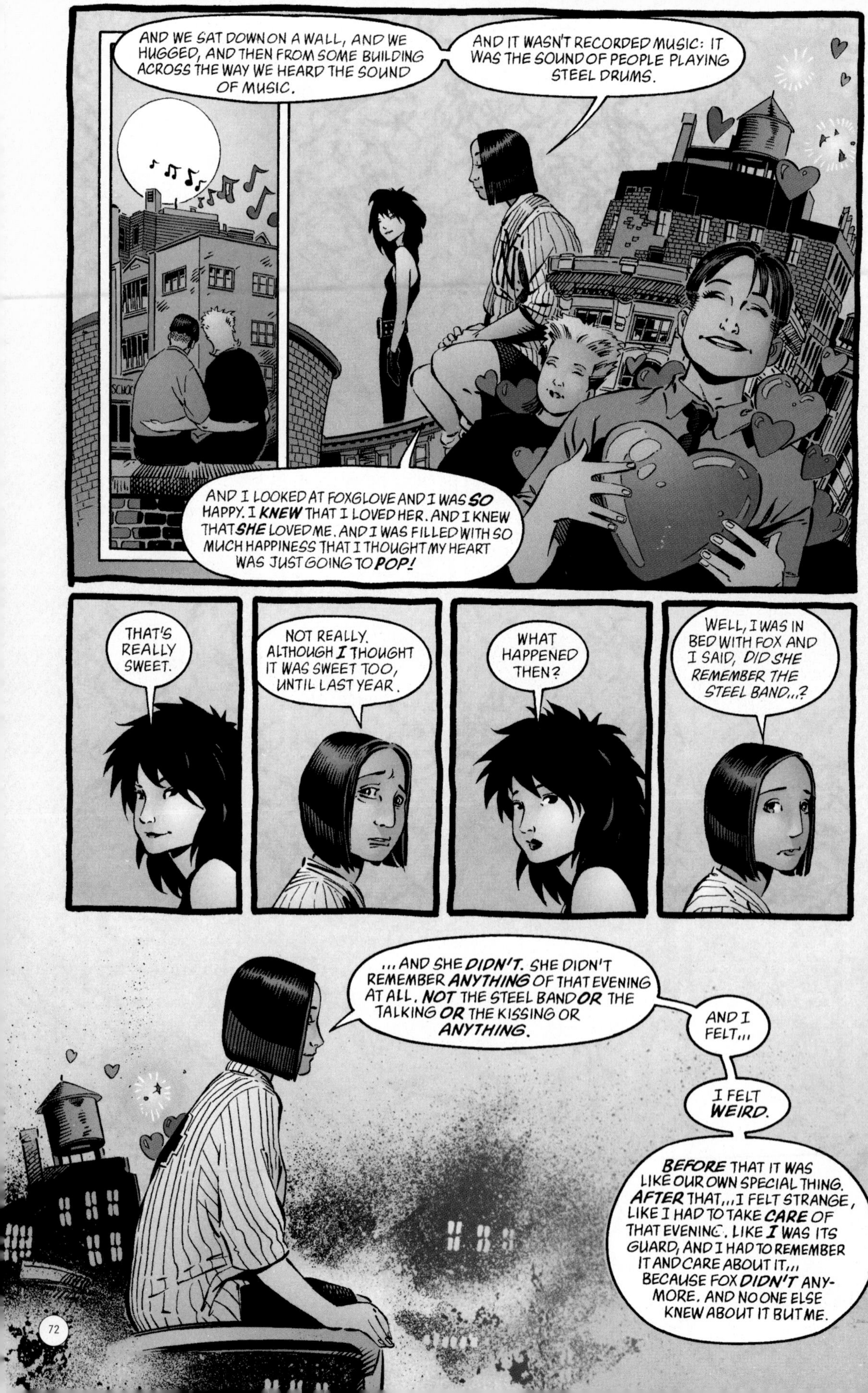

AND WE SAT DOWN ON A WALL, AND WE HUGGED, AND THEN FROM SOME BUILDING ACROSS THE WAY WE HEARD THE SOUND OF MUSIC.
AND IT WASN'T RECORDED MUSIC: IT WAS THE SOUND OF PEOPLE PLAYING STEEL DRUMS.
SCHOO
AND I LOOKED AT FOXGLOVE AND I WAS SO HAPPY. I KNEW THAT I LOVED HER. AND I KNEW THAT SHE LOVED ME. AND I WAS FILLED WITH SO MUCH HAPPINESS THAT I THOUGHT MY HEART WAS JUST GOING TO POP!
THAT'S REALLY SWEET.
NOT REALLY. ALTHOUGH I THOUGHT IT WAS SWEET TOO, UNTIL LAST YEAR.
WHAT HAPPENED THEN?
WELL, I WAS IN BED WITH FOX AND I SAID, DID SHE REMEMBER THE STEEL BAND...?
...AND SHE DIDN'T. SHE DIDN'T REMEMBER ANYTHING OF THAT EVENING AT ALL. NOT THE STEEL BAND OR THE TALKING OR THE KISSING OR ANYTHING.
AND I FELT...
I FELT WEIRD.
BEFORE THAT IT WAS LIKE OUR OWN SPECIAL THING. AFTER THAT... I FELT STRANGE, LIKE I HAD TO TAKE CARE OF THAT EVENING. LIKE I WAS ITS GUARD, AND I HAD TO REMEMBER IT AND CARE ABOUT IT... BECAUSE FOX DIDN'T ANYMORE. AND NO ONE ELSE KNEW ABOUT IT BUT ME.

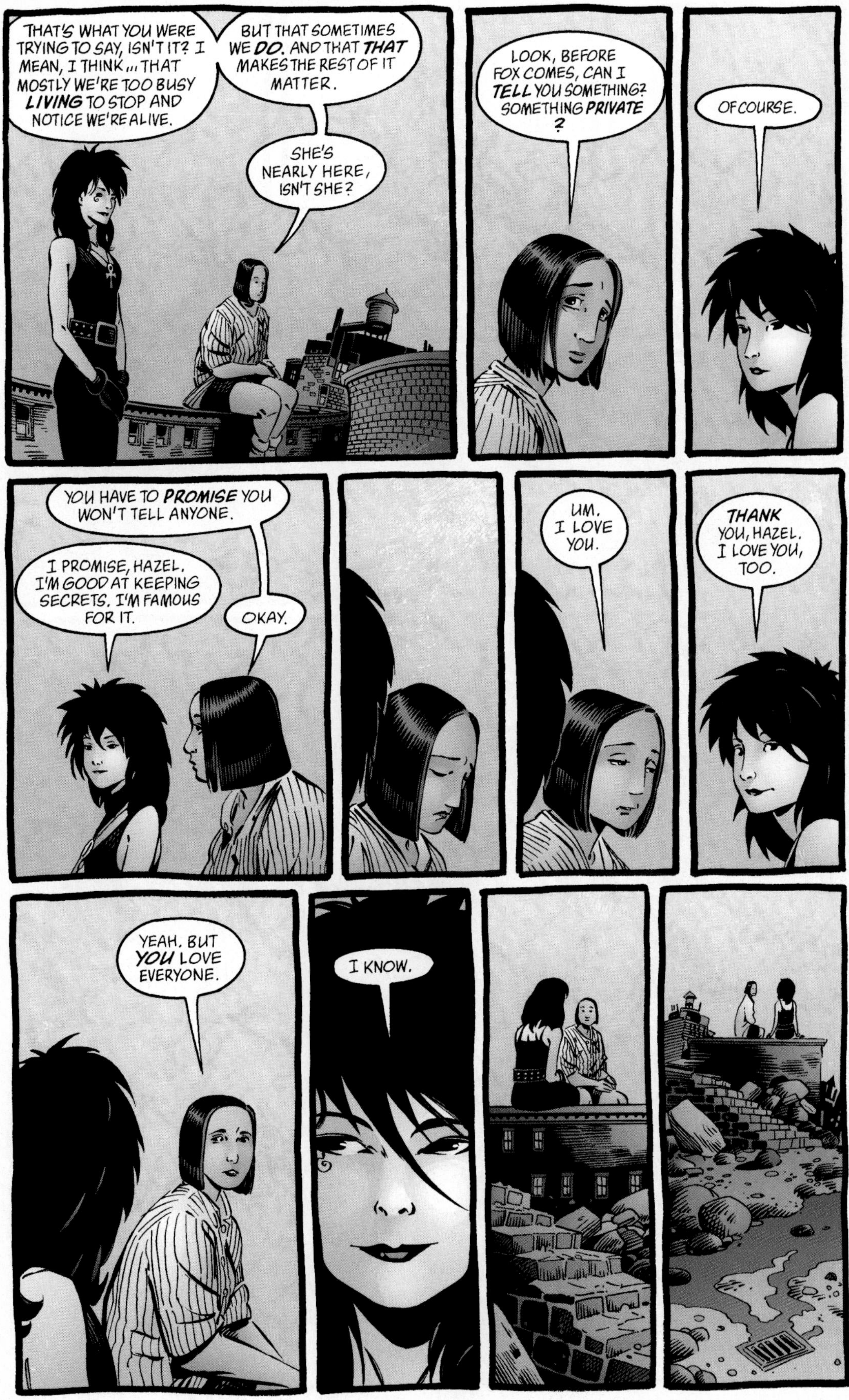
THAT'S WHAT YOU WERE TRYING TO SAY, ISN'T IT? I MEAN, I THINK... THAT MOSTLY WE'RE TOO BUSY LIVING TO STOP AND NOTICE WE'RE ALIVE.
BUT THAT SOMETIMES WE DO. AND THAT THAT MAKES THE REST OF IT MATTER.
SHE'S NEARLY HERE, ISN'T SHE?
LOOK, BEFORE FOX COMES, CAN I TELL YOU SOMETHING? SOMETHING PRIVATE?
OF COURSE.
YOU HAVE TO PROMISE YOU WON'T TELL ANYONE.
I PROMISE, HAZEL. I'M GOOD AT KEEPING SECRETS. I'M FAMOUS FOR IT.
OKAY.
UM. I LOVE YOU.
THANK YOU, HAZEL. I LOVE YOU, TOO.
YEAH. BUT YOU LOVE EVERYONE.
I KNOW.

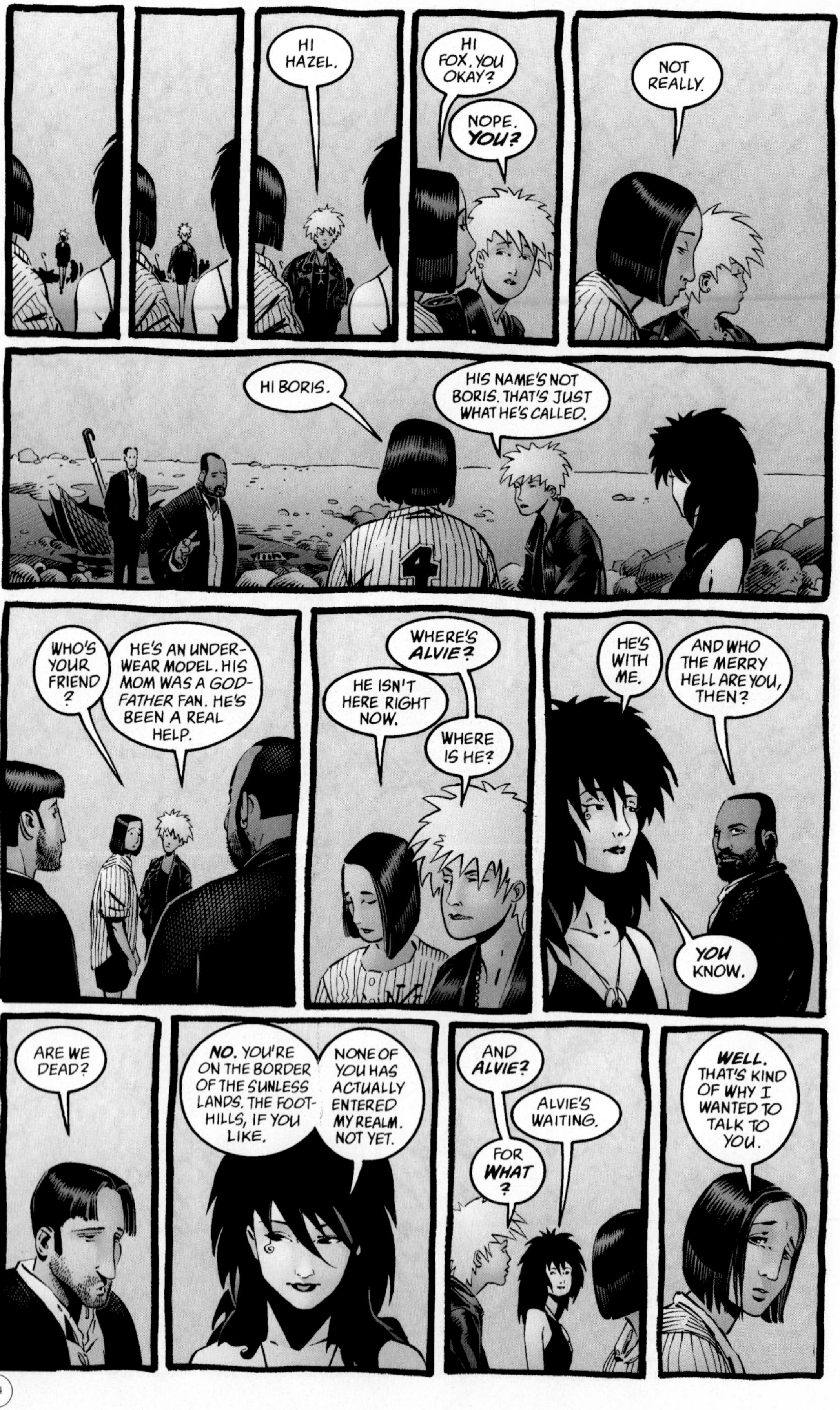
HI HAZEL.
HI FOX. YOU OKAY?
NOPE. YOU?
NOT REALLY.
HI BORIS.
HIS NAME'S NOT BORIS. THAT'S JUST WHAT HE'S CALLED.
WHO'S YOUR FRIEND?
HE'S AN UNDERWEAR MODEL. HIS MOM WAS A GODFATHER FAN. HE'S BEEN A REAL HELP.
WHERE'S ALVIE?
HE ISN'T HERE RIGHT NOW.
WHERE IS HE?
HE'S WITH ME.
AND WHO THE MERRY HELL ARE YOU, THEN?
YOU KNOW.
ARE WE DEAD?
NO. YOU'RE ON THE BORDER OF THE SUNLESS LANDS. THE FOOTHILLS, IF YOU LIKE.
NONE OF YOU HAS ACTUALLY ENTERED MY REALM. NOT YET.
AND ALVIE?
ALVIE'S WAITING.
FOR WHAT?
WELL. THAT'S KIND OF WHY I WANTED TO TALK TO YOU.

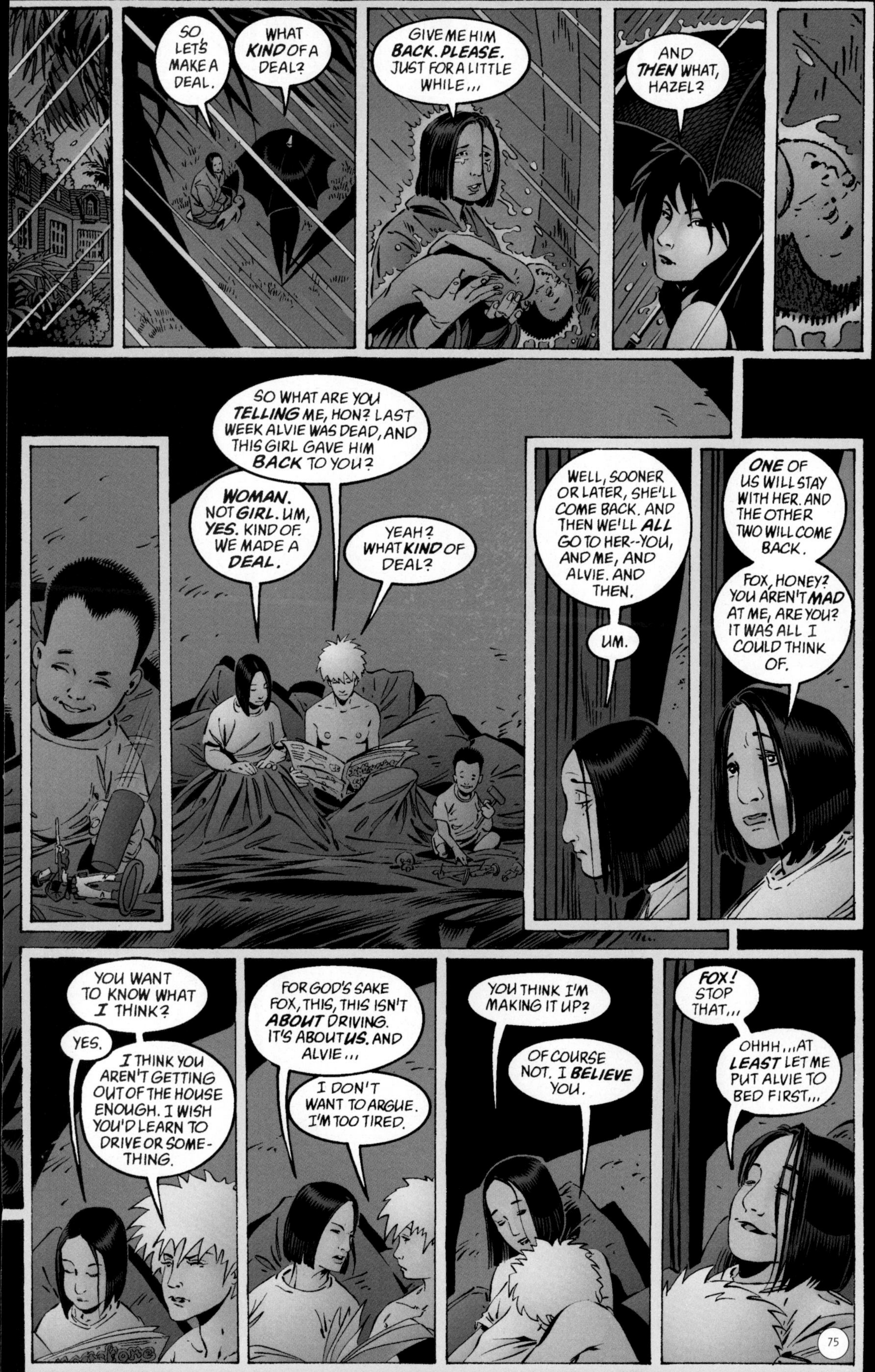

SO, LET'S MAKE A DEAL.
WHAT KIND OF A DEAL?
GIVE ME HIM BACK. PLEASE. JUST FOR A LITTLE WHILE...
AND THEN WHAT, HAZEL?
SO WHAT ARE YOU TELLING ME, HON? LAST WEEK ALVIE WAS DEAD, AND THIS GIRL GAVE HIM BACK TO YOU?
WOMAN. NOT GIRL. UM, YES. KIND OF. WE MADE A DEAL.
YEAH? WHAT KIND OF DEAL?
WELL, SOONER OR LATER, SHE'LL COME BACK. AND THEN WE'LL ALL GO TO HER--YOU, AND ME, AND ALVIE. AND THEN.
UM.
ONE OF US WILL STAY WITH HER. AND THE OTHER TWO WILL COME BACK.
FOX, HONEY? YOU AREN'T MAD AT ME, ARE YOU? IT WAS ALL I COULD THINK OF.
YOU WANT TO KNOW WHAT I THINK?
YES.
I THINK YOU AREN'T GETTING OUT OF THE HOUSE ENOUGH. I WISH YOU'D LEARN TO DRIVE OR SOME-THING.
FOR GOD'S SAKE FOX, THIS, THIS ISN'T ABOUT DRIVING. IT'S ABOUT US. AND ALVIE...
I DON'T WANT TO ARGUE. I'M TOO TIRED.
YOU THINK I'M MAKING IT UP?
OF COURSE NOT. I BELIEVE YOU.
FOX! STOP THAT...
OHHH...AT LEAST LET ME PUT ALVIE TO BED FIRST...

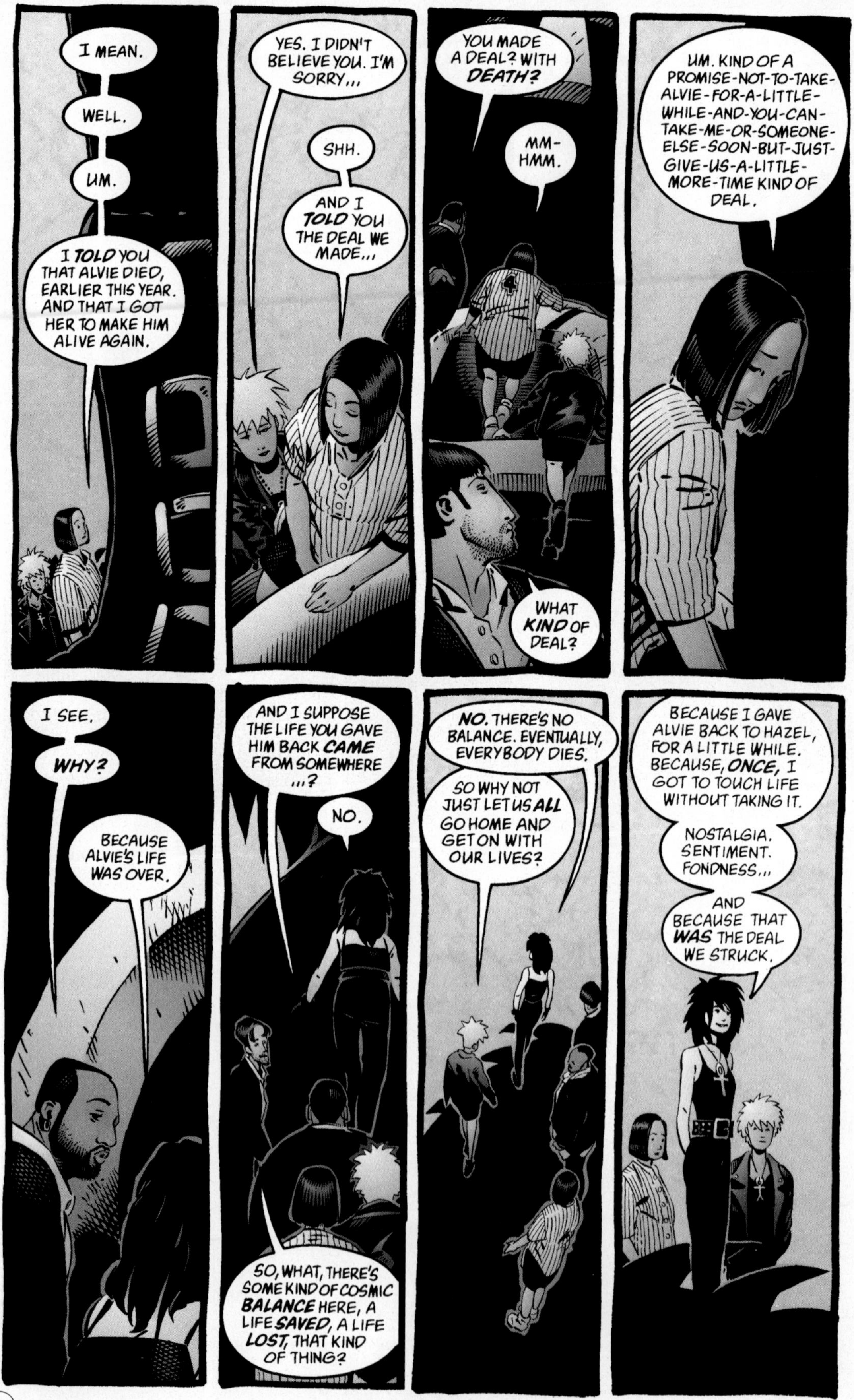
I MEAN.
WELL.
UM.
I TOLD YOU THAT ALVIE DIED, EARLIER THIS YEAR. AND THAT I GOT HER TO MAKE HIM ALIVE AGAIN.
YES. I DIDN'T BELIEVE YOU. I'M SORRY...
SHH.
AND I TOLD YOU THE DEAL WE MADE...
YOU MADE A DEAL? WITH DEATH?
MM-HMM.
WHAT KIND OF DEAL?
UM. KIND OF A PROMISE-NOT-TO-TAKE-ALVIE-FOR-A-LITTLE-WHILE-AND-YOU-CAN-TAKE-ME-OR-SOMEONE-ELSE-SOON-BUT-JUST-GIVE-US-A-LITTLE-MORE-TIME KIND OF DEAL.
I SEE.
WHY?
BECAUSE ALVIE'S LIFE WAS OVER.
AND I SUPPOSE THE LIFE YOU GAVE HIM BACK CAME FROM SOMEWHERE...?
NO.
SO, WHAT, THERE'S SOME KIND OF COSMIC BALANCE HERE, A LIFE SAVED, A LIFE LOST, THAT KIND OF THING?
NO. THERE'S NO BALANCE. EVENTUALLY, EVERYBODY DIES.
SO WHY NOT JUST LET US ALL GO HOME AND GET ON WITH OUR LIVES?
BECAUSE I GAVE ALVIE BACK TO HAZEL, FOR A LITTLE WHILE. BECAUSE, ONCE, I GOT TO TOUCH LIFE WITHOUT TAKING IT.
NOSTALGIA. SENTIMENT. FONDNESS...
AND BECAUSE THAT WAS THE DEAL WE STRUCK.

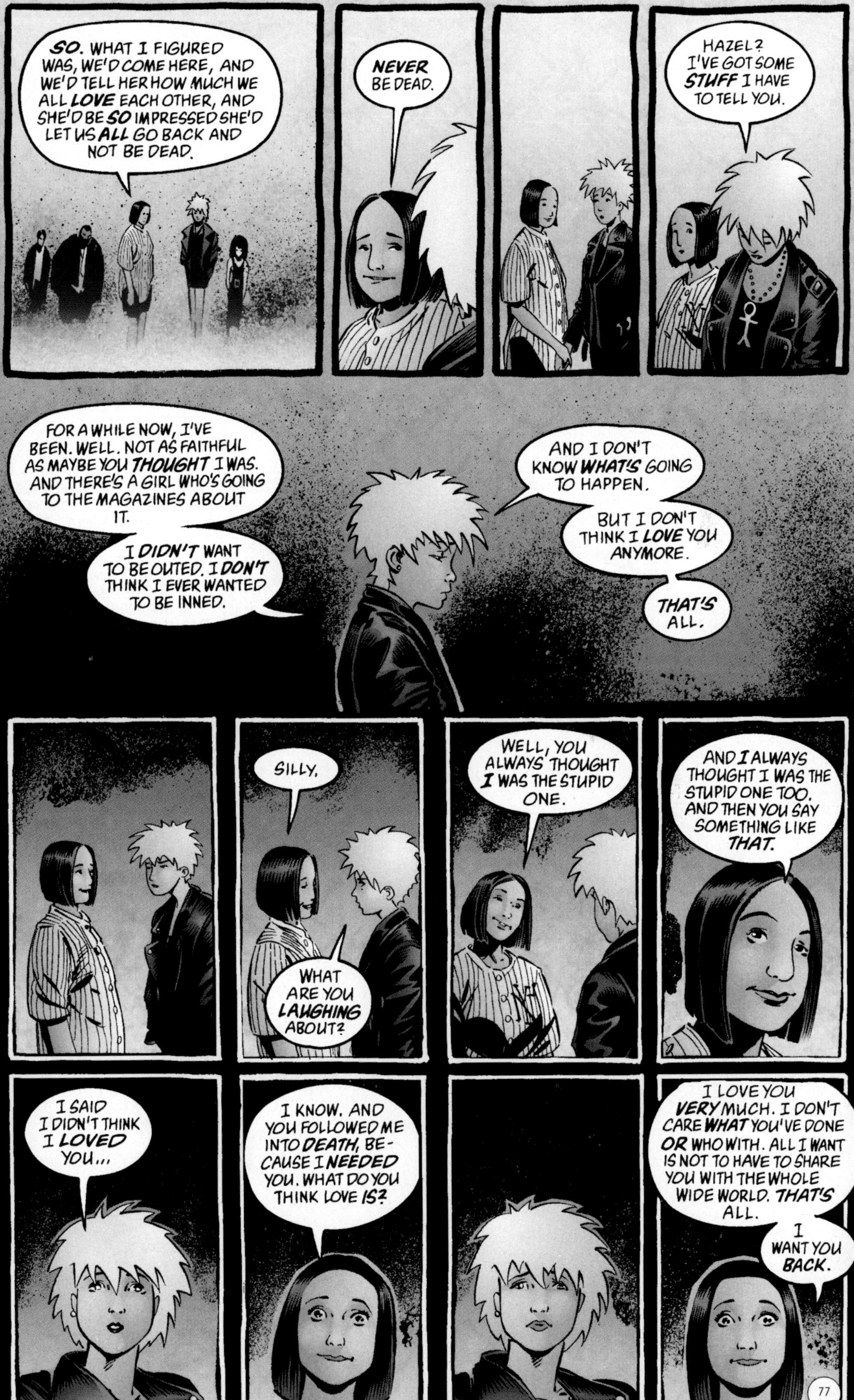
SO. WHAT I FIGURED WAS, WE'D COME HERE, AND WE'D TELL HER HOW MUCH WE ALL LOVE EACH OTHER, AND SHE'D BE SO IMPRESSED SHE'D LET US ALL GO BACK AND NOT BE DEAD.
NEVER BE DEAD.
HAZEL? I'VE GOT SOME STUFF I HAVE TO TELL YOU.
FOR A WHILE NOW, I'VE BEEN. WELL. NOT AS FAITHFUL AS MAYBE YOU THOUGHT I WAS. AND THERE'S A GIRL WHO'S GOING TO THE MAGAZINES ABOUT IT.
I DIDN'T WANT TO BE OUTED. I DON'T THINK I EVER WANTED TO BE INNED.
AND I DON'T KNOW WHAT'S GOING TO HAPPEN.
BUT I DON'T THINK I LOVE YOU ANYMORE.
THAT'S ALL.
SILLY.
WHAT ARE YOU LAUGHING ABOUT?
WELL, YOU ALWAYS THOUGHT I WAS THE STUPID ONE.
AND I ALWAYS THOUGHT I WAS THE STUPID ONE TOO. AND THEN YOU SAY SOMETHING LIKE THAT.
I SAID I DIDN'T THINK I LOVED YOU...
I KNOW. AND YOU FOLLOWED ME INTO DEATH, BE-CAUSE I NEEDED YOU. WHAT DO YOU THINK LOVE IS?
I LOVE YOU VERY MUCH. I DON'T CARE WHAT YOU'VE DONE OR WHO WITH. ALL I WANT IS NOT TO HAVE TO SHARE YOU WITH THE WHOLE WIDE WORLD. THAT'S ALL.
I WANT YOU BACK.

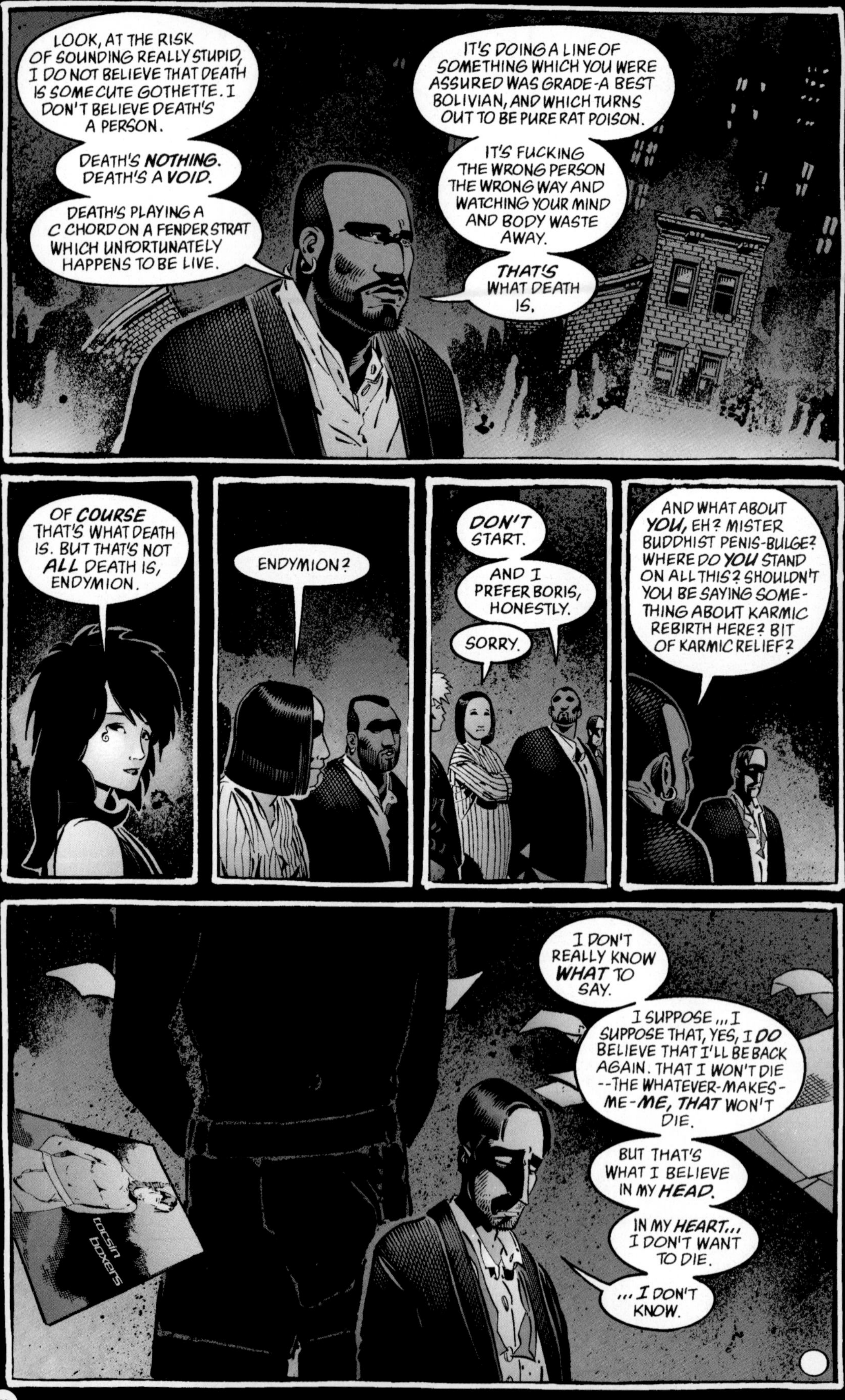
LOOK, AT THE RISK OF SOUNDING REALLY STUPID, I DO NOT BELIEVE THAT DEATH IS SOME CUTE GOTHETTE. I DON'T BELIEVE DEATH'S A PERSON.
DEATH'S **NOTHING**. DEATH'S A **VOID**.
DEATH'S PLAYING A C CHORD ON A FENDER STRAT WHICH UNFORTUNATELY HAPPENS TO BE LIVE.
IT'S DOING A LINE OF SOMETHING WHICH YOU WERE ASSURED WAS GRADE-A BEST BOLIVIAN, AND WHICH TURNS OUT TO BE PURE RAT POISON.
IT'S FUCKING THE WRONG PERSON THE WRONG WAY AND WATCHING YOUR MIND AND BODY WASTE AWAY.
THAT'S WHAT DEATH IS.
OF **COURSE** THAT'S WHAT DEATH IS. BUT THAT'S NOT **ALL** DEATH IS, ENDYMION.
ENDYMION?
DON'T START.
AND I PREFER BORIS, HONESTLY.
SORRY.
AND WHAT ABOUT **YOU**, EH? MISTER BUDDHIST PENIS-BULGE? WHERE DO **YOU** STAND ON ALL THIS? SHOULDN'T YOU BE SAYING SOMETHING ABOUT KARMIC REBIRTH HERE? BIT OF KARMIC RELIEF?
I DON'T REALLY KNOW **WHAT** TO SAY.
I SUPPOSE ... I SUPPOSE THAT, YES, I **DO** BELIEVE THAT I'LL BE BACK AGAIN. THAT I WON'T DIE --THE WHATEVER-MAKES-ME-**ME, THAT** WON'T DIE.
BUT THAT'S WHAT I BELIEVE IN MY **HEAD**.
IN MY **HEART**... I DON'T WANT TO DIE.
... I DON'T KNOW.
tocsin boxers

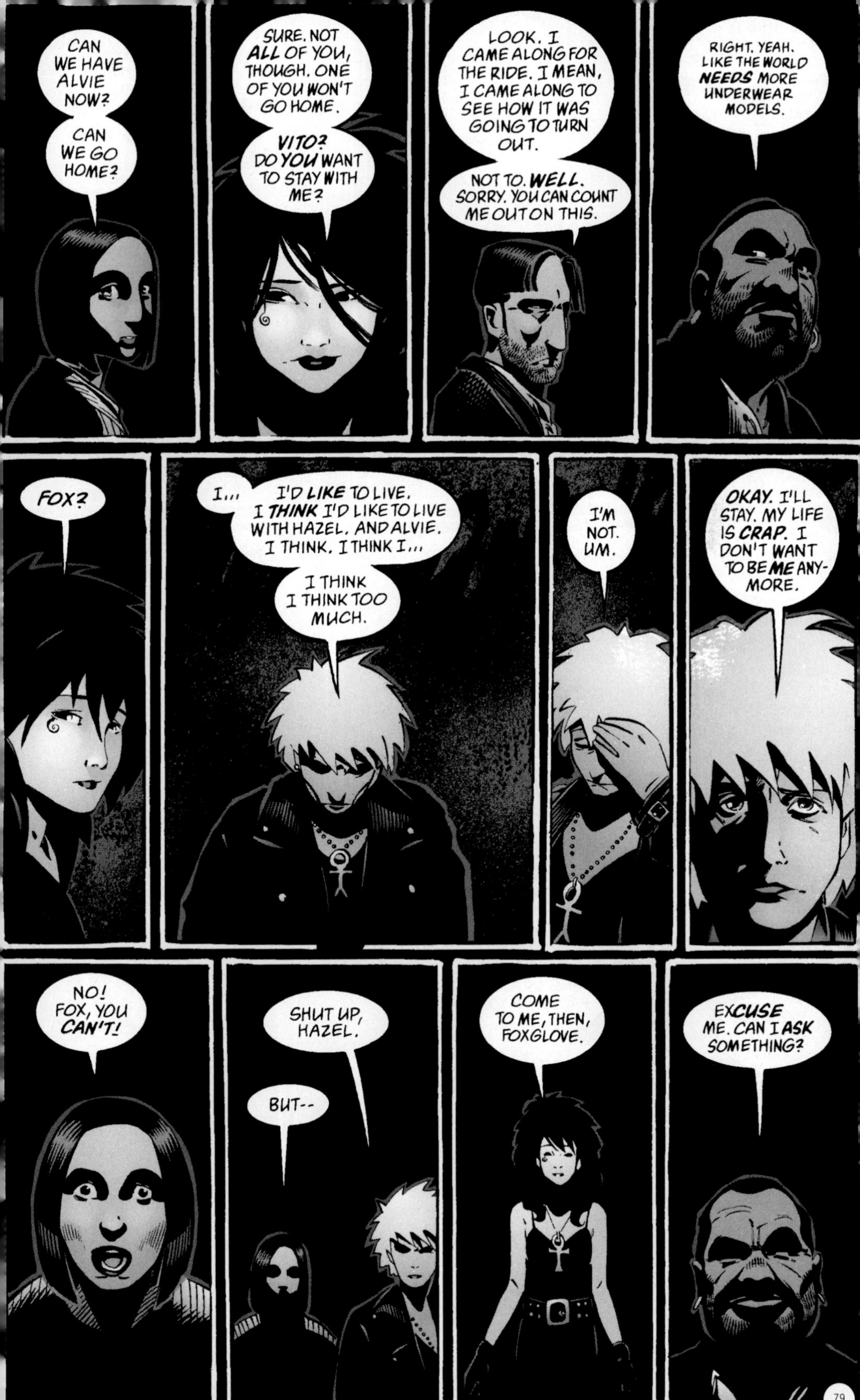
CAN WE HAVE ALVIE NOW?
CAN WE GO HOME?
SURE. NOT ALL OF YOU, THOUGH. ONE OF YOU WON'T GO HOME.
VITO? DO YOU WANT TO STAY WITH ME?
LOOK. I CAME ALONG FOR THE RIDE. I MEAN, I CAME ALONG TO SEE HOW IT WAS GOING TO TURN OUT.
NOT TO. WELL. SORRY. YOU CAN COUNT ME OUT ON THIS.
RIGHT. YEAH. LIKE THE WORLD NEEDS MORE UNDERWEAR MODELS.
FOX?
I...
I'D LIKE TO LIVE. I THINK I'D LIKE TO LIVE WITH HAZEL. AND ALVIE. I THINK. I THINK I...
I THINK I THINK TOO MUCH.
I'M NOT. UM.
OKAY. I'LL STAY. MY LIFE IS CRAP. I DON'T WANT TO BE ME ANYMORE.
NO! FOX, YOU CAN'T!
SHUT UP, HAZEL.
BUT--
COME TO ME, THEN, FOXGLOVE.
EXCUSE ME. CAN I ASK SOMETHING?

UM. THIS *ISN'T* A DREAM, *IS* IT? IT'S *REAL*. YEAH?

I'M AFRAID SO.

THAT WAS WHAT I THOUGHT.

I DON'T KNOW. YOU'RE *HOPELESS*, THE *LOT* OF YOU. *ESPECIALLY* YOU, FOX.

SO. LET ME SEE IF I'VE GOT THIS ONE STRAIGHT.

ON THE *ONE* HAND, YOU'VE GOT THE GIRLS AND THE KID AND ME AND HIM, AND ON THE *OTHER* HAND, SOMEBODY'S GOT TO STAY BEHIND.

ISN'T THAT RIGHT?

YES. BUT FOX HAS ALREADY VOLUNTEERED.

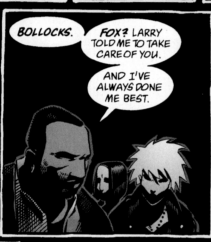
BOLLOCKS.

FOX? LARRY TOLD ME TO TAKE CARE OF YOU.

AND I'VE ALWAYS DONE ME BEST.

SO IT'S GOING TO HAVE TO BE ME.

BORIS? WHY?

BECAUSE IT'S MY *DUTY*, I SUPPOSE.

BECAUSE IT'S MY *JOB*.

GO AND TAKE *CARE* OF YOURSELF, FOX LOVE. HAVE A *PROPER* LIFE. BRING UP ALVIE TO BE PROUD OF YOU. ALL THAT.

I DON'T THINK YOU WERE EVER CUT *OUT* TO BE A POP STAR. IT'S *NO* FIT LIFE FOR A HUMAN BEING.

AND YOU ONLY LIVE *ONCE*.

IF *THAT*.

ENDYMION? ARE YOU CERTAIN?

I REALLY *DO* PREFER BORIS, IF YOU DON'T MIND.

NO, I DON'T MIND.

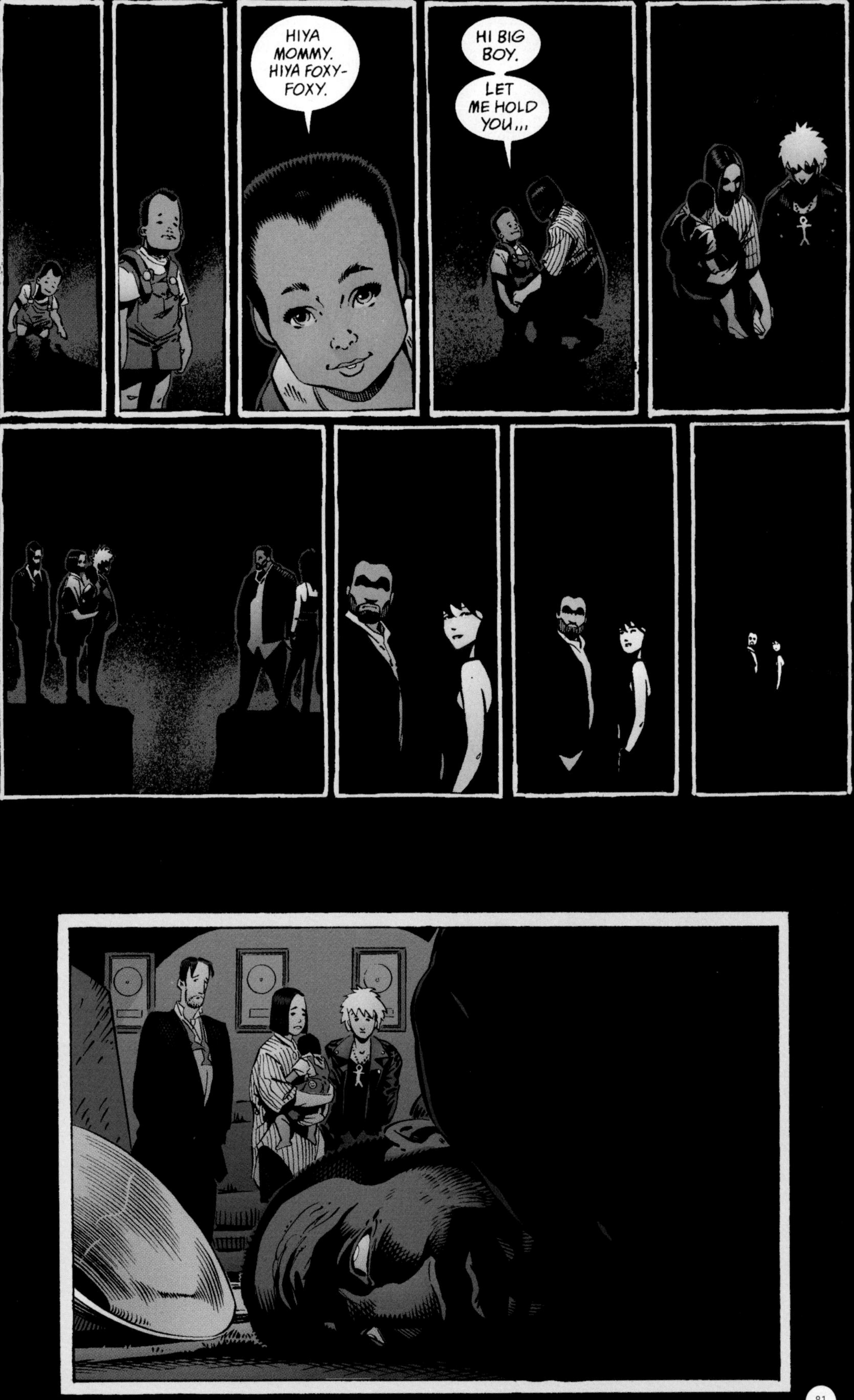
HIYA MOMMY. HIYA FOXY-FOXY.
HI BIG BOY.
LET ME HOLD YOU...

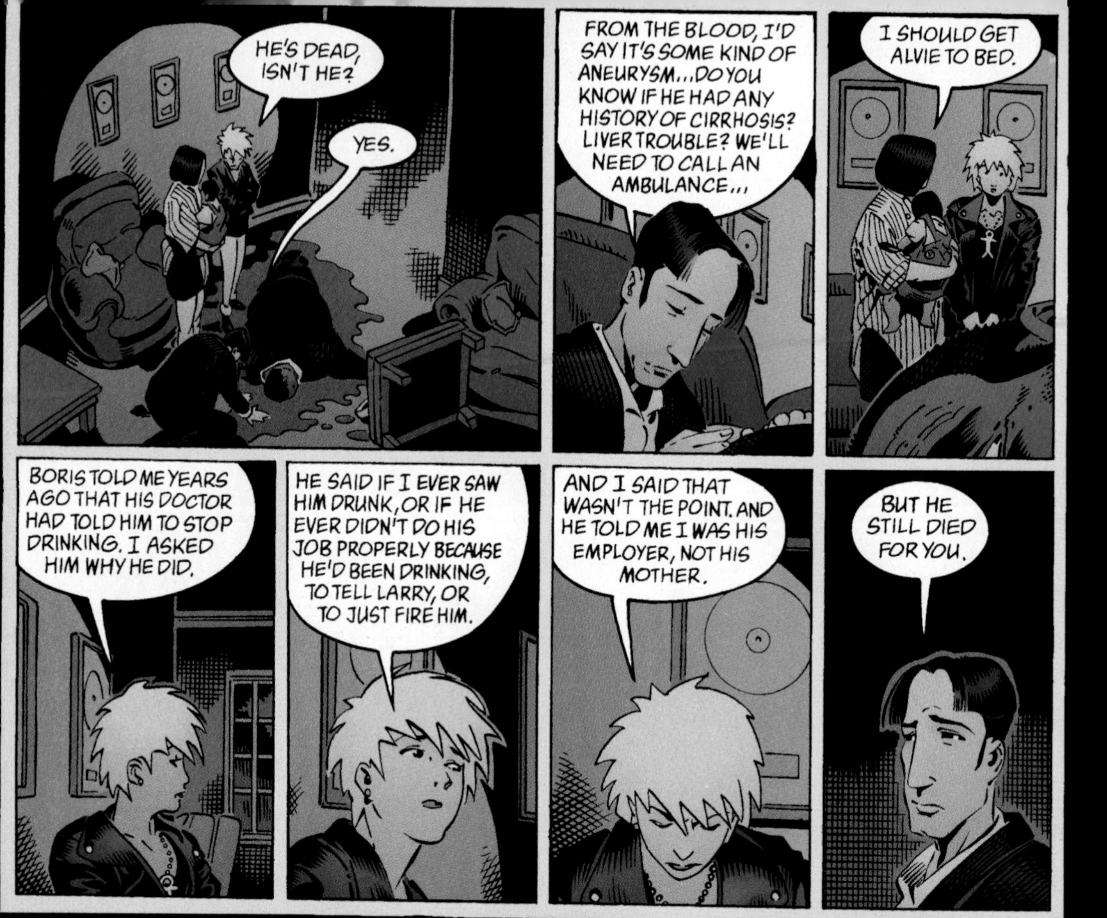
HE'S DEAD, ISN'T HE?
YES.
FROM THE BLOOD, I'D SAY IT'S SOME KIND OF ANEURYSM...DO YOU KNOW IF HE HAD ANY HISTORY OF CIRRHOSIS? LIVER TROUBLE? WE'LL NEED TO CALL AN AMBULANCE...
I SHOULD GET ALVIE TO BED.
BORIS TOLD ME YEARS AGO THAT HIS DOCTOR HAD TOLD HIM TO STOP DRINKING. I ASKED HIM WHY HE DID.
HE SAID IF I EVER SAW HIM DRUNK, OR IF HE EVER DIDN'T DO HIS JOB PROPERLY BECAUSE HE'D BEEN DRINKING, TO TELL LARRY, OR TO JUST FIRE HIM.
AND I SAID THAT WASN'T THE POINT. AND HE TOLD ME I WAS HIS EMPLOYER, NOT HIS MOTHER.
BUT HE STILL DIED FOR YOU.

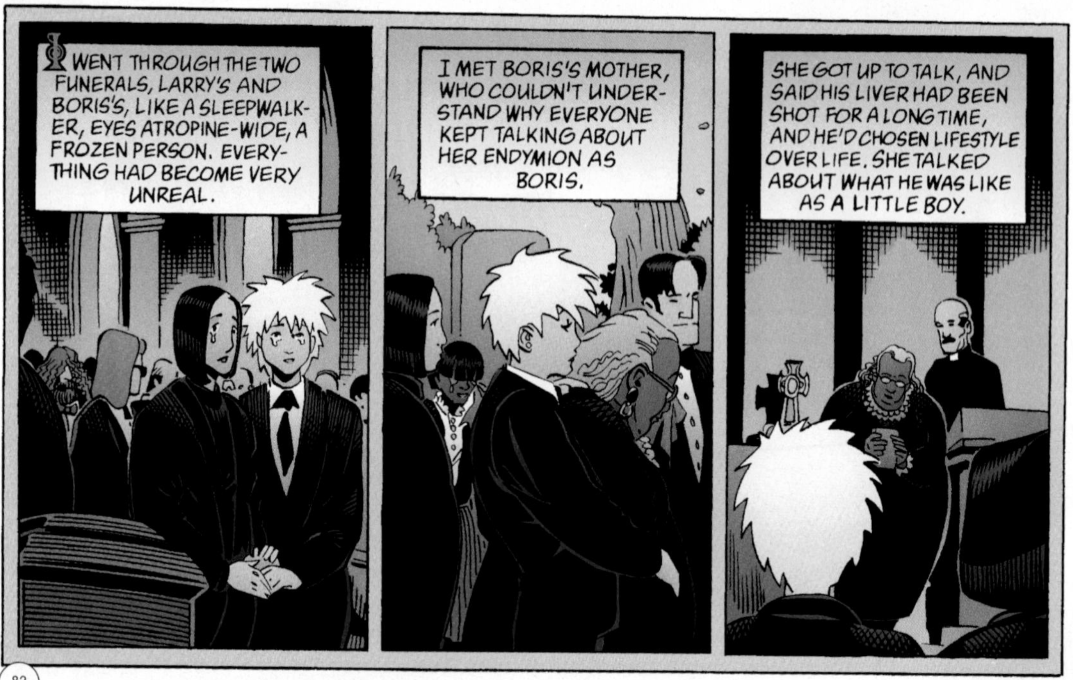
I WENT THROUGH THE TWO FUNERALS, LARRY'S AND BORIS'S, LIKE A SLEEPWALKER, EYES ATROPINE-WIDE, A FROZEN PERSON. EVERYTHING HAD BECOME VERY UNREAL.
I MET BORIS'S MOTHER, WHO COULDN'T UNDERSTAND WHY EVERYONE KEPT TALKING ABOUT HER ENDYMION AS BORIS.
SHE GOT UP TO TALK, AND SAID HIS LIVER HAD BEEN SHOT FOR A LONG TIME, AND HE'D CHOSEN LIFESTYLE OVER LIFE. SHE TALKED ABOUT WHAT HE WAS LIKE AS A LITTLE BOY.

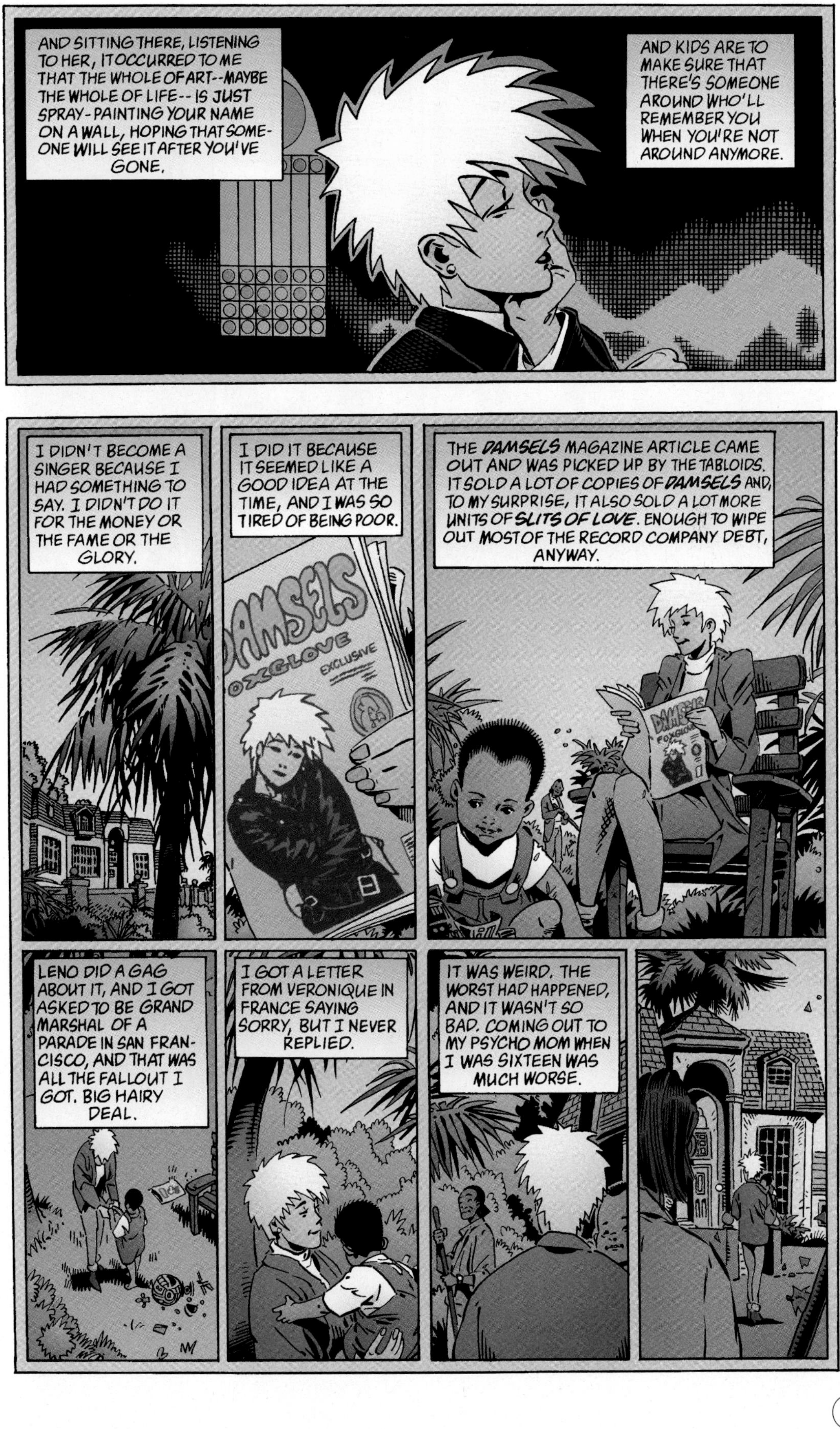
AND SITTING THERE, LISTENING TO HER, IT OCCURRED TO ME THAT THE WHOLE OF ART--MAYBE THE WHOLE OF LIFE-- IS JUST SPRAY-PAINTING YOUR NAME ON A WALL, HOPING THAT SOMEONE WILL SEE IT AFTER YOU'VE GONE.
AND KIDS ARE TO MAKE SURE THAT THERE'S SOMEONE AROUND WHO'LL REMEMBER YOU WHEN YOU'RE NOT AROUND ANYMORE.
I DIDN'T BECOME A SINGER BECAUSE I HAD SOMETHING TO SAY. I DIDN'T DO IT FOR THE MONEY OR THE FAME OR THE GLORY.
I DID IT BECAUSE IT SEEMED LIKE A GOOD IDEA AT THE TIME, AND I WAS SO TIRED OF BEING POOR.
DAMSELS
FOXGLOVE
EXCLUSIVE
THE DAMSELS MAGAZINE ARTICLE CAME OUT AND WAS PICKED UP BY THE TABLOIDS. IT SOLD A LOT OF COPIES OF DAMSELS AND, TO MY SURPRISE, IT ALSO SOLD A LOT MORE UNITS OF SLITS OF LOVE. ENOUGH TO WIPE OUT MOST OF THE RECORD COMPANY DEBT, ANYWAY.
LENO DID A GAG ABOUT IT, AND I GOT ASKED TO BE GRAND MARSHAL OF A PARADE IN SAN FRANCISCO, AND THAT WAS ALL THE FALLOUT I GOT. BIG HAIRY DEAL.
I GOT A LETTER FROM VERONIQUE IN FRANCE SAYING SORRY, BUT I NEVER REPLIED.
IT WAS WEIRD. THE WORST HAD HAPPENED, AND IT WASN'T SO BAD. COMING OUT TO MY PSYCHO MOM WHEN I WAS SIXTEEN WAS MUCH WORSE.

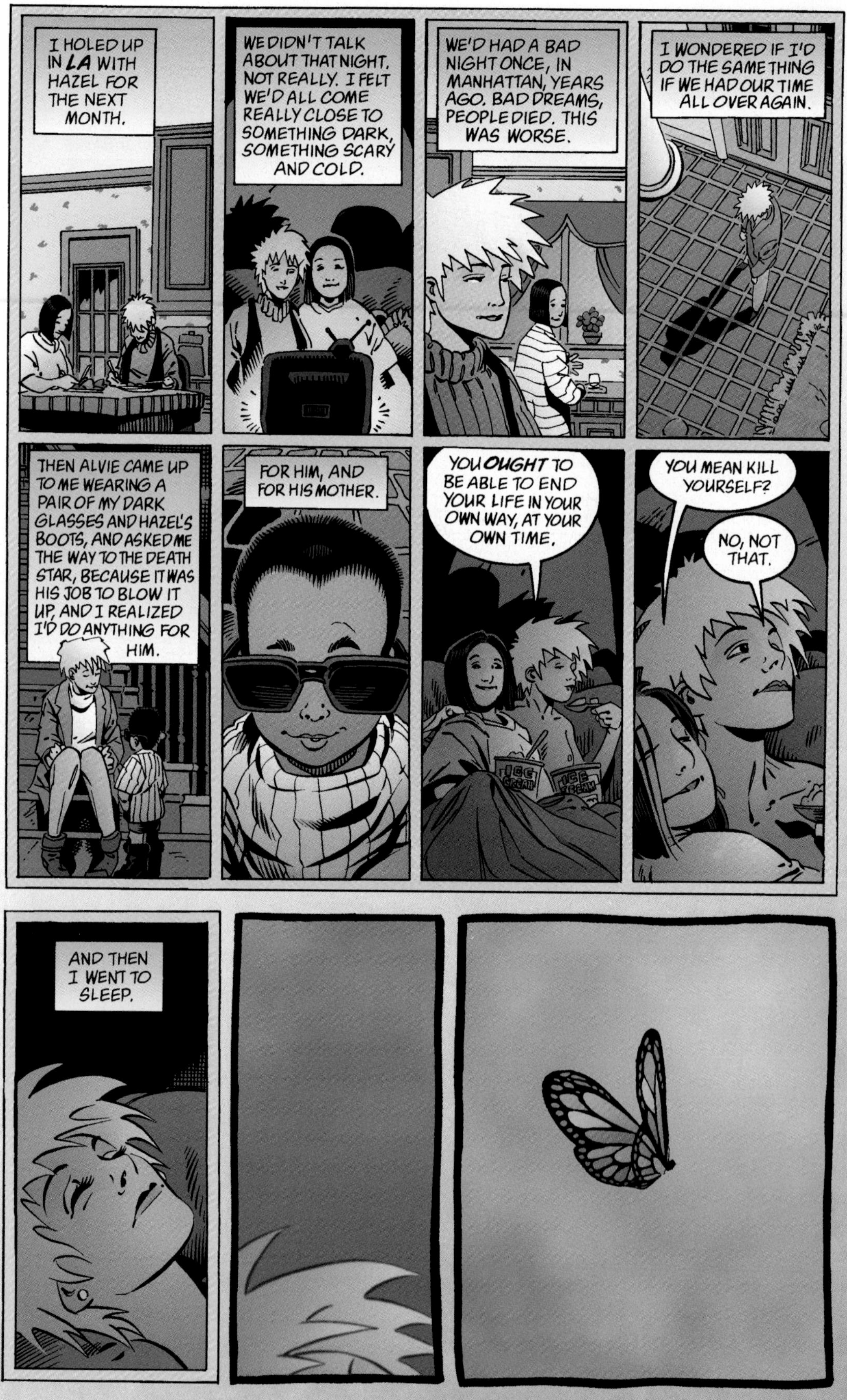
I HOLED UP IN LA WITH HAZEL FOR THE NEXT MONTH.
WE DIDN'T TALK ABOUT THAT NIGHT, NOT REALLY. I FELT WE'D ALL COME REALLY CLOSE TO SOMETHING DARK, SOMETHING SCARY AND COLD.
WE'D HAD A BAD NIGHT ONCE, IN MANHATTAN, YEARS AGO. BAD DREAMS, PEOPLE DIED. THIS WAS WORSE.
I WONDERED IF I'D DO THE SAME THING IF WE HAD OUR TIME ALL OVER AGAIN.
THEN ALVIE CAME UP TO ME WEARING A PAIR OF MY DARK GLASSES AND HAZEL'S BOOTS, AND ASKED ME THE WAY TO THE DEATH STAR, BECAUSE IT WAS HIS JOB TO BLOW IT UP, AND I REALIZED I'D DO ANYTHING FOR HIM.
FOR HIM, AND FOR HIS MOTHER.
YOU OUGHT TO BE ABLE TO END YOUR LIFE IN YOUR OWN WAY, AT YOUR OWN TIME.
YOU MEAN KILL YOURSELF?
NO, NOT THAT.
AND THEN I WENT TO SLEEP.

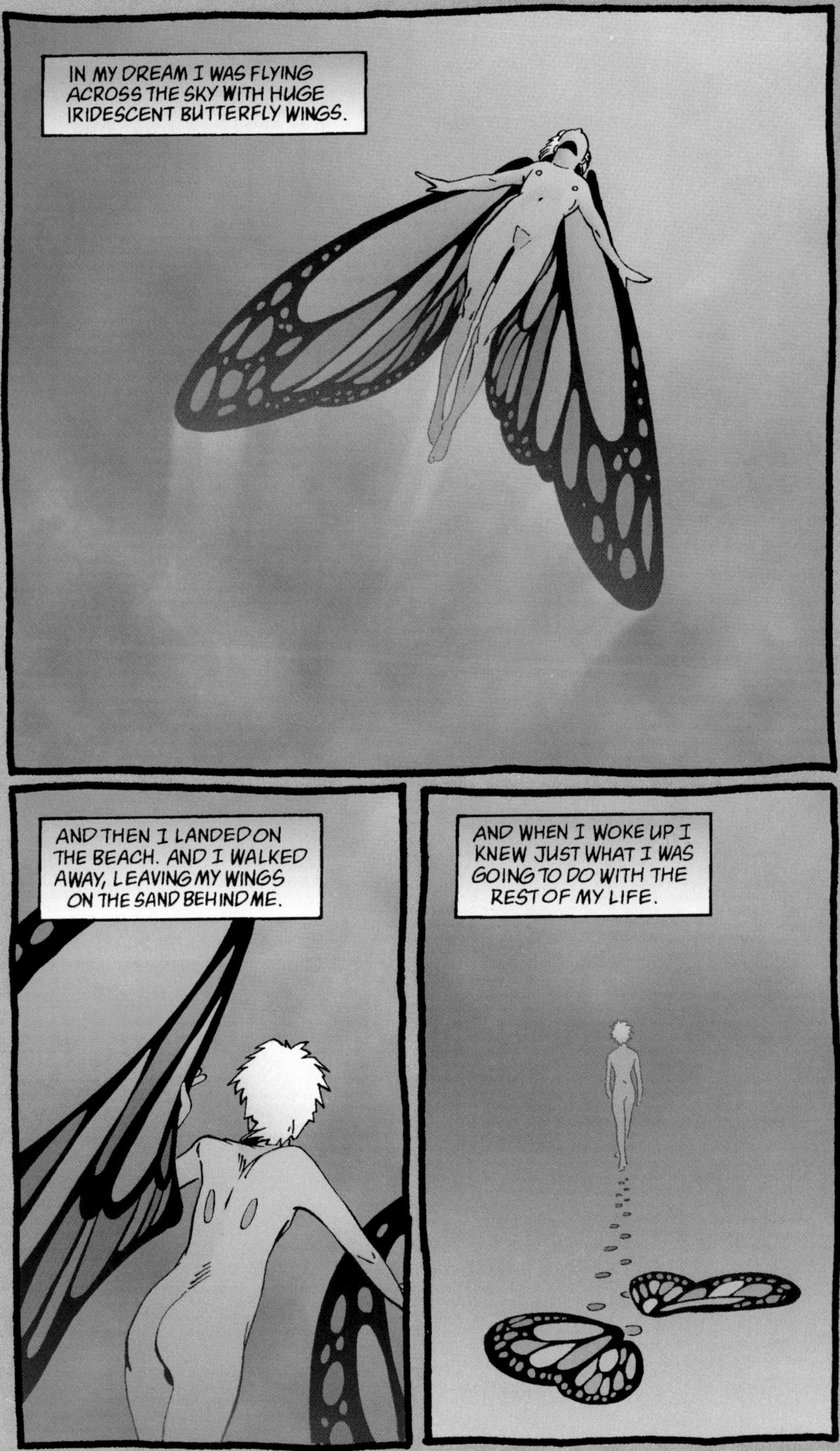
IN MY DREAM I WAS FLYING ACROSS THE SKY WITH HUGE IRIDESCENT BUTTERFLY WINGS.
AND THEN I LANDED ON THE BEACH. AND I WALKED AWAY, LEAVING MY WINGS ON THE SAND BEHIND ME.
AND WHEN I WOKE UP I KNEW JUST WHAT I WAS GOING TO DO WITH THE REST OF MY LIFE.

EPILOGUE

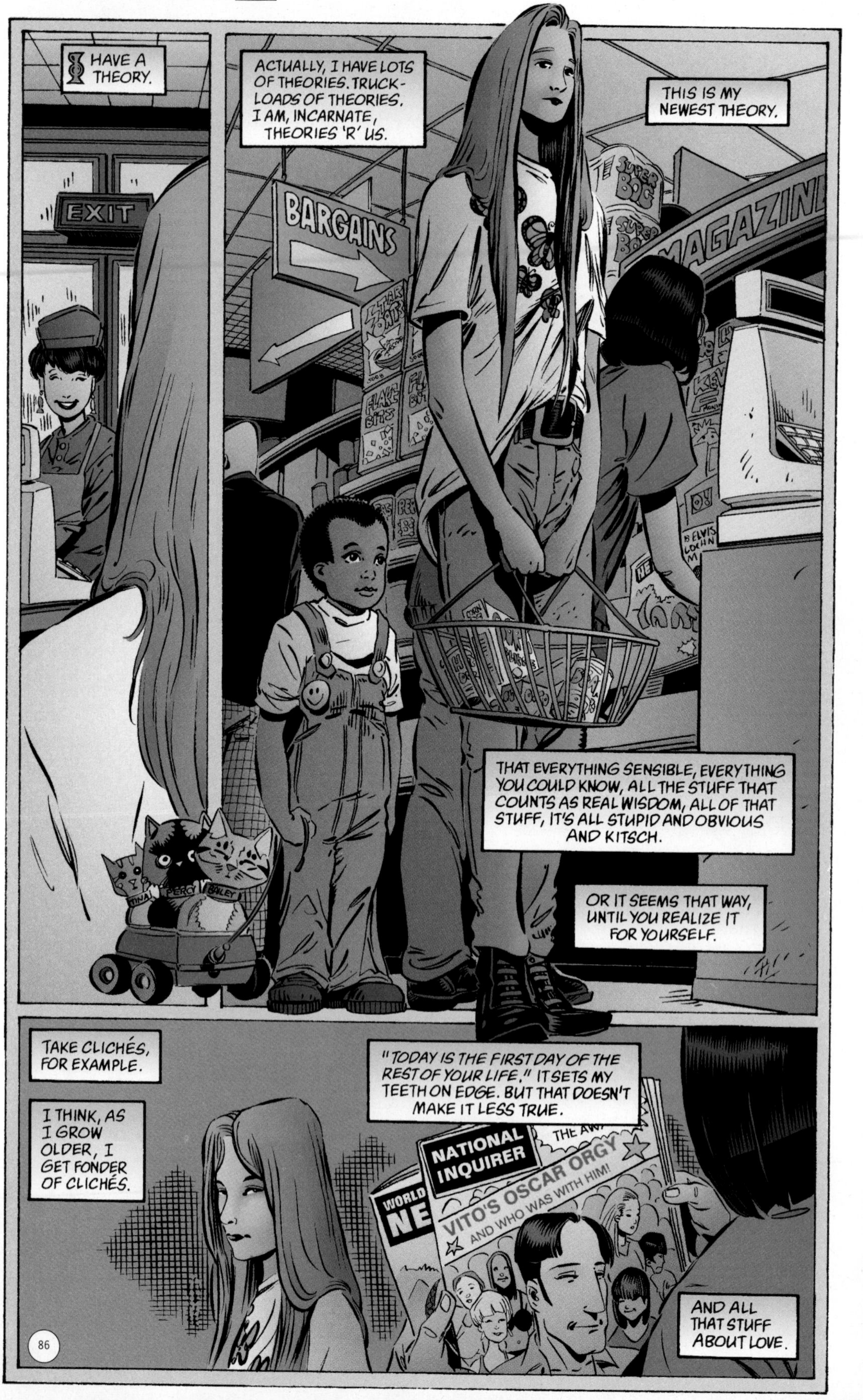

I HAVE A THEORY.
ACTUALLY, I HAVE LOTS OF THEORIES. TRUCK-LOADS OF THEORIES. I AM, INCARNATE, THEORIES 'R' US.
THIS IS MY NEWEST THEORY.
EXIT
BARGAINS
MAGAZIN
FLAKE BITS
TINA
PERCY
BAILEY
THAT EVERYTHING SENSIBLE, EVERYTHING YOU COULD KNOW, ALL THE STUFF THAT COUNTS AS REAL WISDOM, ALL OF THAT STUFF, IT'S ALL STUPID AND OBVIOUS AND KITSCH.
OR IT SEEMS THAT WAY, UNTIL YOU REALIZE IT FOR YOURSELF.
TAKE CLICHÉS, FOR EXAMPLE.
I THINK, AS I GROW OLDER, I GET FONDER OF CLICHÉS.
"TODAY IS THE FIRST DAY OF THE REST OF YOUR LIFE," IT SETS MY TEETH ON EDGE. BUT THAT DOESN'T MAKE IT LESS TRUE.
NATIONAL INQUIRER
VITO'S OSCAR ORGY
AND WHO WAS WITH HIM!
AND ALL THAT STUFF ABOUT LOVE.

WHAT DOES IT *MEAN*, WHEN YOU MOVE FROM THE *NATIONAL INQUIRER* TO THE *WORLD WEEKLY NEWS*?

IS *ELVIS* THE LOCH NESS MONSTER?

WORLD WEEKLY NEWS

EXCLUSIVE

I SUPPOSE IT MEANS YOU'RE NOT A CELEBRITY ANY-MORE. YOU'RE NOW A *LEGEND*, OR A *DREAM*. WHY?

MM. WELL, SAYS *HERE* THAT YOU'VE BEEN DOING GIGS WITH BUDDY HOLLY.

IS ELVIS LOCHN MON

WORLD WEEKLY NEWS

BUDDY HOLLY AND FOXGLOVE
DESERT DUO?

y others, and in oung people sh approach to of calm reality nd the appeal wider audience

e so many es that:
oing a h sphere
R to o
m. Lik
ss ple

BUDDY HOLLY AND FOXGLOVE.
MISSING ARTISTS IN SECRET CONCERT
A WORLD WEEKLY NEWS EXCLUSIVE

ELVIS

REALLY? *WHERE?*

IN AN ABANDONED GHOST-TOWN MOTEL IN THE ARIZONA DESERT.

WORLD WEEKLY IS

WHY ARIZONA ?

IT DOESN'T SAY.

HOW *COOL.*

UH-OH. I GET TO DRIVE, REMEMBER?

OKAY.

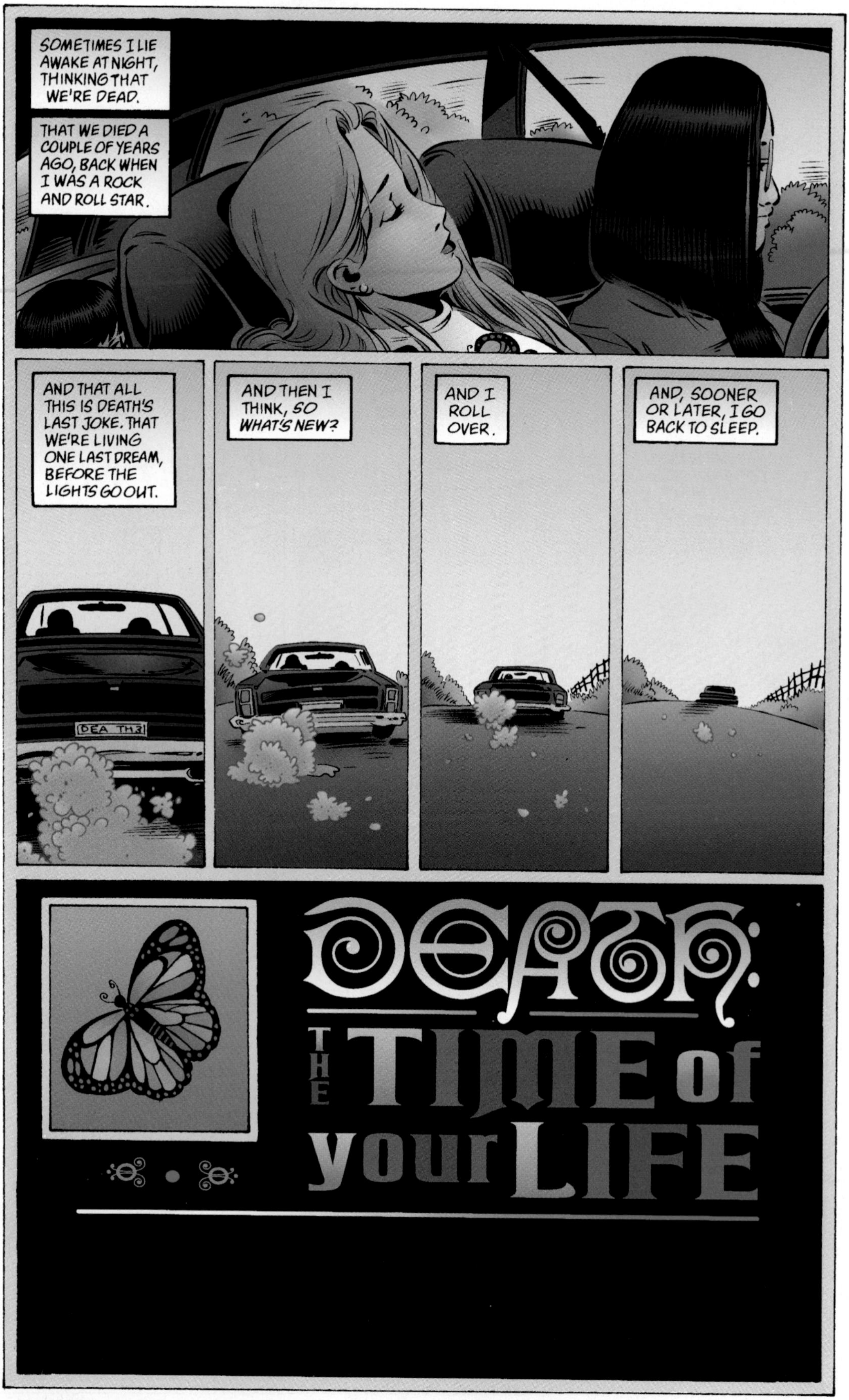
SOMETIMES I LIE AWAKE AT NIGHT, THINKING THAT WE'RE DEAD.
THAT WE DIED A COUPLE OF YEARS AGO, BACK WHEN I WAS A ROCK AND ROLL STAR.
AND THAT ALL THIS IS DEATH'S LAST JOKE. THAT WE'RE LIVING ONE LAST DREAM, BEFORE THE LIGHTS GO OUT.
DEA TH3
AND THEN I THINK, SO WHAT'S NEW?
AND I ROLL OVER.
AND, SOONER OR LATER, I GO BACK TO SLEEP.
DEATH:
THE TIME of your LIFE

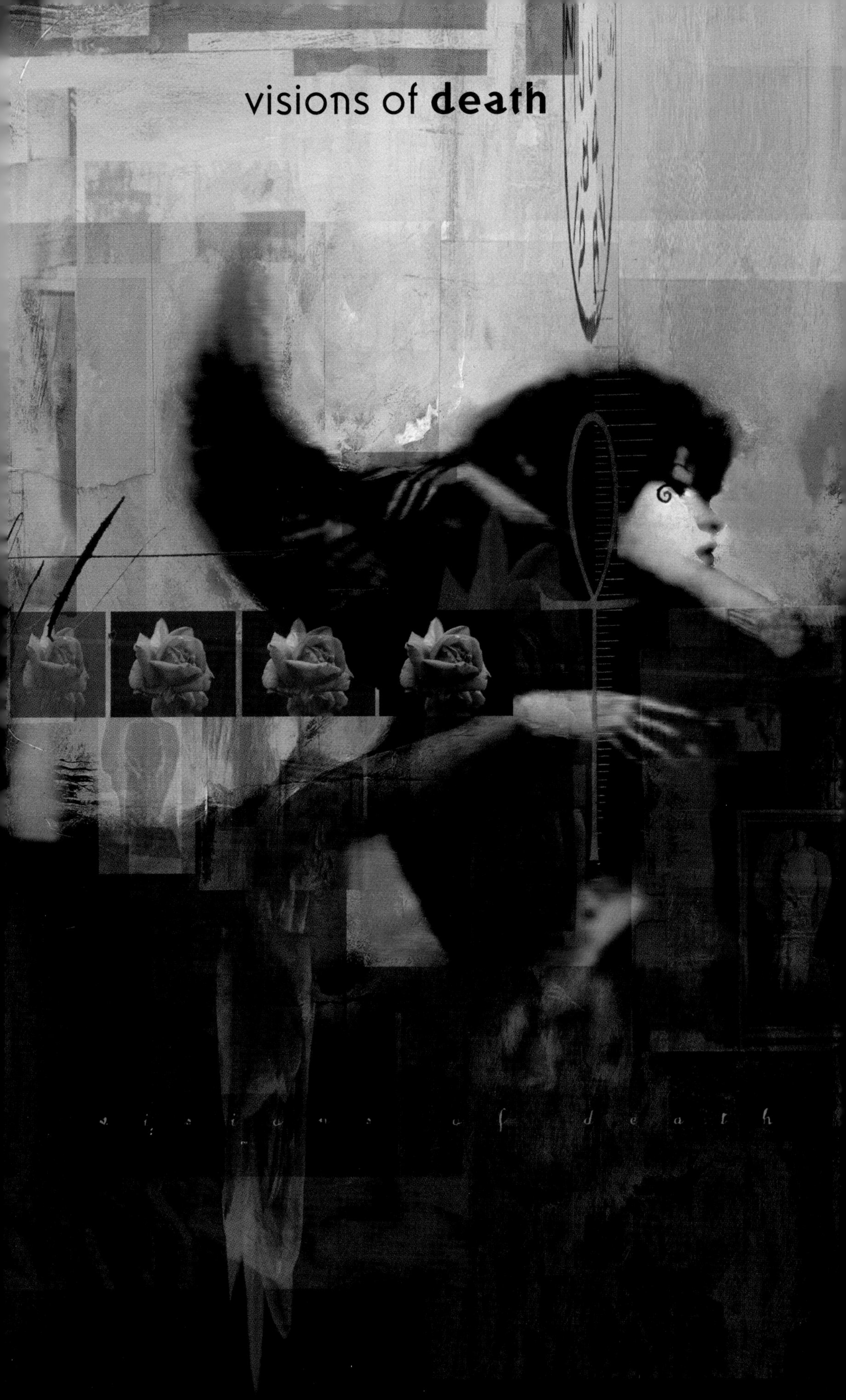
visions of death
visions of death

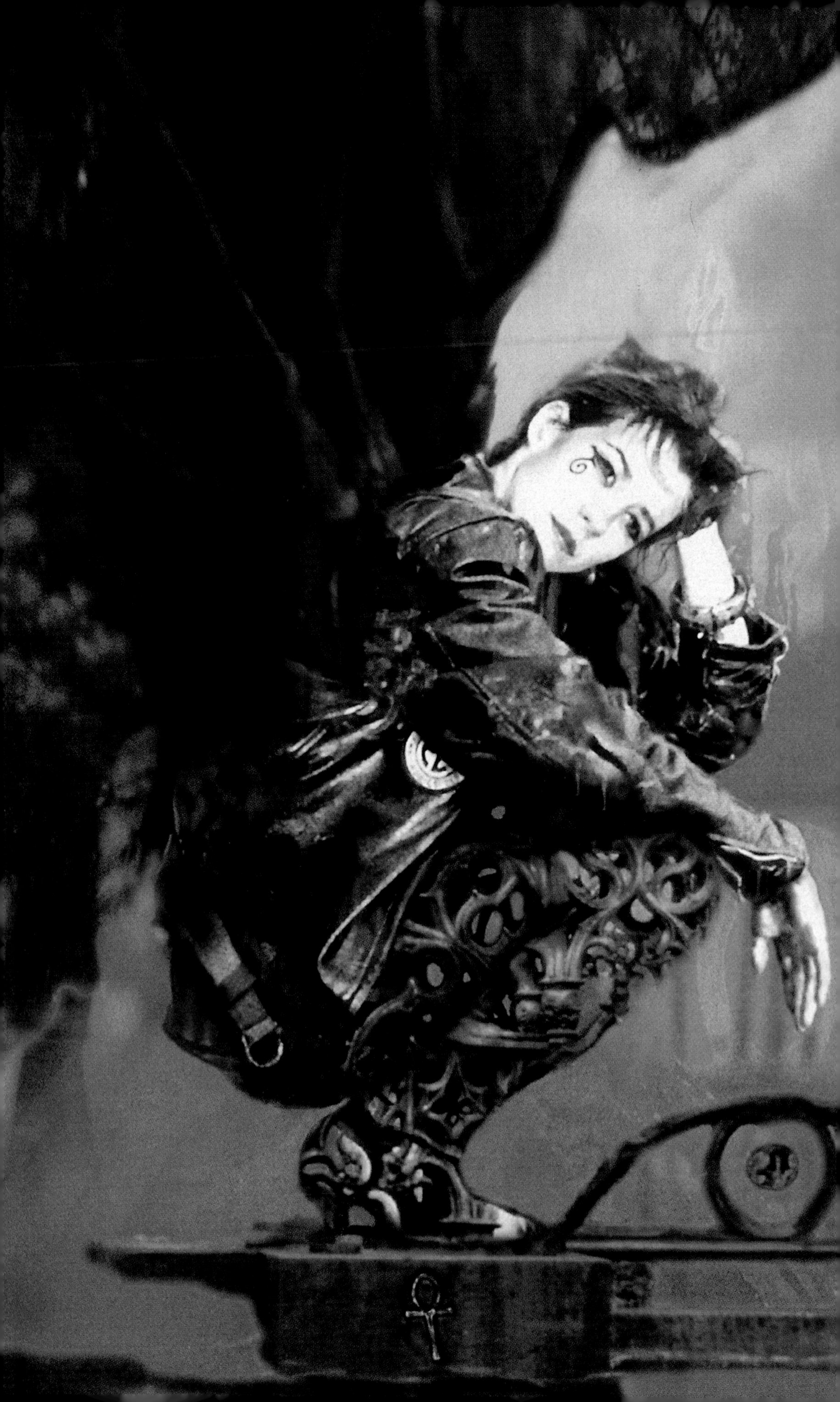

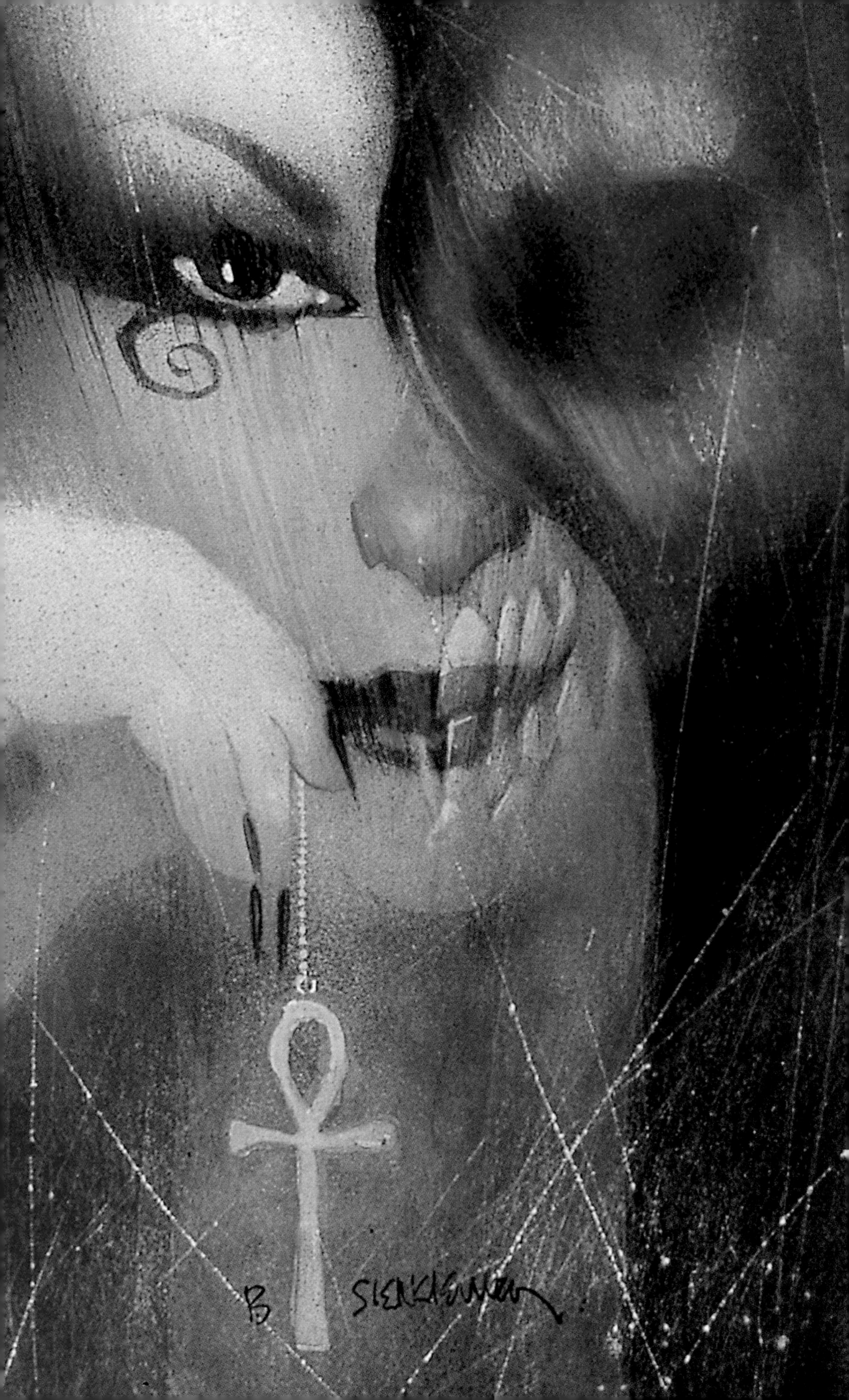

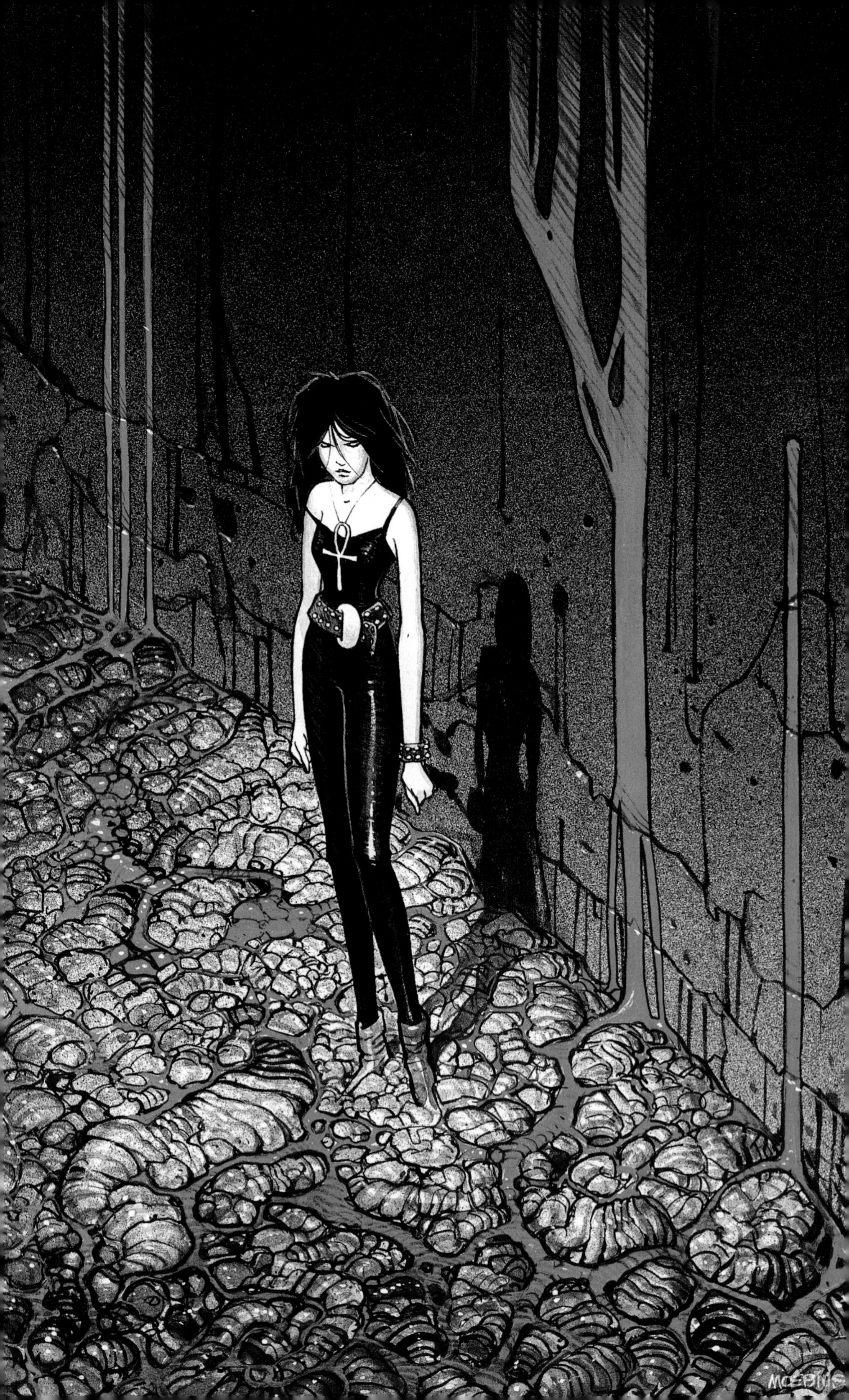
MŒBIUS

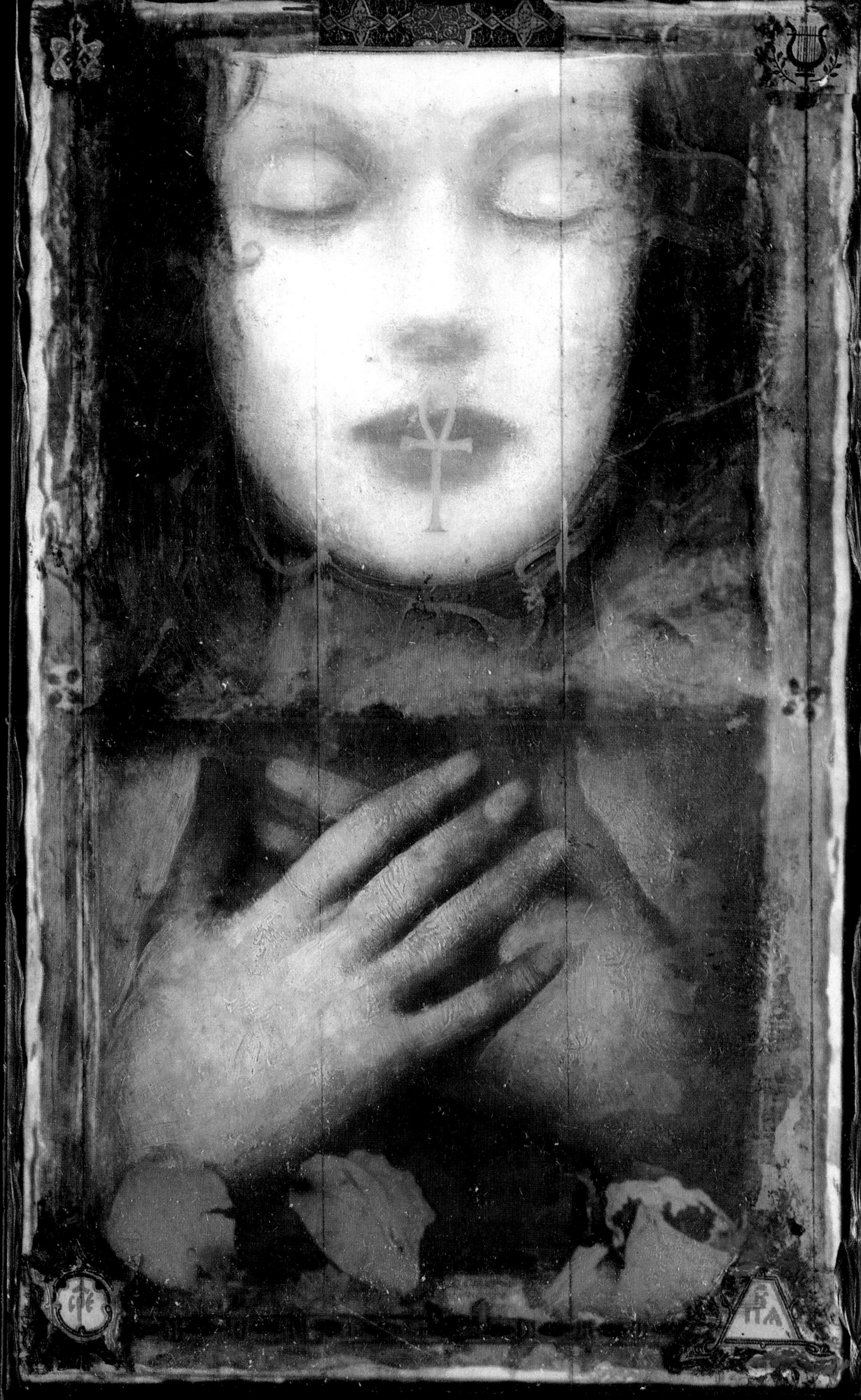

afterword.
neil gaiman

Life and Death, as Welsh musician and iconoclast John Cale once pointed out, are just things you do when you're bored.

Yes.

I am relearning things I had forgotten, these days. It comes of having a two-year-old daughter, which means that I have begun, once more, to tell stories aloud. Or rather, having told one story aloud, I find myself having to tell that story over and over again.

Bedtime stories, when told to toddlers, are tales of a very specific type. The story needs to be the same as the night before — often, in parts, word for word the same — but with room for contribution from the child (the color of a monster, what the darkness tastes like, the name of the Queen's horse, all these change from night to night, according to her whim). The tales need to be flexible enough to include any new passions (a birthday party at the end of the story has now become a grand feast at Cinderella's palace), but unchanging enough that each recounting of the story is a visit from a beloved and constant friend, not an awkward and unwelcome stranger.

As a professional teller of tales one treads a similar path, knowing that one's audience wants — if not the same story it got last time, then at least the same feeling it got from reading the last story. But one also suspects that, unless one is going off and trying new things and making a fool of oneself, then one has stopped growing and begun to die. Living and ceasing to live, Andre Breton is reputed to have said, are imaginary solutions. Existence lies elsewhere.

One tries to love one's stories as one loves one's children — unreservedly, without playing favorites, while not being blind to their problems and their faults. For a variety of reasons, this story was somewhat truncated on its original appearance, which left it with less resemblance to the tale in my head when I began than it should have had. It's only a little longer now, but I'm much happier with it than I was.

I suppose that, now I come to think of it, this is also a bedtime story, although the night is long, and the dawn is always uncertain.

I'd like to thank Karen Berger for her patience, and for giving us the extra few pages we did not have in the monthly comic, and to thank Mark Buckingham for his help, then and now

Neil Gaiman
December 1996, having the Time of My Life (or, as Elvis Costello sang, something quite like it...)

Christopher

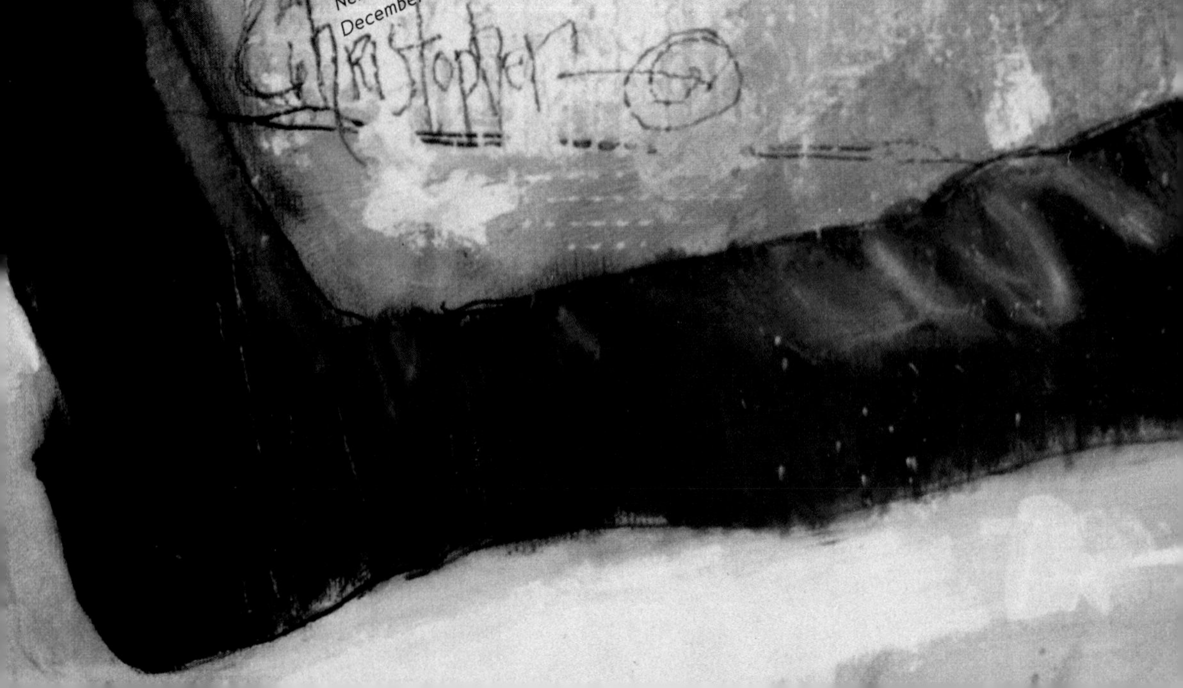

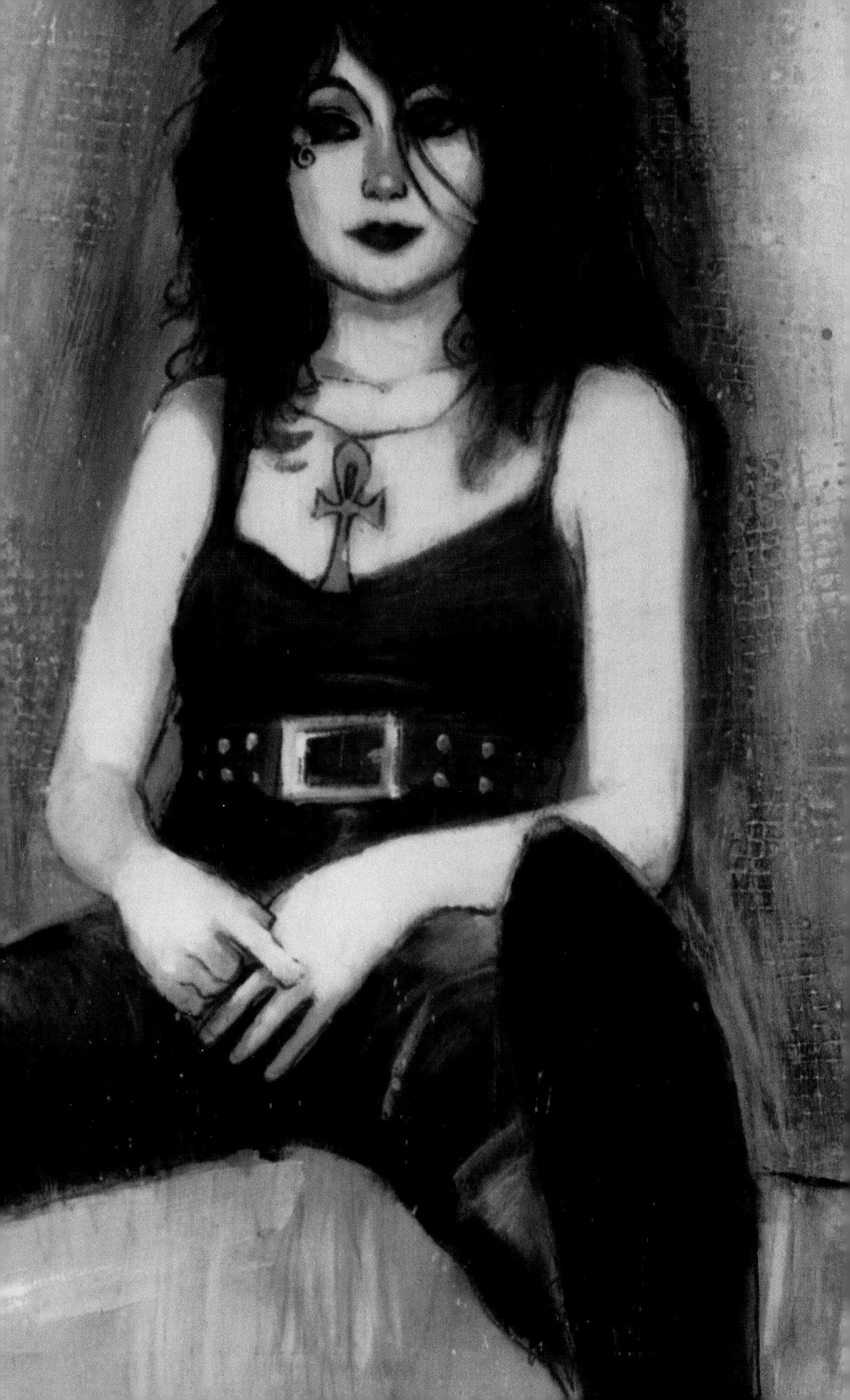

ELEVEN DEFINITIVE GRAPHIC NOVELS THAT REVEAL
THE STORY OF MORPHEUS AND THE ENDLESS,
HIS UNIQUELY DYSFUNCTIONAL FAMILY:

VOLUME 1: PRELUDES & NOCTURNES
Dream of the Endless, also known as the Sandman, had been
imprisoned for 70 years. After his escape, the Sandman must
reclaim his realm, The Dreaming, as well as his articles of power.

VOLUME 2: THE DOLL'S HOUSE
Rose Walker finds more than she bargained for — including
long lost relatives, a serial killers' convention and, ultimately,
her true identity — with the help of the Sandman.

VOLUME 3: DREAM COUNTRY
Four chilling and unique tales, including the World Fantasy Award-
winning story of the first performance of Shakespeare's *A Midsummer
Night's Dream* with art by Charles Vess. Also contains Gaiman's original
comic book script for *Calliope.*

VOLUME 4: SEASON OF MISTS
Ten thousand years ago, the Sandman condemned his one true love
to the pits of Hell. When his sister Death convinces him this was an
injustice, Dream journeys to Hell to rescue his lost lover — just as
Lucifer Morningstar decides to abdicate his throne, leaving the Key
to Hell in the hands of the Sandman.

VOLUME 5: A GAME OF YOU
Barbie used to dream of being a princess in a private kingdom with
strange animals as her subjects. But Barbie has stopped dreaming
and now her imaginary world and the real world entwine in a riveting
story about gender and identity.

VOLUME 6: FABLES & REFLECTIONS
From the mists of the past to the nightmares of the present, Dream
touches the lives of the king of ancient Baghdad and Lady Johanna
Constantine, among others, in nine remarkable self-contained stories.

VOLUME 7: BRIEF LIVES
Delirium, youngest of the Endless, prevails upon her brother Dream
to help find their missing brother, Destruction. Their odyssey through
the waking world also leads the Sandman to resolve his painful
relationship with his son, Orpheus.

VOLUME 8: WORLDS' END
Caught in the vortex of a reality storm, wayfarers from throughout
time, myth, and the imagination converge on a mysterious inn. In
the tradition of Chaucer's *Canterbury Tales*, the travelers wait out
the tempest that rages around them by sharing stories.

VOLUME 9: THE KINDLY ONES
Unstoppable in their mission of vengeance, the Kindly Ones will not
rest until the crime they seek to punish has been washed clean with
blood. Now Dream of the Endless, his acquaintances, and his family
find themselves caught up in this dark conspiracy.

VOLUME 10: THE WAKE
Ancient gods, old friends, and even enemies gather to remember and
pay tribute in the strangest wake ever held. And, at the end of his
life, William Shakespeare fulfills his side of a very strange bargain.

VOLUME 11: ENDLESS NIGHTS
Seven dark and beautiful tales — one each for the Sandman and his
siblings — are illustrated by an international dream team of artists.

FROM THE WORLD OF THE SANDMAN:

THE SANDMAN: THE DREAM HUNTERS
NEIL GAIMAN/YOSHITAKA AMANO
Set in Japan and told in illustrated prose, this adult fairy tale
featuring the Lord of Dreams is beautifully painted by legendary
artist Yoshitaka Amano.

DEATH: THE HIGH COST OF LIVING
NEIL GAIMAN/CHRIS BACHALO/MARK BUCKINGHAM
A solo story of Death, who, for one day every century, assumes
mortal form to learn more about the lives she must take.

DEATH: THE TIME OF YOUR LIFE
NEIL GAIMAN/CHRIS BACHALO/MARK BUCKINGHAM/MARK PENNINGTON
A young lesbian mother strikes a deal with Death for the life of her
son in a story about fame, relationships, and rock and roll.

DESTINY: A CHRONICLE OF DEATHS FORETOLD
ALISA KWITNEY/VARIOUS
In a doomed town in the year 2009, a handful of survivors awaiting
the final coming of the Plague are visited by a stranger claiming to
carry the Book of Destiny.

THE LITTLE ENDLESS STORYBOOK
JILL THOMPSON
This tale of a diminutive version of the Endless is written and painted
by acclaimed SANDMAN artist Jill Thompson.

DEATH: AT DEATH'S DOOR
JILL THOMPSON
It's the party from Hell — literally — in this fanciful retelling of
SEASON OF MISTS. Executed in a flawless *Manga* style by Jill Thompson.

DUST COVERS — THE COLLECTED SANDMAN COVERS 1989-1997
DAVE MCKEAN/NEIL GAIMAN
A complete portfolio of Dave McKean's celebrated SANDMAN cover art,
together with commentary by McKean and Gaiman.

THE QUOTABLE SANDMAN
NEIL GAIMAN/VARIOUS
A mini-hardcover of memorable quotations from THE SANDMAN
accompanied by a host of renditions of Morpheus and the Endless.

THE SANDMAN COMPANION
HY BENDER/VARIOUS
A treasury of artwork, essays, analysis, and interviews about
THE SANDMAN.

OTHER BOOKS BY NEIL GAIMAN FROM VERTIGO:

BLACK ORCHID
NEIL GAIMAN/DAVE MCKEAN
In the tradition of Alan Moore's SWAMP THING, Gaiman and McKean's
first comics collaboration reimagines the character of Black Orchid in
a lushly painted story of identity and betrayal.

THE BOOKS OF MAGIC
NEIL GAIMAN/JOHN BOLTON/SCOTT HAMPTON/CHARLES VESS/PAUL JOHNSON
A quartet of fallen mystics (John Constantine, the Phantom Stranger,
Dr. Occult, and Mister E) introduce the world of magic to young Tim
Hunter, who is destined to become the world's most powerful magician.

MR. PUNCH
NEIL GAIMAN/DAVE MCKEAN
Gaiman and McKean reunite to create a unique vision of nostalgia
and remembrance.

NEIL GAIMAN'S MIDNIGHT DAYS
NEIL GAIMAN/MATT WAGNER/TEDDY KRISTIANSEN/VARIOUS
A collection of Gaiman stories from other VERTIGO titles, featuring
Swamp Thing, John Constantine, and the Golden Age Sandman.

NEIL GAIMAN AND CHARLES VESS' STARDUST
NEIL GAIMAN/CHARLES VESS
A Victorian-era tale of the magic and romance between a young man
and a shooting star, told in prose with lavish painted illustrations.